01209 616182

college

Camborne Pool Redruth College

Library

the **SOUND ON SOUND** book of

live sound
for the
performing musician

CORNWALL COLLEGE
LIBRARY

CP000623

CORNWALL COLLEGE

CORNWALL COLLEGE
LEARNING CENTRE

Cover design: The Whole Hog Design Company

Design: David Houghton

Printed by: Redwood Books Ltd

Published by: Sanctuary Publishing Limited, The Colonnades, 82 Bishops Bridge Road, London W2 6BB

Copyright: Paul White, 1998

All rights reserved. No part of this book may be reproduced in any form or by any electronic or mechanical means, including information storage or retrieval systems, without permission in writing from the publisher, except by a reviewer who may quote brief passages.

ISBN: 1-86074-210-6

the **SOUND ON SOUND** book of

live sound
for the
performing musician

paul white

contents

CHAPTER 4

CHAPTER 5

CHAPTER 9

introduction

At last there is a book designed to provide practical guidance and advice to musicians working in small- to medium-sized venues. *Live Sound For The Performing Musician* covers every aspect of enhancing your performance, from choosing a PA system, the basic principles on which it operates, plus tips for getting the best possible sound in various real-life situations. Back-line miking and instrument amplification are also covered.

Talent is important, but good sound matters too, and the quality of sound achieved is dictated not only by the equipment available, but also by how that equipment is utilised. Properly used, even relatively inexpensive equipment can produce exceptionally good results, but without the right knowledge, even the best systems can let you down. *Live Sound For The Performing Musician* shows how to get the best out of your own PA system, and how to approach the demanding job of mixing. This includes a full tour of a typical live sound mixer, an explanation of what all the different microphone types do and a guide to using effects and signal processors.

All this is accomplished in plain English with clear diagrams, and any necessary jargon is explained both in the text and in a comprehensive glossary. Topics covered include all the components of a typical PA set-up, tuning, instrument miking, DI techniques, radio mics, basic wiring information, amplifier and loudspeaker principles, and how to approach live mixing. There are also tips to help you make the best of difficult situations and workarounds to use when something goes wrong.

introduction to PA

The purpose of this chapter is to provide a brief introduction to the subjects which will be covered in depth later in the book. It also describes the main components of a typical PA system along with some basic advice on their operation.

Though we tend to take PA systems for granted, the technology has actually changed quite a lot since the early days of sound systems. Big systems have got even bigger, but the new technology also allows portable systems to be made smaller, lighter and more powerful, which is good news for gigging bands with limited transport capacity, or for those playing small venues.

In the early days of touring bands, the PA system was likely to comprise a mono mixer amplifier of around 100 watts driving a couple of 4x10 or 4x12 speaker columns with no tweeters, no crossovers and no off-stage mixing. Effects were limited to spring reverb or tape-loop echo, and the microphones employed ranged from dynamic models by the likes of Beyer or Shure to fragile ribbon mics such as the ubiquitous Rezlo. Concepts such as flat frequency response, controlled directivity or stage monitoring were entertained only by the most visionary of audio pioneers. Much has changed since then.

Despite the increased sophistication of modern PA systems, the underlying aim is still the same as it every was, and the purpose of this book is to look at the equipment involved, the principles on which it operates, and the best way to use it in a real-world gigging/touring environment. Even the best system can perform poorly if set up incorrectly.

role of the pa system

PA, or Sound Reinforcement as it is sometimes called, might best be described as a system that helps increase the volume of existing back line instruments and vocals or, in larger venues, provides the bulk of the front-of-house sound. PA is also used to describe a system used to carry announcements in a public place, such as a shopping mall or railway station, but that particular application is (I'm sure you'll be relieved to hear!), outside the scope of this book.

For larger venues or tours, it's usual to hire in a PA system and a mix engineer, but for pubs, clubs, smaller college venues and so on, it's normal for bands to have their own system and either to have their own mix engineer or to mix the sound themselves from on stage. A modern, stereo PA system capable of delivering several hundreds of watts of power can be small enough to fit into the back of a hatchback car or small van, but it's important to choose the right type of system for your application, especially when it comes to loudspeakers and amplifiers. For example, if you're a solo folk singer working with just voice and guitar, there's no point in getting a system with powerful bass bins that go down to 30Hz as you'll only be carrying around heavy and expensive equipment designed to reproduce very low frequencies that you are simply not producing. Conversely, if you want to amplify an entire rock band, create powerful dance music, or handle a synthesiser setup that is generating deep bass and drum sounds, then you need to have a system that can reproduce low frequencies at high sound levels without distortion.

the band pa's function

The role of a concert PA system is fairly easily understood, in that it has to amplify the whole band and project the sound to fill a large auditorium. But in a club environment, the PA plays more of a reinforcement role, augmenting the sound of the on-stage, back-line amplification as well as carrying the vocals. For example, in a typical pub gig, the guitarist's amplifier is likely to produce as much volume as is required, so little or no help is needed from the PA system. The PA system still needs to be able to handle a wide audio spectrum, but its main job will be to lift the vocals over the level of the back-line and drums. If space or budget is tight, a smaller system with a less extended bass response will handle vocals perfectly adequately, but you'll have to rely on the bass player's own amplification and the natural acoustic sound of the drums to project the bass end of the mix.

sound control

One of the benefits of a larger PA system is that you can gain more control over what your audience hears, and it follows that if you want your sound engineer to have a reasonable degree of control over a mix in a small venue, it is helpful to use modestly-powered back-line amplification and then mic it up. Not only does this give the mix engineer more leeway to turn things up, it also reduces the amount of spill from the back-line amplifiers into the vocal mics, resulting in a clearer sound all round. This can be a major problem in real-world venues and various strategies for improving on-stage sound will be discussed later in the book. For typical pub work, guitar combo amplifiers rated at around 50 watts each and bass/keyboard amplifiers rated at around 100 watts are usually adequate. Using a 200-watt guitar stack in a pub leaves the sound engineer with virtually no control.

basic pa principles

In some ways, you can consider a PA as equivalent to a giant hi-fi system, but because it often has to work in a less than ideal acoustic environment, it must be specifically designed to cope with the coloured-sounding or reverberant rooms that are so often encountered on the gig circuit. This includes the type of equalisation provided and the directivity of the loudspeakers. If the room is very reverberant, obtaining an intelligible vocal sound can be very difficult and a basic understanding of the relationship between the room acoustics and acoustical properties of the loudspeakers is essential.

Loudspeaker and microphone placement will be covered in detail later in the book, but a basic fact of physics is that in any room, the direct sound from the loudspeakers will become quieter as you move further back in the room. This is related to something called the "inverse square law", a mathematical expression describing how sound waves get weaker as they move outwards, simply because their energy is dissipated over a wider area. By contrast, any reverberant or reflected sound will not follow the inverse square law, as it does not emanate from a single point source but rather bounces off every hard surface in the room. Consequently, the nominal level of the reverberant sound is likely to be more or less the same, regardless of whereabouts you are in the room.

the critical distance

From these two simple facts, it follows that as you move further from the loudspeakers, the direct sound gets weaker compared to the reverberant sound, until you reach a point when both direct and reverberant sound are equal in intensity. This is known as the "critical distance", and beyond this point, the reverberant sound predominates, making it progressively harder to define detail in the direct sound. In a situation where vocal intelligibility is important, this can be a significant problem.

You might think that the critical distance depends entirely on the room acoustics, but fortunately, that isn't entirely true. The amount of reverberant sound depends on how much sound reaches the walls and ceilings in the first place, and if your speakers produce a more tightly focused "beam" of sound, then it's possible to increase the critical distance by directing more sound onto the audience and less onto the walls. In a given room, the more directional the PA system, the further the critical distance from the loudspeaker, but the directional characteristics of the speaker also have to be chosen so as to provide acceptable coverage of the audience. The choice and positioning of loudspeakers will be discussed later, but it helps to be aware of this very important factor early on.

the pa mixer

At its simplest, a PA system comprises loudspeaker cabinets, power amplifiers, and some means of mixing several microphone signals to feed those amplifiers. This job is handled by the mixing console, or in the case of a combined mixer/amplifier, by the preamp section of mixer amp. A PA mixer need not be complex, but it should be fitted with basic tone controls and should have provision to connect external effects units and signal processors such as equalisers, limiters and so on. It is also desirable to have some means of feeding a stage monitoring system. As a rule, even fairly basic stand-alone mixers will have more comprehensive features than the mixer sections of most mixer amplifiers. Figure 1.1 shows the components of a typical small PA system based around a stereo mixer.

Digital effects units are commonly used to add reverb and echo to live performances, and the use of more sophisticated effects is by no means unusual – if it can be done in the studio, it is only natural to want to be able to recreate it live. Again, effects and signal processors are covered in depth later in this book.

stage monitoring

A portable PA system needs to be very rugged, both electrically and mechanically, and it must be easy to set up and take down. Correct positioning of the speakers is critical to minimise the risk of acoustic feedback and to maximise audience coverage, and for all but the smallest systems, some form of on-stage monitoring or foldback is desirable. Note that in PA circles, the terms "monitoring" and "foldback" are generally interchangeable.

A foldback system may be considered as an independent sound system, comprising power amplifiers and speakers, running from a foldback (pre-fade send) output on the mixing console. Foldback is needed because, with a well-designed PA system, the majority of the sound is projected towards the audience, which may leave the performers struggling to hear

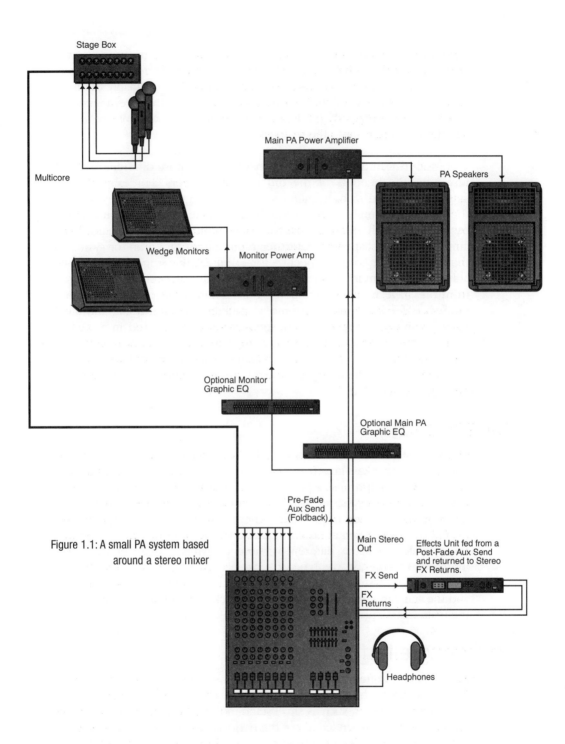

Stage Box

Multicore

Main PA Power Amplifier

PA Speakers

Wedge Monitors

Monitor Power Amp

Optional Monitor
Graphic EQ

Optional Main PA
Graphic EQ

Pre-Fade
Aux Send
(Foldback)

Main Stereo
Out

Effects Unit fed from a
Post-Fade Aux Send
and returned to Stereo
FX Returns.

FX Send

FX
Returns

Headphones

Figure 1.1: A small PA system based
around a stereo mixer

themselves sing or play. An effective foldback system provides the performers with a suitable mix (which may be quite different to the front-of-house mix), to help them keep in time and in tune. Arguably the most important job of a small foldback system is to ensure that the singers can hear themselves properly, but in a larger system, it is commonplace also to add the instruments into the foldback mix.

More sophisticated PA mixers can provide two or more different foldback mixes for the benefits of the different performers. For example, the singers may need to hear each other more than anything else, whereas the bass player might need to hear the drummer and the drummer the bass player. Each different foldback mix requires a separate foldback amplifier and loudspeaker. A further requirement of a monitor system is that its coverage is quite specific; for example, the singer shouldn't be able to hear too much of the guitarist's monitor speakers, and the output from the stage monitors shouldn't get back into the performer's mics, otherwise feedback may become a problem. Conventional monitors usually comprise a two-way loudspeaker system mounted in a wedge-shaped cabinet which can be aimed upwards at the performer. If the monitor cabinet is placed in the dead zone of a cardioid or hypercardioid microphone, unwanted spill can be minimised. Naturally all these topics are covered later.

monitor quality

Monitor systems are often chosen on the basis of low price, but poor quality monitor loudspeakers greatly increase the chance of acoustic feedback and can seriously compromise a performance. Touring PA companies have very elaborate foldback systems, usually controlled by a separate engineer from a position at one side of the stage. These systems utilise special monitor mixing consoles which are quite separate to the front-of-house mixer and can provide numerous different versions of a mix over several different monitors. By contrast, the type of console used by a typical gigging band with their own system generally has to handle both the front-of-house mix and the stage monitor mix, so all the foldback mixing has to be done from the main mixing position.

monitoring alternatives

Stage monitors often take the form of floor-standing wedges containing a bass/mid driver, a horn tweeter and some form of crossover network, but there are alternatives, such as small stand-mounted loudspeakers, full-range speaker systems suspended above the performers, side-fills or sophisticated in-ear systems. Side-fills are similar to full-range PA loudspeakers, but they are positioned at either side of the stage, facing the performers.

In-ear monitoring systems use specially designed miniature earpieces to provide the performers with a stereo foldback mix, usually via a radio link to avoid cabling, and the benefits include excellent isolation as well as keeping the stage clear. In-ear monitoring is increasing in popularity and will be more fully explained in the chapter on monitoring.

loudspeakers

PA loudspeakers vary in complexity from simple, passive two-way systems incorporating a 12-inch speaker and a horn tweeter, to huge multi-way, multi-cabinet active systems comprising separately amplified sub-bass, bass, mid-range and high frequency enclosures. The majority of small, portable systems are based around passive two-way designs, though advances in design technology means that smaller systems can now benefit from active crossovers, and some manufacturers are building the power amplifiers and active crossovers in to the speaker cabinets to save space and to make setting up easier. There's also a move towards moulded plastic speaker enclosures for smaller systems, and these are often much lighter than their wooden counterparts. However, their irregular shape can make them difficult to stack in a car or van.

power amplifiers

Power amplifiers should be chosen with enough power to deliver a clean signal at the full rated power of the loudspeakers. You might think that choosing smaller amplifiers will protect your speakers from damage in the case of overload, but the truth is the exact opposite. Once an amplifier is driven into distortion, it produces a lot of high frequency harmonics, which can fry a tweeter in seconds! As a rule, loudspeakers are quite tolerant of the occasional peak overload as long as the amplifier isn't driven into distortion.

Because most conventional power amplifiers are only around 60% efficient at best, they also generate a lot of heat when they are working hard, so adequate ventilation is essential. For every kilowatt of power fed to the speakers, something like 400 watts is lost as heat – and 400 watts is about the same heat as produced by half an electric fire bar! A rack system with an integral fan is recommended for systems rated above a kilowatt or so, and when mounting several amplifiers in one rack, unless they are individually fan-cooled, it is wise to leave a space between the amplifiers to allow some air flow.

Because modern power amplifiers can be very heavy, rear supports should be included when mounting them in a rack. Care should also be taken to shield the amplifiers' output terminals so that they can't be touched by accident as it is possible to get a significant electric shock from the speaker output of a high power amplifier while it is being used.

amplifier loading

To achieve the maximum power from an amplifier, it should be run into the lowest impedance load that it can safely handle, which is usually four ohms, though some larger professional models will drive loads of only two ohms. If an amplifier rated at 200 watts into four ohms is used with an eight-ohm speaker system, you may not be able to get more than 100 watts out of it. To get the right amplifier loading, it is helpful to understand series and parallel loudspeaker connection, which will be covered in the section on loudspeakers.

cabling

For very small PA systems, a combined mixer and amplifier can be very convenient, the main disadvantage being that long leads are often required to feed the loudspeakers. Separate mixers and amplifiers allow power amplifiers to be placed close to the loudspeakers, enabling shorter cable runs to be used. This is important, as all cable has a finite electrical resistance, and in loudspeaker applications where the speakers themselves have a low electrical resistance, you can end up in a situation where a significant part of your amplifier power is being wasted warming up the cables! Not only that, you'll find that if your cables are inadequately rated, the sound quality will suffer, noticeably at the bass end where sounds will be less well defined.

The rule is to use the heaviest gauge cable possible, and the higher the power of your system, the more carefully you need to consider the type of cable. Similarly, long cables need to be made from thicker cable than shorter leads to provide the same level of performance. Guitar leads or other coaxial screened cables are simply not suitable for use with any loudspeaker system, as their electrical resistance is too high, though having said that, if you have a very small system and you turn up at a gig having left your speaker leads at home, you can get by using a short instrument lead if you're prepared to accept compromised sound quality.

If the mixing console is remote from the stage, as it generally is if you're not mixing and playing at the same time, the microphone cables have to be routed to the mixer, and this is normally accomplished via a multicore cable, sometimes called a "snake", with a stage box housing mic sockets at one end and connectors for the mixing desk at the other. Essentially, a multicore cable comprises several individually screened cable pairs in one flexible outer sheath, and is usually rolled onto a drum or reel when not in use. Good multicore cable is, unfortunately, expensive, but there's no cheap alternative.

microphones

Dynamic cardioid or hypercardioid mics tend to be the mainstay of live sound because they are tough, they produce a hard-hitting sound, and their cardioid response helps prevent sound leakage and feedback. In addition to being used extensively for stage vocals, dynamic mics produce a punchy drum sound and are the preferred choice for miking basses and guitars. Capacitor microphones are more sensitive and may be used in some critical applications such as miking acoustic instruments, but in pop applications, the potential feedback problems associated with miking quiet instruments have led to the widespread use of transducer pickup systems, especially in the case of acoustic guitars and other stringed instruments. Brass instruments, on the other hand, tend to produce high levels of sound and can be miked with little difficulty.

The microphone techniques employed on stage often differ from those used in the studio because sound separation rather than absolute accuracy takes priority. For this reason, it may be necessary to use equalisation to improve a fundamentally imperfect sound whereas in the studio the first recourse would normally be to move or change the microphone.

microphone impedance

Live mixing consoles (other than some budget mixer amplifiers) are designed to work with balanced, low-impedance mics because they can be used with long lead lengths and have good immunity to interference. This is essential when stage-to-mixer multicores can be hundreds of feet long and where electronic lighting systems are being used; the latter can generate a significant amount of electromagnetic interference that can be picked up as a buzz or hum on inadequate sound systems.

Systems that use high impedance microphones are limited to cable lengths of around 10 feet or so before the sounds starts to lose level and become dull.

acoustic feedback

During a live performance, the microphones pick up not only the sounds of the instruments or singers at which they are directed, but also other sound from around the room, including the sound of the PA system itself – either directly or reflected from the room's surfaces. You might expect that a cardioid microphone with a unidirectional pickup pattern would reject sound from other directions, but in practice, the amount of isolation that can be achieved is quite limited. If too much of the sound from the PA speakers leaks back into the microphone, it will circulate around the system growing louder all the time, quickly building up into a continuous whine or whistle known as "feedback".

There is always one frequency that has slightly more gain than the others, either because of the EQ settings, the loudspeaker characteristics, the microphone characteristics or the room acoustics, which is why feedback results in a whistle of a specific pitch. If a system has unwanted peaks in its frequency response, then it will be especially susceptible to feedback at those frequencies – that's why it is very important that both the PA and stage monitor speakers have flat frequency responses. Various strategies for reducing feedback problems are discussed throughout the book.

Traditionally, glossaries are always at the ends of books, but because this introduction occupies its conventional place at the front of the book, it inevitably includes terminology that has not yet been explained. For that reason, I've including a mini glossary here to explain some of the more commonly used PA jargon.

introductory mini glossary

acoustic feedback:

A loud audible howling sound caused by the sound from a loudspeaker being picked up by a microphone and re-amplified.

active:

A circuit that uses electrical power to amplify or otherwise process signals.

back-line:

On stage instrument amplification.

audio spectrum:

That part of the sound spectrum audible to humans, generally held to range from around 20Hz to 20kHz.

bass bin:

A type of loudspeaker enclosure, usually quite large, designed to reproduce bass frequencies.

capacitor microphones:

Microphones that work on the principle of changing electrical capacitance between a stationary electrode and a moving, electrically conductive diaphragm. Capacitor microphones require power to polarise the capacitive pickup element and to run the internal preamplifier.

cardioid, also unidirectional:

A term usually applied to microphones meaning a microphone designed to pick sound over a relatively narrow angle.

coaxial screened cable:

Cable comprising one or more central wires surrounded by a conductive, tubular screen, usually fabricated from woven metal, metal foil or conductive plastic. This outer conductive sheath provides a path by which interference can be drained away to ground. An insulating outer sheath is normally fitted.

crossover:

An electrical or electronic circuit designed to route only high frequencies to the tweeters and low frequencies to the bass speakers or "woofers".

critical distance:

The distance from a loudspeaker where the direct sound is equal in intensity to the reverberant sound.

directivity:

Describes the angle of coverage of a loudspeaker system, both in the vertical and horizontal planes. Higher directivity equates to a narrower angle of coverage.

dynamic microphones:

Microphones that work on the principle of a coil of wire, attached to a thin diaphragm, moving in a magnetic field.

equalisation:

A specialised form of tone control.

flat frequency response:

Describes the performance of a system which applies an equal amount of gain to all frequencies. In practice, a small amount of deviation is permitted within specified limits.

foldback system:

See Stage Monitoring system.

horn tweeter:

A high frequency loudspeaker which has a horn-shaped flare fixed to the front in order to increase the acoustic efficiency and better control the directivity.

hypercardioid

Refers to a unidirectional or cardioid microphone with a very narrow pickup angle.

impedance:

A simplistic definition is a circuit's "resistance" to alternating current.

in-ear monitoring:

A relatively recent innovation that uses miniature, in-ear phones in place of on-stage monitor loudspeakers.

limiter:

A device that limits the maximum level of an audio signal to prevent it from exceeding a pre-defined level.

mix engineer:

Sound engineer experienced in mixing live music.

mixer/amplifier:

A single unit containing both mixer and power amplifier(s).

mixer:

A device which accepts a number of microphone or line-level signal sources and mixes them together to form a composite signal.

multicore cable:

The type of cable used to connect stage microphones to a remote mixer comprises several individually screened cable pairs within a single flexible outer sheath.

passive two-way:

Refers to a loudspeaker system comprising a bass driver and a tweeter fed from a passive crossover filter network comprising capacitors, resistors and inductors.

power amplifier:

Amplifier designed to accept line-level signal and boost them to the high power levels necessary to drive loudspeakers. Most (but not all) professional power amplifiers have two channels for stereo operation.

reverberant:

Describes a space or room where the natural level of reflected sound gives rise to a reverberation or multiple echo effect.

speaker columns:

Type of loudspeaker enclosure where the loudspeakers are arranged in a vertical row.

stage monitoring:

A system of amplifiers and loudspeakers that enables the performers on stage to hear what they are playing and singing.

spill:

Unwanted leakage of sound from loudspeakers or other sources into live microphones.

stage box:

A box fitted with multiple connectors, usually XLRs, enabling microphones to be fed into a multicore.

tweeter:

Type of loudspeaker specifically designed to reproduce high frequencies.

chapter 2

loudspeakers and enclosures

The loudspeaker is one of the main components of any PA system, and both the design of the speaker, and the enclosure in which it is mounted, have a profound effect on the performance of that system. As you will discover, there's more to good PA than simply buying a powerful speaker and bolting it into a box that happens to be the right size to fit into the back of your car!

The essential job of any loudspeaker is to convert electrical energy to acoustic energy as accurately and efficiently as possible. Though our hearing range decreases with age (and with exposure to damagingly high sound levels), the human hearing range is usually considered to be 20Hz to 20kHz, and this is generally accepted as being the frequency range over which a well designed audio system should operate. However, the laws of physics conspire to make it very difficult for a single loudspeaker to cover the entire audio spectrum with any degree of efficiency. Physically small loudspeakers may well be able to accurately cover the mid and high frequencies, but they're incapable of generating the high levels of bass and lower mid-range required in most PA applications. Even so, there are several commercially available compact designs that utilise multiple small speakers of modest power rating to produce full range systems suitable for use in smaller venues.

To reproduce low frequencies effectively where we may be dealing with wavelengths of 40 feet or longer, it is necessary to move a lot of air, which is why conventional bass speakers have larger diameters than high-frequency or mid-range speakers. Another general rule is that larger diameter drivers tend to require larger cabinets, which partly explains why bass enclosures tend to be large and heavy.

While large-diameter loudspeakers can be designed to reproduce low frequencies quite effectively, their high-moving mass and large physical dimensions make them relatively poor at reproducing higher frequencies, so in most practical systems, the audio range is shared between speakers of

CORNWALL COLLEGE
LIBRARY

different sizes so that each can handle the section of the audio spectrum with which it is most comfortable. To this end, some circuitry needs to be added in order to route the required part of the audio spectrum to the appropriate speakers. This is called a crossover.

introducing crossovers

A crossover is used to send just the relevant part of the audio spectrum to each speaker, and depending on the size of the system, the spectrum may be divided into two or more frequency bands. The simplest type of crossover comprises passive filtering circuitry and it is usually built into the speaker cabinet. Electrically, the passive crossover comes between the power amplifier and the speakers. In a two-way system, the bass is handled by a low-frequency driver, also known as a woofer, and the treble by a high-frequency driver or tweeter. In larger systems, there may be one or more additional speakers handling the mid-range, and these are called mid-range drivers.

Before looking more closely at how these various loudspeakers work together, it is useful to examine the mechanics of their operation as this provides clues to their strengths and limitations.

drivers

A chassis loudspeaker without a box or cabinet is called a driver, and virtually all drivers used in PA systems work on the same electric motor principle established during the formative years of audio engineering. Designs have been improved over the years, and new materials have been developed, but the basic principle remains the same.

The familiar "cone" loudspeaker comprises a stiff cone of doped paper or synthetic material suspended in a rigid cage or chassis by means of a flexible surround, as shown in Figure 2.1. The narrow end of the cone is fixed onto a parallel-sided tube, or former, onto which is wound a coil of thin wire, and the coil is positioned in a slot between the poles of a powerful magnet. Whenever a current is passed through the coil, a force is set up between it and the magnet, causing the cone of the driver to move either backwards or forwards from its neutral position, depending on the polarity of the electric current. This is exactly the same principle as an electric motor, except the motion developed is linear rather than rotational. If the electric current passed through the coil is an audio signal, then sound is produced from the cone.

The driver is fed from the output of a power amplifier, whose job it is to amplify (make larger) the small audio signal from a mixing desk or other

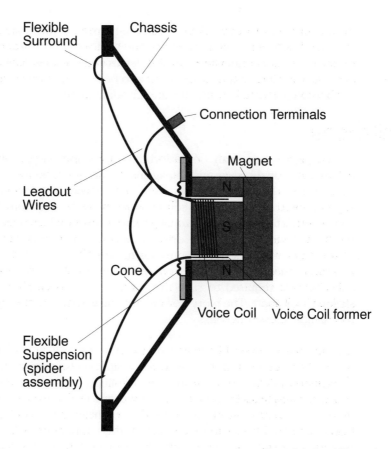

Figure 2.1: Cone driver schematic

source. A dynamic microphone works in almost the exact opposite way to a loudspeaker, so what happens in practice is that the tiny movements of the microphone diaphragm are recreated on a much larger scale by the loudspeaker cone.

driver distortion

From Figure 2.1, it is evident that the cone can only move so far before it reaches a physical limit, where either the suspension will permit no more travel or the voice coil will be driven out of the gap. As the cone approaches these limits, its movement becomes more restricted with the result that the physical movement of the cone is no longer exactly proportional to the electrical input. The result is distortion, where distortion is defined as any difference between the input signal and the output signal other than in amplitude (level). In reality, all systems distort to some extent, but providing the amount of distortion is kept small, the human hearing system perceives the sound as being accurate or clean. Audible levels of distortion result in a fuzzy or unclear sound where musical details and vocal intelligibility tend to become lost. Note that distortion will also occur if the original audio signal has become distorted during the amplification process.

limitations

A loudspeaker cone can only reproduce the input signal faithfully if it behaves as a rigid piston pushing against the air – if it bends or vibrates in other ways, distortion will result as any unwanted vibrations will be superimposed on the wanted sound. Much research goes into cone shape and materials to reduce distortion, but some distortion is inevitable. After all, the basic principle of a cone driver is very crude and all the movement comes from magnetic forces pushing against the voice coil. This places enormous mechanical stresses on the components, and very advanced adhesives are required to stop the speaker cone assembly from literally shaking itself apart. The more power handling is required, the greater these mechanical stresses become.

Another major physical limitation on the power handling of a loudspeaker is the heat generated in the voice coil. Loudspeakers are relatively inefficient devices, so most of the amplifier power fed into them is converted into heat. Because any voice coil has an electrical impedance, the more power that's put in, the more the coil heats up, and if more heat is being generated than can be dissipated, the temperature will continue to increase and the coil will eventually burn out. Before burnout occurs, however, the increased temperature of the voice coil and magnet system will reduce the loudspeaker's efficiency – a phenomenon known as power compression. It is important to be aware of power compression, otherwise when the system loses power through getting too hot, there's a temptation to feed in even more power to compensate. As you might expect, this can lead to driver failure. For this reason, high-power loudspeakers need to be designed with cooling very much in mind, and in recent years, several imaginative solutions have been implemented, including PA drivers with heavy cast spokes in front of the cone.

The main obstacle to cooling is that the voice coil is mounted on a lightweight tubular former within an air gap, so there's no easy way to conduct the heat away. Most heat is lost by radiation into the magnet and chassis metalwork, but some high-frequency devices use a liquid to fill the air gap, the most common being Ferrofluid. Ferrofluid comprises a colloidal suspension of magnetic material in a lubricating liquid and can help conduct heat away from the coil.

bass drivers

A driver required to deliver high levels of bass needs to have a relatively large diameter, but the larger the cone, the more rigid it has to be to prevent bending or deforming under load, and that in turn results in a heavier cone assembly. The mass of a large-diameter voice coil capable of handling the high powers encountered in PA bass applications is also significant. Simple mechanics tells us that when we try to accelerate a large mass, it requires far more energy than accelerating a small mass. The faster you try to move the cone, the higher the inertial resistance to that movement, and in audio terms, this means the higher the frequency, the harder the cone is to move. This is one reason why large bass drivers cannot faithfully reproduce high frequencies.

Another reason why large bass drivers can't reproduce high frequencies effectively is their diameter. If you imagine an 18-inch diameter bass driver that has, somehow, been built with an infinitely light, infinitely rigid cone and an infinitely powerful magnetic motor, it might seem that it should be able to function as a high-frequency driver. However, even if these impossible criteria were achievable, the driver performance would still be compromised by its very geometry. The diameter of the cone would simply be too large compared with the wavelengths of the high-frequency sounds being reproduced, and while this doesn't affect the ability of the driver to project sound forward, consider what happens if you move slightly to one side.

Referring to Figure 2.2, it can be appreciated that sound originating from the side of the cone nearest you will reach your ears before sound from the further side, and the same is true of all the points in between. The result is phase cancellation, and the further you move away from the main axis of the loudspeaker, the more serious this becomes. The practical outcome is that large-diameter drivers tend to concentrate their high-frequency output into a relatively narrow beam, whereas lower frequencies are propagated with a much wider dispersion angle. The higher the frequency, the more serious this "beaming" effect, which not only prevents the system from providing an even audience coverage, it also invites feedback as it is highly likely that a reflection from one of these tightly beamed, high-frequency sounds will find its way back into a stage microphone.

cone breakup

Yet another problem occurs at high frequencies because the cone of the driver ceases to behave as a perfect piston – it starts to vibrate or break up. The term "loudspeaker breakup" describes the way the cone assembly

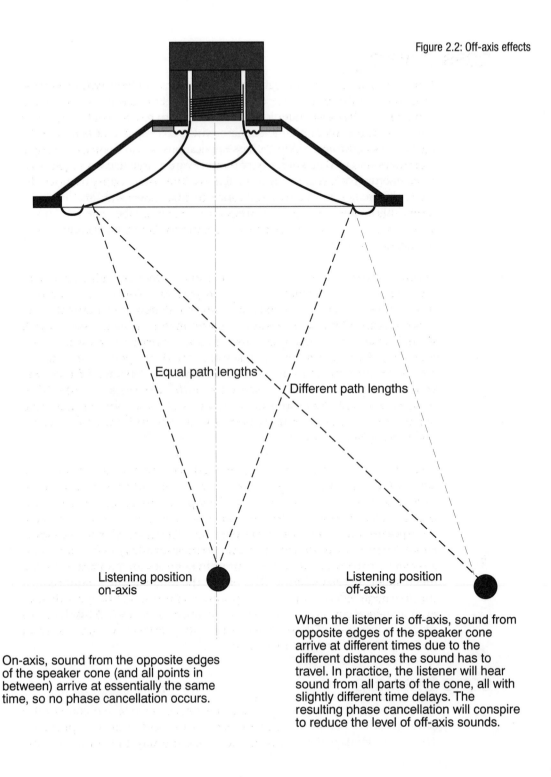

Figure 2.2: Off-axis effects

Equal path lengths

Different path lengths

Listening position
on-axis

Listening position
off-axis

On-axis, sound from the opposite edges
of the speaker cone (and all points in
between) arrive at essentially the same
time, so no phase cancellation occurs.

When the listener is off-axis, sound from
opposite edges of the speaker cone
arrive at different times due to the
different distances the sound has to
travel. In practice, the listener will hear
sound from all parts of the cone, all with
slightly different time delays. The
resulting phase cancellation will conspire
to reduce the level of off-axis sounds.

vibrates or ripples under load and does not imply mechanical failure. Indeed, guitar speakers are designed to break up in certain ways so as to produce a characteristic sound coloration. Some hi-fi speakers use complex damping or bracing to minimise distortion due to cone breakup, but this in turn tends to increase the mass of the cone resulting in a further decrease in efficiency. In PA applications, high efficiency is important, not just to minimise the amplifier power needed, but perhaps more importantly, to minimise the amount of power dissipated as heat inside the loudspeaker drivers. The trick is to design a driver where there are no significant breakup problems within the frequency range that the driver will be expected to handle.

mid-range and beyond

As you may have inferred from the previous section, the usual solution to driver beaming problems is to use progressively smaller diameter loudspeakers to handle the higher frequencies. In other words, mid-range drivers are smaller than bass drivers, while high-frequency drivers are even smaller still.

Mid-range drivers are usually cone drivers, similar in construction to bass drivers, but physically smaller, and they may be mounted in a different type of cabinet or enclosure. High-frequency drivers, on the other hand, need to be so small that the direct radiating area may be only one or two square inches, and while this is fine for domestic hi-fi applications, such a driver would be incapable of providing the level necessary for live sound. Unfortunately, you can't simply mount a dozen or so dome tweeters on the front of a cabinet because then you get the same phase cancellation problems you'd get with a large-diameter, single driver.

In a properly designed PA system, each high-frequency speaker radiates into its own section of space producing minimum overlap with other high-frequency drivers in other cabinets – that's one of the reasons speaker cabinets are arrayed at an angle to each other. Having ruled out hi-fi-style dome tweeters for high-power PA use, there is some constructional similarity between a hi-fi tweeter and a PA high-frequency driver, so it's worth looking at how hi-fi speakers are put together.

Hi-fi tweeters often employ small, dome-shaped diaphragms in place of cones, and these may be fabricated from a variety of materials including plastic, treated fabric and even metals such as aluminium or titanium. The diaphragm is driven by a voice coil arrangement similar to that employed in the cone loudspeaker, although the distance of travel is very much smaller.

horn-loaded tweeters

In PA applications, horn-loaded tweeters are almost always used because of their higher efficiency. These comprise a compression driver, not unlike an industrial grade hi-fi tweeter, feeding into a flared horn. Using a horn has two main advantages, firstly in that it significantly increases acoustic efficiency by matching the driver to the air in the room more efficiently (think of it as an acoustic gearbox), and secondly, the horn shape controls the directivity or angle of coverage of the sound, enabling it to be focused more precisely. If you can control the output from a tweeter to concentrate it into a narrow angle, then it's reasonable to assume that you'd get a higher sound level than from spreading the same amount of sound energy over a wider angle. This also makes it easier to "array" multiple cabinets at slightly different angles so as to cover a wider overall area without allowing the tweeter coverage to overlap significantly. Figure 2.3 shows both a conventional, direct radiating tweeter and a compression-driven horn.

It's also possible to feed a single horn from two or more compression drivers by using a kind of Y manifold shape at the rear of the horn, a technique sometimes used where very high power levels are needed. A more recent development is the constant directivity horn, where the profile of the horn is designed to prevent the lower end of the high frequency spectrum from being radiated over too wide an angle (with a non-constant directivity system, the dispersion angle narrows as the frequency increases). This artificial tailoring of the directivity tends to make the very top end of the high-frequency band too quiet when compared with the lower end (because it's being spread out over a larger angle), so some filtering has to be introduced in the crossover circuitry to compensate. This subject will be covered in more depth later.

Horns are also often employed to increase the efficiency, and to control the directivity, of mid-range drivers, but because of the larger dimensions of the horn required to handle the longer wavelengths, it will probably be built from wood, glass fibre or rigid foam.

more about crossovers

We've established that bass driver cones move relatively slowly, but over quite large distances, whereas high-frequency driver diaphragms move over a more limited distance but more quickly. High-frequency drivers, therefore, have to be protected from potentially damaging low-frequency signals outside their range. Similarly, bass and mid drivers must be prevented from receiving frequencies higher than they are designed to reproduce, not

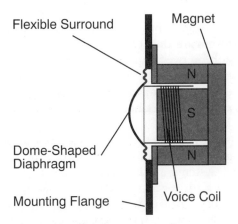

Flexible Surround

Magnet

Dome-Shaped Diaphragm

Mounting Flange

Voice Coil

Direct Radiating Dome Tweeter

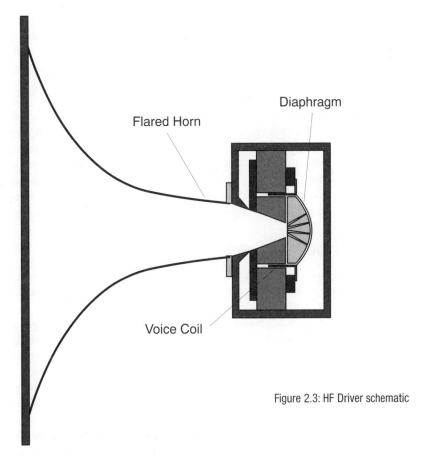

Diaphragm

Flared Horn

Voice Coil

Figure 2.3: HF Driver schematic

Compression Driver with Horn

because they will be damaged, but to prevent high-frequency beaming. Furthermore, most drivers are only capable of producing a flat frequency response and low distortion over a specific part of the audio spectrum, so feeding a driver with frequencies it was never designed to handle will seriously compromise the quality and accuracy of the overall sound. That's why the crossover is such an important part of the system.

At its simplest, a crossover is a series of passive electrical filters, comprising resistors, capacitors and inductive coils wired between the amplifier output and the drivers. Such systems are invariably located inside the speaker cabinets themselves. In a three-way speaker system comprising bass, mid and tweeter units, the bass speaker would be fed via a so-called low-pass filter – a filter that only allows through frequencies below a certain limit. This ensures that the bass speaker never has to deal with frequencies higher than those it was designed to reproduce.

A mid-range speaker has both upper and lower limits of safe operation, so it has to be fed by both high- and low-pass filters to ensure that it receives only mid-range frequencies. Too low frequencies will cause damage and distortion whereas high frequencies will again result in beaming and coloration.

High-frequency drivers are fed via a high-pass filter to ensure they receive frequencies only above a certain limit, so it's important to select bass, mid and high drivers that overlap slightly in terms of the frequency ranges they can cover. Figure 2.4 shows how the three crossover bands are arranged so that one filter slopes away as the next one rises, ensuring a smooth transition from one driver to the next.

passive crossovers

The type of crossover described is known as a passive crossover, because the only circuitry needed comprises passive filters. Such designs are generally reliable and cost-effective, but they are best suited only to relatively low power applications. Some of the amplifier power is absorbed by the passive crossover circuit, resulting in a loss of efficiency, and unless all three drivers are equally efficient at turning electrical energy into acoustic energy (most unlikely), the more efficient drivers have to be fed with attenuated or reduced signals to bring them down to the level of the least efficient driver in the system. In other words, you have to deliberately waste power to get a flat frequency response across the audio spectrum. An accurate system must have a flat frequency response – which simply means that all frequencies within the audio range are treated equally, rather than some being amplified more more than others.

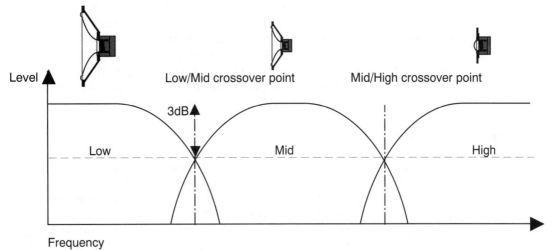

Figure 2.4: Three-way crossover characteristic

crossover slopes

Because of the restrictions of passive circuitry, the filter characteristic of a passive crossover can't be made particularly steep without wasting power and using a lot of expensive components. A filter doesn't simply block all frequencies beyond its cutoff point but rather has a sloping response that reduces frequencies beyond the cutoff point by so many dBs per octave. The more dBs per octave, the sharper the response of the filter is said to be. Simple passive filters usually have slopes of six or 12dB per octave, and in practical terms, this means that the drivers still receive significant amounts of power outside their ideal range. For example, with a 6dB per octave filter, the signal voltage is only halved for every octave you go beyond the cutoff point, whereas a 24dB per octave filter will reduce the signal to one sixteenth of the original for each octave beyond the cutoff frequency.

As well as making sure each driver covers only its designated frequency range, a steep filter also minimises the area of overlap between drivers handling adjacent frequency bands. This is usually desirable, because a wide overlap can lead to phase problems as both drivers struggle to deliver a slightly different version of what's going on in the crossover's overlap region.

active crossovers

PA as we now know it was revolutionised by the introduction of the active crossover, a device that allows an audio signal to be split into different frequency bands before the power amplifiers. This enables separate power amplifiers to be used to drive the bass, mid- and high-frequency loudspeakers, and because the filtering occurs before the amplifiers, no amplifier power is lost in the crossover circuit. Figure 2.5a shows a simple three-way passive crossover system, while in 2.5b, the same three-way speaker system is driven from an active crossover system feeding separate power amplifiers.

active advantages

Because the active crossover circuits deal with low level audio signals rather than the massive amounts of power needed to drive loudspeakers, the filters can be built using active electronic circuitry, permitting much greater flexibility and precision in design. What's more, the system performance is no longer restricted by the driver with the least efficiency as the amplifier powers and gains can be optimised by providing more power to less efficient speakers. This gives the designers far more flexibility when selecting drive units for use in a system, and the ability to design steeper filters helps minimise the amount of "out of band" signal that each driver receives.

Active crossovers considerably reduce the risk of driver damage, because an overload in one part of the audio spectrum won't necessarily cause an overload in the other areas. With typical pop music programme material, the energy at the bass end of the spectrum far exceeds that at the high end, and in a passive system, this can pose a danger to the tweeters. Imagine what happens when something like a dance record is played too loud so that the amplifier is driven into clipping distortion. Every time a loud bass note or drum beat is played, the amplifier clips, producing square waves rich in high-frequency harmonics. These pass through the crossover in just the same way as legitimate high frequency signals, so they reach the tweeter. If these artificially-generated harmonics are high enough in level and long enough in duration, they may cause mechanical damage, or result in voice coil burnout through overheating.

Looking at the same scenario in an active system where the crossover comes before the amplifiers, an overload at the bass end will be confined to the bass amplifier. The mid-range drivers and tweeters still receive clean signals from their own amplifiers. Crossovers will be covered in more detail in the chapter covering signal processors.

driver abuse

As explained earlier, a loudspeaker has both mechanical and thermal limits beyond which damage occurs. A loudspeaker cone (or tweeter diaphragm) can only move a finite distance before it reaches the physical limits of the

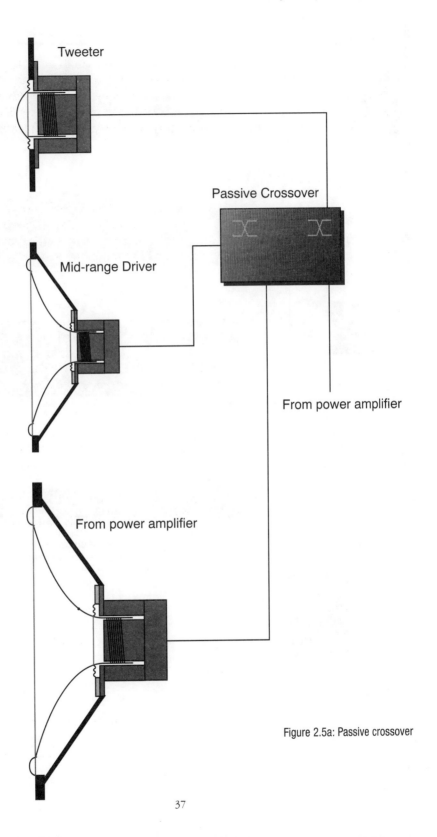

Tweeter

Passive Crossover

Mid-range Driver

From power amplifier

From power amplifier

Figure 2.5a: Passive crossover

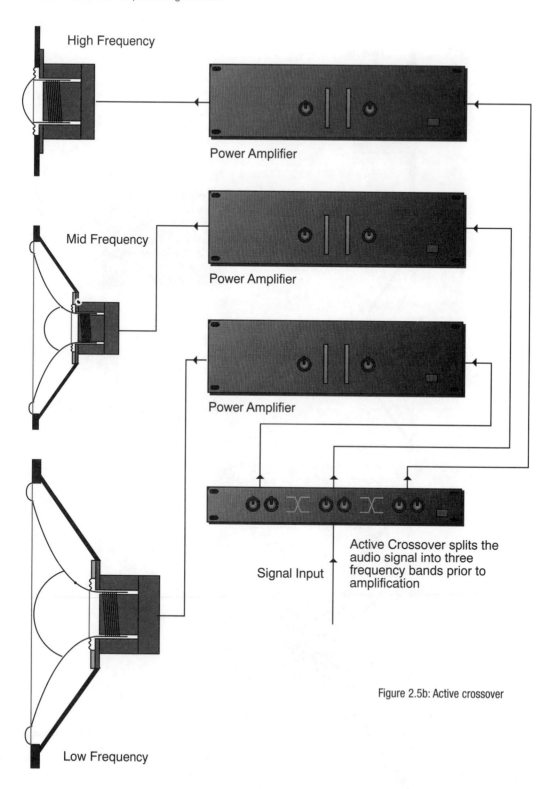

High Frequency

Power Amplifier

Mid Frequency

Power Amplifier

Power Amplifier

Signal Input

Active Crossover splits the audio signal into three frequency bands prior to amplification

Figure 2.5b: Active crossover

Low Frequency

suspension system, and the voice coil – the outer edge of a loudspeaker cone is attached to a cast or pressed metal chassis via a flexible surround designed to hold the cone central while impeding its movement as little as possible. The voice coil assembly at the narrow end of the cone is centred by means of a flexible corrugated surround, known as a spider, and again the degree of movement is limited. If too much signal is applied to the loudspeaker, either the suspension will run out of travel or the voice coil will be driven out of the magnetic gap, and as the cone approaches these limits, the physical movement is no longer proportional to the electrical input because as the suspension becomes stretched, it produces a force opposing the cone's motion. Furthermore, as more of the voice coil is driven out of the magnetic gap, there is less magnetic flux available to drive the cone. The result is that louder sounds become compressed and progressively more distorted.

Ultimately, the speaker cone may be forced against the limits of the suspension system, sometimes referred to as "hitting the end stops". If this is allowed to continue for any length of time, damage is almost certain.

the effects of heat

Power compression is a feature of all moving coil loudspeakers, and heat is an inevitable bi-product of normal operation. However, excessive power being fed into a speaker continually will eventually result in the temperature of the voice coil rising beyond safe limits. The first symptom is usually significant power compression as the efficiency of the speaker drops, and if the power isn't reduced to safe limits, the temperature will continue to rise until the coil fails or the heat distorts the coil former to such an extent that it rubs on the sides of the magnetic gap. This produces a rattling, distorted sound that can only be cured by having the speaker re-coned. A similar result occurs if the coil becomes detached from the former due to adhesive failure. Eventually, complete failure occurs as the coil wire wears away on the side of the gap causing the speaker to go open circuit. Another potential mechanical weak spot is the speaker lead-out wires – the flexible conductors joining the moving coil to the stationary connector strip or terminal on the chassis. Excessive or violent cone excursions can cause these to break!

speaker power ratings

Most loudspeakers are rated on the assumption that the music fed into them will comprise both loud peaks and some quieter sections between, but the use of compressors and limiters reduces the dynamic range of the input considerably. By increasing the average signal level in this way, thermal problems are more likely, so published loudspeaker power ratings can't always be taken at face value.

Non-thermal related damage is most likely when the speaker is driven with a heavily-clipped signal from an underpowered amplifier. In effect, the speaker is trying to respond to a square wave and the voice coil assembly, as well as heating up, can quite literally shake itself apart. As a rule, speakers tolerate short periods of undistorted overload much better than prolonged periods of clipped input.

loudspeakers and loudness

The rated power of a loudspeaker tells you how much electrical power the speaker can handle, but it doesn't tell you how much acoustic power is produced – in other words, it doesn't tell you how much of the input power is converted into sound. Even the most efficient loudspeakers only convert a few per cent of the electrical input into sound, but there's quite a difference between the most efficient and least efficient speakers around. While cabinet design also affects efficiency to a huge extent, a chassis speaker should have a published rating that tells you how many dBs SPL you can expect from it at a distance of one metre when fed by a fixed level signal, usually one watt. These measurements are done on plane baffles (no horn loading), and provide a useful means of comparing speaker performance. Even then, the figures don't tell you the whole story because they only let you know how efficient the speaker is at low powers – they don't tell you anything about the severity of any power compression effects.

The maximum SPL the speaker can produce is a useful figure to know, but again, this can be misleading as the figures are sometimes calculated rather than measured, and often take no account of power compression. It's often better to buy a speaker by reputation rather than relying entirely on what the spec sheet says.

loudspeaker enclosures

Loudspeakers are of little use without an enclosure or cabinet, and the reason is fairly evident when you consider what would happen if you tried to use a loudspeaker driver on its own as shown in Figure 2.6. Whenever a loudspeaker cone moves forward it compresses the air directly in front of it, while the pressure of the air behind the cone is reduced. When it moves back, the opposite happens. In the absence of an enclosure, there's nothing to prevent the high-pressure air in front of the cone from simply flowing around the edge of the speaker into the low-pressure region at the rear, which is exactly what happens. In other words, instead of the loudspeaker driver projecting acoustic energy into the room, much of the energy is wasted.

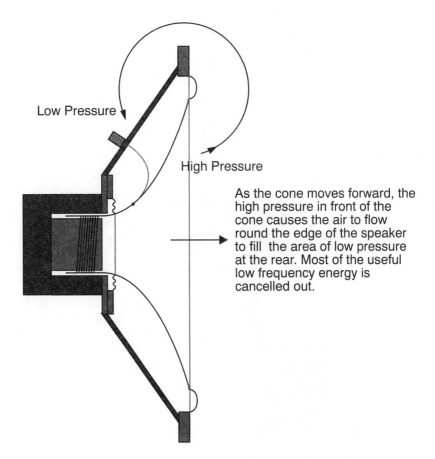

Low Pressure

High Pressure

As the cone moves forward, the high pressure in front of the cone causes the air to flow round the edge of the speaker to fill the area of low pressure at the rear. Most of the useful low frequency energy is cancelled out.

Figure 2.6: Performance of an unmounted driver

The lower the frequency, the more time the air has to move around the edge of the speaker before the cone changes direction, which means that at bass frequencies, virtually all the energy is wasted pumping air from the front of the driver to the back and vice versa. In effect, instead of generating a sound wave that can be projected into the room, the driver is creating a localised pocket of turbulence with radiated sound as a by-product.

What's needed is some way to stop the air leaking around the sides of the driver, and one way is to mount it on a baffle or board as shown in Figure 2.7. Here we see a driver mounted in a cutout at the centre of a large, flat plate or baffle. If the baffle is large enough compared to the wavelength of sound at low frequencies, the air won't have time to move from the front of the baffle to the back before the cone changes direction. As a result, the acoustic efficiency is much improved, especially at low frequencies, and if you look at the way the sound is projected, it's evident that this arrangement

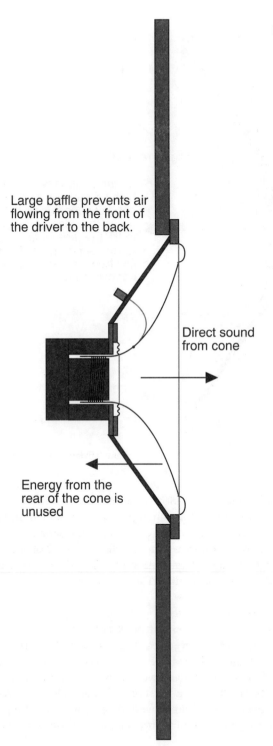

Figure 2.7: Driver fitted to flat baffle

Large baffle prevents air flowing from the front of the driver to the back.

Direct sound from cone

Energy from the rear of the cone is unused

works as a dipole. In other words, a lobe of sound is projected from the front of the baffle and an equal and opposite lobe is created at the rear, rather like a figure-of-eight mic in reverse. If you were to stand edge-on to the baffle, the front and rear sounds would cancel out leaving a dead spot.

Assuming that no sound actually passes through the baffle, all the sound generated by the rear of the speaker cone is wasted as far as the listener in front of the speaker is concerned. A huge baffle isn't a practical way of mounting loudspeakers for live performance, so the next logical step is to fold the baffle into the shape of a box, then use absorbent material inside the box to soak up the unwanted power from the rear of the driver. This is known as an "infinite baffle" enclosure, and now the sound only comes out of the front (though at low frequencies, sound tends to become almost omnidirectional because of the long wavelengths involved). However, the box may need to be fairly large to obtain a good low-frequency response, and because half of the sound energy is being absorbed inside the box, the acoustic efficiency is not great. Note that whenever the front of the cone couples directly with the air in the room rather than feeding a horn flare, it is known as a direct radiator.

pa enclosures

For PA applications, it is desirable to generate as much acoustic energy as possible from the smallest practical enclosure, and that usually means choosing an electrically efficient driver and mounting it in a so-called ported or vented enclosure, an example of which is shown in Figure 2.8. The type of enclosure shown is a direct radiating, ported system where the port causes the box to resonate at a certain frequency, much as a milk bottle will resonate at a fixed note when you blow over its neck. If the enclosure/port is tuned so that this "note" occurs where the natural bass end of the speaker starts to roll off, the bass response can usefully be extended downwards by making constructive use of the energy that is normally absorbed inside the box. The frequency of resonance depends on the volume of air inside the box, the dimensions of the port and the mechanical "springiness" of the loudspeaker.

internal reflections

A potential problem still exists due to sound reflecting from the internal walls of the enclosure, and to combat this, enclosures are often lined with acoustic wadding or other damping material. Large amounts of porous damping materials affect the speed of propagation of sound within the enclosure and thereby influence the frequency at which the enclosure resonates. Because of this, the effect of introducing damping material on

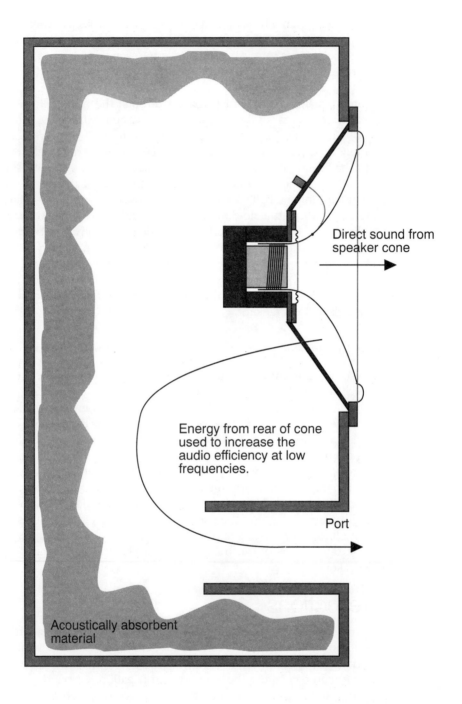

Direct sound from
speaker cone

Energy from rear of cone
used to increase the
audio efficiency at low
frequencies.

Port

Acoustically absorbent
material

Figure 2.8: Ported enclosure

enclosure tuning has to be considered at the design stage. Furthermore, care must be taken over the choice of enclosure parameters – tuning the enclosure to too narrow a frequency band will result in a peaky, coloured low-frequency response. It is also important not to feed frequencies into the speaker that are below the cutoff frequency of the cabinet as below the resonant frequency of the box, the air in the cabinet no longer loads the speaker cone. Without an air load to push against, the speaker cone will be free to move to the limits of its mechanical excursion where damage can occur.

As a general rule, the larger the driver diameter, the larger the volume of enclosure it will require, though enclosure size is also a function of the mechanical properties of the driver. You can't, for example, take an enclosure designed to work with one kind of 12-inch speaker and expect it to work properly with a different model of 12-inch speaker. As a consequence, both sealed box (infinite baffle) and ported enclosures designed for 15-inch and 18-inch drivers can be quite large.

horn loading

Even with the benefits of porting, direct radiating loudspeaker systems are relatively inefficient. Loudspeaker cones are very effective at pushing hard against small volumes of air, but what we actually want is to move a large volume of air over a shorter distance. Transferring energy from a moving driver cone to the air in an efficient manner involves mechanical matching, and a significant improvement in matching can be obtained by placing the driver at the end of an exponential horn as shown in Figure 2.9. Horns are regularly used to increase the efficiency of high-frequency units, but they may also be used with mid and bass drivers.

A horn can be thought of as the mechanical equivalent of a gearbox or a transformer, matching the capabilities of a power source to the needs of its load. Not only does a horn improve the mechanical coupling between the loudspeaker cone and the air, it also helps direct the sound over a narrower area, enabling designers to construct enclosures with well-defined coverage patterns. This is important when it comes to using multiple enclosures in an array, as the greatest efficiency is produced when the overlap between adjacent enclosures is kept to a minimum.

Short horns with square or rectangular section flares are often used in the design of mid-range PA loudspeakers, because they are simple to construct from plywood, and they can be used to help project sound to the back of a large auditorium. More advanced designs use materials such as fibreglass to create more precisely-shaped horns with no sharp corners.

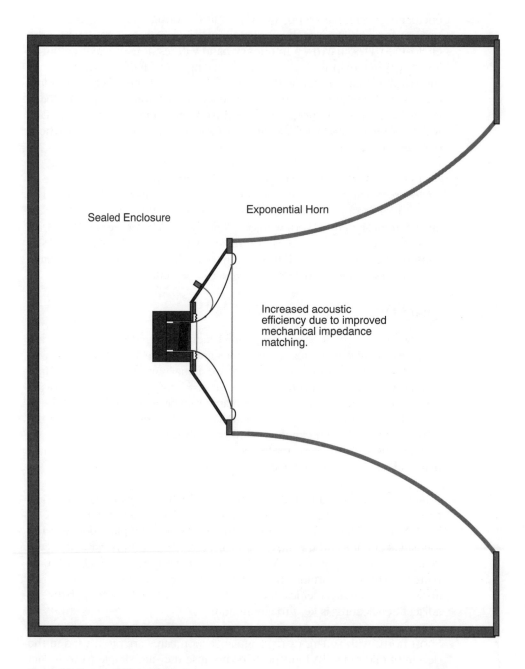

Sealed Enclosure

Exponential Horn

Increased acoustic
efficiency due to improved
mechanical impedance
matching.

Figure 2.9: Exponential horn loading

horn cut-off frequency

The shape and size of a horn dictates the frequency down to which it will work properly, and if frequencies below this cutoff frequency are fed to the driver, there is a real risk of driver damage, as the cone is no longer "loaded" by the air in the horn and will tend to move too far – rather like a car engine over-revving when the wheels spin. This is exactly the same problem as described relating to ported bass speaker cabinets being run below their cut-off frequency. For this reason, electronic high-pass filtering is generally included in the system to prevent potentially-damaging low frequencies from reaching the drivers.

For effective operation, the diameter of the horn mouth should – in theory – be at least a quarter of the wavelength of the lowest note to be reproduced. At 50Hz, for example, the wavelength is approximately 20ft, so a horn with a diameter of at least 5ft would be required. Furthermore, sub-bass systems capable of going down to 25Hz would need to be 10ft across – clearly impractical in a touring rig!

stacking the odds

Getting a sufficiently large horn aperture to work effectively at low frequencies might seem like an impossible requirement to meet, but it turns out that stacking several low-frequency boxes is acoustically equivalent to using one very large enclosure. In big concert systems, large numbers of enclosures are stacked to provide very efficient low-frequency arrays, but even in smaller systems, stacking two or four bass boxes together can produce a few welcome extra dBs of low end.

folded horns

The lower the frequency you want to work to, the larger the horn, but horn length also affects efficiency, and as a rule, the longer the horn, the better the mechanical matching of the driver to the air in the room. For deep bass frequencies, a straight horn would be impractically long and bulky, so enclosures are often designed which resemble a horn that has been folded to make it physically more compact. While internal reflections would compromise the performance of such a horn at high frequencies, the long wavelengths involved in reproducing deep bass mean that folded low-frequency horns can work almost as well as straight horns.

There are several methods of designing a folded horn bass enclosure, some of which make use of the sound from both sides of the cone, and some of which do not. Several variations of the folded horn are shown in Figure 2.10.

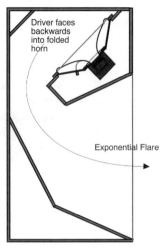

Folded Horn
"Scoop" Bin

Driver faces
backwards
into folded
horn

Exponential Flare

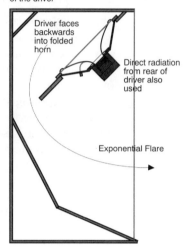

Folded Horn Bin
using both sides
of the driver

Driver faces
backwards
into folded
horn

Direct radiation
from rear of
driver also
used

Exponential Flare

Figure 2.10: Some folded horn enclosures

Alternative W-Bin

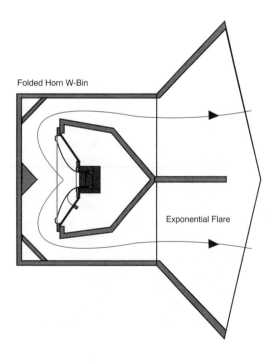

Folded Horn W-Bin

Exponential Flare

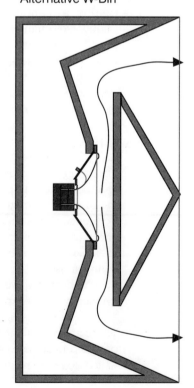

practical systems

During the seventies and early eighties, a typical concert PA was likely to comprise a stack of horn-loaded bass enclosures (or bins as they were often called), stacks of mid-range, horn-loaded boxes, and separate high-frequency, horn-loaded compression drivers perched on top. Constant directivity horns were also introduced during this period where specially calculated flare shapes were used to produce a relatively consistent directivity pattern over the entire frequency range covered by the horn. Constant directivity horns are currently very popular and it's also possible to design high-frequency horns for different degrees of directivity in the horizontal and vertical planes, thus enabling system designers to create enclosures that provide the optimum sound coverage when used in large arrays.

The various enclosures in such a PA system are fed from racks of high-power amplifiers, usually located close to the loudspeakers so as to minimise cable lengths. The amplifiers are fed from an active crossover and safety limiters are generally employed to prevent the power amplifiers from being driven into clipping. The problem with having all the enclosures separate is that setting up takes a long time, and a great deal of expertise is required to array the enclosures in the most effective way. There are also mechanical stability problems with multi-box systems, especially if the different elements come from different manufacturers.

integrated solutions

In recent years, we've moved away from totally separate boxes to integrated systems comprising multi-way, full-range enclosures supplemented by separate sub-bass enclosures. The full-range enclosures are often three-way affairs combining horn-loaded (or direct radiating in smaller systems), bass and mid-range units with compression-driven, high-frequency horns. As with older PA systems, these full-range enclosures are generally fed from separate power amplifier racks, but the crossover units are now more sophisticated, sometimes designed for specific loudspeaker systems. Most of these will include their own limiters, and the more sophisticated DSP-based "processor"-type electronic crossovers may combine the roles of crossover, protection limiting, system specific EQ, time alignment delay and other parameters.

Although the performance of a full-range enclosure can be impressive, most touring systems use separate sub-bass enclosures, which may be slung from the ceiling in carefully angled arrays along with the full-range cabinets, stacked beneath the stage, or stacked at the sides of the stage beneath the full-range enclosures. Talking about concert systems may seem a little esoteric if you're playing pub gigs using whatever you can get into the back of a car, but many of the modern gigging systems bear a strong resemblance to a scaled-down concert system. For example, compact full-range systems often include built-in power amps and active crossovers, and there are numerous systems on the market where compact full-range enclosures can be augmented by surprisingly compact sub-bass enclosures to produce concert sound in miniature at smaller venues. While concert systems are generally "flown" from overhead gantries or roof supports using steel cables and complicated mounting hardware, the majority of small gigging systems are either floor standing or rely on tripod stands to get the speakers up to the necessary height. In both cases, the overall system performance is significantly influenced by where the speakers are positioned.

compact pa

The type of PA system most commonly used for small gigs is built around compact two or three-way integrated speaker cabinets where the bass end is generally handled by a 12- or 15-inch loudspeaker and the high end by a horn-loaded compression driver. Three-way systems may have a direct radiating or horn-loaded mid-range driver, and both active and passive systems are to be found. For systems rated at a few hundred watts, passive crossovers provide a cost-effective and technically acceptable solution, and there's the advantage that only one power amplifier is required to drive the cabinet rather than the two or three needed for an active system.

The other down side of conventional active systems is the significant amount of wiring between the crossovers, power amps and speaker cabinets, which is probably one reason why more manufacturers are building integrated active systems, where the crossover and power amps are fitted inside the speaker cabinet. This would obviously be impractically heavy for most large concert systems, but for smaller systems, it provides a very convenient solution. A number of manufacturers have used moulded plastic cabinets to house such systems, often formed into complex shapes, but though these shapes may be acoustically beneficial, it can make stacking the cabinets difficult during transport.

multiple driver cabinets

Earlier in the chapter, I mentioned that some manufacturers use multiple identical, small-diameter drivers to produce compact full-range systems, the most well known probably being Bose (TM). If a driver is physically small in diameter, it can cover a very wide frequency range, which is why small radios, TV sets and similar domestic audio products can produce reasonable audio quality with just a single speaker. Advances in technology have

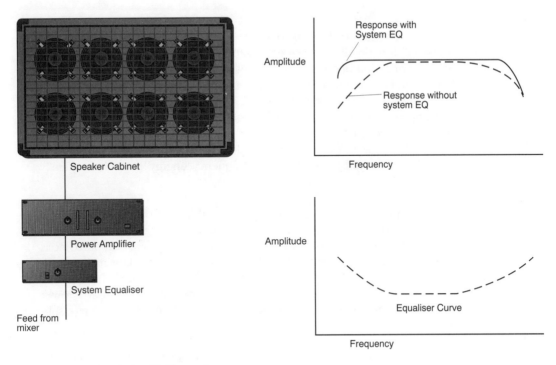

Figure 2.11: A typical multi-driver system

enabled small speakers to be made relatively powerful, and if they are used in multiples, they can handle sufficient power for small and medium-sized PA applications. The most well known speaker of this type is probably the Bose 802, which uses eight identical drivers in a ported, moulded plastic cabinet about the size of a TV set. Figure 2.11 shows a typical compact speaker enclosure with multiple identical drivers.

A properly designed driver of three or four inches in diameter can handle most of the audio spectrum, though the bass doesn't go so deep as with a dedicated bass bin, and the top end doesn't extend quite as high as a good tweeter. Even so, for general purpose applications, where the main requirement is to amplify vocals, they have adequate range and the results can be surprisingly good, not least because there's no crossover to introduce tonal artifacts at the crossover point.

small-driver limitations

Though small diameter cone speakers can cover a wide frequency range, the laws of physics dictate that they are still less efficient at the very low and very high ends of the audio spectrum than they are in the mid-range. Because the response of these small speakers tends to fall off at either end of the audio spectrum, it is possible to use equalisation to compensate by boosting the bass and high end of the spectrum while leaving the mid-range unchanged. Most manufacturers provide a dedicated, preset equaliser which is wired in between the mixer and power amplifier to provide a flatter overall response. This improves the perceived sound quality considerably, but because of the amount of boost added at the low and high ends of the spectrum, there's less headroom left at these extremes than there is in the mid-range. Most music has a limited amount of high-frequency energy, so high frequency overload is rarely a concern.

The main problem area is the bass end, and if 6dB of bass boost has been applied to make the response flat, it stands to reason that the bass will have 6dB less headroom compared with the mid-range. The practical outcome is that such speaker systems work best when they're handling mainly mid-range sound, such as vocals, where they combine reasonably high power with a clean sound. For full-range work, they need to be used at a lower overall level, or in combination with an active crossover and a separate sub-bass speaker.

Speaker enclosures built on the above principles can be made both light and compact, but apart from their lack of headroom at the bass end, they also tend to be less efficient than conventionally-designed speakers, the outcome of which is that you need a large power amplifier to drive them. At one time this could have been a problem, but these days, high-power amplifiers are less heavy and less expensive than used to be the case.

sub-bass in small systems

Where more bass power is needed, and where bass reproduction is required to extend to a lower frequency than compact PA cabinets can manage, the alternatives are either to move to larger full-range cabinets, or to add one or more sub-bass speakers to the existing compact system. Whether the existing speakers use multiple small-diameter drivers or conventional bass/mid drivers augmented by horns, the principle is the same. The small mid/high cabinets are often known as satellite systems as they are mounted separately to the larger sub-bass cabinets. Compact cabinets may be stand-mounted to provide optimum coverage, while the sub-bass speakers may be set up at floor level so as not to obstruct the audience's sight line. Because of the long wavelengths involved in bass reproduction, it is possible to site the bass speakers away from the mid/high boxes without compromising the sound in any significant way. Furthermore, because low frequencies are essentially omnidirectional, it's possible to use just a single mono sub-bass cabinet as part of a stereo system, without losing the stereo image.

sub-bass crossover

For such a system to work effectively, a crossover must be used to remove bass frequencies from the mid/high feed and to remove mid and high frequencies from the sub-bass feed. Depending on the system, this may be achieved using passive crossovers located within the sub-bass cabinet or by means of a two-way active crossover and separate power amplifiers. If only a single sub-bass speaker is to be used, it will be necessary to use an active crossover that can provide a mono sub-bass output, and of course additional amplification will be needed for any sub-bass enclosure fed from an active crossover.

In small venue situations where it is necessary to amplify a bass instrument or drum kit via the main PA, or to reproduce full-range backing tracks, the sub-bass speaker approach is very attractive. It also has the advantage that for very small venues, the system may be operated without the sub-bass speaker. Figure 2.12 shows a satellite system using separate sub-bass speakers with integral passive crossovers. Note that the sub-bass speakers have both inputs and outputs so that the satellite speakers can be fed from the integral passive crossover using a single short speaker cable.

sub-bass placement

Where possible, the sub-bass speaker or speakers should be placed in line with the main speakers to keep the two sound sources time aligned with each other. If the bass speaker is placed a long way forward of the satellite speakers, the bass energy will arrive before the rest of the sound, whereas placing the bass speakers too far back will cause the bass to be delayed. How serious this is depends on the room acoustics and on the crossover frequency being used, but it's good practice to keep the alignment as accurate as possible.

boundary effect

As a rule, mounting a sub-bass speaker on the floor, close to a solid wall will increase the amount of bass that can be obtained from the system because of something known as the boundary effect. At very low frequencies, a bass speaker sends sound in all directions, and if the cabinet is standing away from the wall, sound emitted from the rear of the cabinet will reflect from the wall, then combine with the sound coming from the front of the cabinet. Because of the time taken for the sound to reach the wall and bounce back again, it will be out of phase with the direct sound at some frequencies, causing cancellation. The outcome is a loss of energy at some frequencies, resulting in uneven bass.

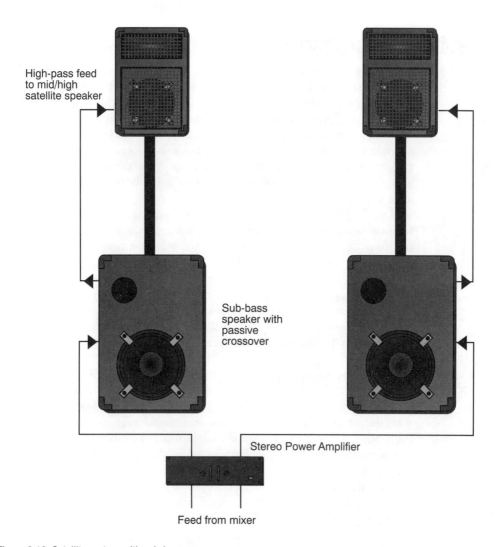

High-pass feed
to mid/high
satellite speaker

Sub-bass
speaker with
passive
crossover

Stereo Power Amplifier

Feed from mixer

Figure 2.12: Satellite system with sub-bass

By placing the bass speaker close to the wall, all the reflected sound from the rear of the cabinet will be very nearly in-phase with the sound from the front of the speaker, resulting in an overall increase in bass level. Standing sub-bass cabinets in corners can produce a further rise in bass efficiency as the sound now reflects from two walls, so if you're short on power and want to get physics on your side, this dodge can sometimes help squeeze a little more out of a marginal system.

enclosure practicalities

A theoretically ideal loudspeaker would radiate acoustic energy only from the cones of the drivers and the cabinet ports, but any physical structure can be made to vibrate, which in the case of loudspeaker enclosures, results in unwanted sound coloration. To minimise this unwelcome artifact, enclosures must be as rigid as possible, plus they may be acoustically damped.

Most commercial loudspeaker enclosures are built from plywood, though chipboard and MDF are sometimes used, as well as moulded plastic. Internal bracing is used to increase the rigidity of the enclosures and panel resonances may be reduced by applying bitumen damping panels to the inner surface. However, heavy panels are difficult to damp, so surface damping is most effective in lightweight, portable systems.

Many designers now believe that enclosure panel resonances are far less of a problem than sound reflections that occur inside the box, and that can interact with the rear of the driver cone to produce an audible effect on the sound. Such internal reflections may be minimised by the use of careful cabinet geometry and by the use of acoustically absorbent materials.

It is important that enclosures are airtight, otherwise the box tuning may change, and in any event, the sound of air being forced in and out through a small gap can be loud enough to be annoying. Joints are often caulked with silicone rubber and the drivers themselves are mounted using gaskets. If you're interested in building your own loudspeakers, many of the major driver manufacturers can provide enclosure construction details.

time alignment

In a multi-way loudspeaker system, it is imperative that the sound from the bass, mid and high frequency drivers reaches the audience at the same time, otherwise the phase integrity of the original signal will not be preserved and the sound will not appear natural. What's more, if the sound from, say, the mid-range driver is delayed very slightly with respect to that coming from the HF unit, problems will arise in the crossover region where the coverage of the two drivers overlaps. On-axis sounds will suffer cancellation, causing a fall in level, while at some angle off-axis, the signals will add in phase causing frequencies in the crossover region to be beamed downwards. Conversely, if the HF unit was "late", the sound would be beamed upwards, where the greater the timing discrepancy, the greater the angle of deviation.

Mounting all the drivers on the same baffle isn't a solution, because in reality, the effective sound source of a driver is in the vicinity of its voice coil, not its front rim, so the deeper the driver, the later the sound reaches the baffle line. What's more, fitting a horn to a driver also modifies its effective sound source position, and in hi-fi systems, you may have noticed designs with stepped baffles to help overcome this problem. By contrast, PA systems are more likely to rely on a crossover design that introduces the right amount of phase shift to bring the sources back into line. Either of these techniques go by the name "time alignment", and when multiple enclosures are used together, it's important that they are properly lined up for the same reason.

Sub-bass units operate at such a long wavelength that time alignment isn't so critical, but efforts should still be made to get the acoustic centres of the sub-bass enclosures somewhere near to those of the full-range cabinets.

microphone types

All microphones convert sound into electrical energy, but there are many different types of microphone, each designed to meet a specific range of needs. Part of the live sound engineer's job is to know which mic is best for use on drums, which for vocals, which for electric guitar and so on, so it helps enormously to have a basic knowledge of the different types and how they work.

In the recording studio, a wide range of dynamic and capacitor models are used, but in most live sound applications, especially at the lower end of the market, dynamic mics are the most commonly used because of their affordability and robust construction. However, there are capacitor and back-electret capacitor microphones that offer advantages in certain live applications, and some are surprisingly inexpensive.

However a microphone works, one common factor is that the mechanical vibration of the air must be transferred to a lightweight mechanical component such as a diaphragm in order for an electrical output to be generated. The alternating positive and negative air pressure changes which we perceive as sound are converted by the microphone into analogous positive and negative fluctuations in electrical current, but for that to happen accurately, the diaphragm has to be able to follow the airborne vibrations very precisely. No microphone is perfect, and indeed, modern physics tells us that nothing can be observed or measured without in some small way affecting the activity being measured. Certainly a microphone diaphragm constitutes a slight disturbance to the very sound it's trying to collect, but despite the implications of Heisenberg's uncertainty principle, a good modern microphone can still be extremely accurate.

low and high impedance

Microphones are generally available as either high-impedance, unbalanced or low-impedance, balanced. Virtually all serious audio equipment uses the low-impedance, balanced format, and if your microphone connects via a three-pin XLR at the base of the body, it almost certainly falls into this category. Conversely, a mic with a fixed cable terminating in a single-pole jack plug is

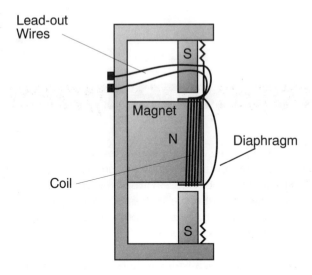

Figure 3.1: Dynamic mic schematic

likely to be high-impedance, unbalanced. High-impedance mics are used mainly with older all-in-one mixer amplifiers and cable lengths should not exceed 15 feet or so, otherwise the high end will suffer and interference may become a problem. Low-impedance, balanced microphones can be used with much longer cables with no loss of signal quality.

dynamic mics

Dynamic mics are relatively inexpensive, mechanically robust, and require no electrical power to operate, which makes them attractive for both recording and live sound applications. At the heart of the dynamic microphone is a rigid, lightweight diaphragm attached to a coil of extremely thin insulated wire. This coil is suspended within a magnetic field created by a permanent magnet, much like a loudspeaker voice coil, and as the diaphragm assembly moves backwards and forwards in response to sound, a small electrical current is generated. Because the diaphragm is vibrating in response to sound, the output signal is a direct electrical representation of that sound. The diaphragm, voice coil and magnetic assembly are incorporated into a single unit known as the microphone capsule, and this is usually visible if the protective wire basket is removed.

The sound energy has to move both the microphone's diaphragm and the coil attached to it, and because the assembly has a finite mass, the faster it tries to move, the more it is opposed by its own inertia. Inertia resists acceleration and a vibrating microphone diaphragm has to accelerate and decelerate many times each second as the diaphragm moves first one way and then the other. In practice, this places an upper frequency limit on dynamic mics of around 16kHz, though some ingenious designs have managed to push this figure a little higher. Figure 3.1 shows a typical dynamic mic schematic.

dynamic efficiency

A dynamic microphone is really a tiny electrical generator where the sound source provides the power, but because the amount of sound energy reaching the microphone is so small, the electrical output is also very limited and the signal needs to be amplified many times before it is large enough to be usable. The more you have to amplify a signal, the more electrical background noise is added, which means that when working with quiet or distant sound sources, dynamic microphones can run into noise problems. However, for most PA applications, the sound sources are relatively loud and usually quite close to the microphones.

ribbon mics

Ribbon microphones are rather specialised devices used mainly for classical recording, though they may occasionally be used for miking live classical performances. The ribbon mic is another form of dynamic microphone where the diaphragm and voice coil are replaced by a thin metal ribbon suspended in a magnetic field. The ribbon moves in response to sound energy and the resulting electrical signal is induced in the ribbon itself. The ribbon is lighter than the combined voice coil and diaphragm assembly of a conventional dynamic microphone, which makes it slightly better able to cope with high frequencies, though the main advantage of ribbon microphones is their smooth, detailed sound. In all types of dynamic microphone, it is common to find a transformer within the microphone body that matches the output of the capsule to the requirements of the mixer or preamp into which it will be fed.

capacitor mics

Capacitor microphones, sometimes known as condenser mics, are generally considered to be the most accurate type of microphone as they are able to respond to very high audio frequencies, and they can be made sensitive enough to work with quiet or more more distant sound sources. Capacitor mics don't have voice coils but they still need a diaphragm, though this can be made much thinner and lighter than that of a dynamic mic, which is why the mic can respond to high frequencies more effectively.

A typical capacitor mic diaphragm is just a few microns thick, often made from mylar or some other synthetic material with a thin metal coating to make it electrically conductive. This diaphragm forms one plate of a capacitor where the other is a fixed metal back-plate, parallel to, and close to the diaphragm. Holes are drilled in the back-plate to prevent air being trapped between the plate, and a high sensitivity amplifier is used to translate changes of electrical capacitance into an output signal. The result is a very sensitive microphone capable of resolving high frequency detail right up to the limits of human hearing and beyond.

capacitor principle

As the diaphragm vibrates, its distance from the stationary metal plate varies, and if a fixed electrical charge is applied between the diaphragm and the plate, a corresponding change in electrical voltage is produced. This voltage change is amplified by circuitry within the microphone, which is why capacitor microphones need electrical power to operate. Power is also needed to provide the electrical charge on the diaphragm as shown in Figure 3.2.

Capacitor mics can be built with different size diaphragms, diaphragms can be made of different materials, and the back-plate design also differs from one model to another. Small-diaphragm models can be designed to sound extremely accurate while the capsule resonance characteristics of large-diaphragm models often produce a warm, flattering sound, especially on vocals.

capacitor benefits

Capacitor mics are much more sensitive than dynamic models and they have a better high-end frequency response, but they're also more complicated. They need an internal preamplifier in order to amplify the signal from the capsule, and to provide impedance matching, which adds to the cost, and a source of power is needed to run the preamp and to sustain the electrical charge on the diaphragm. The most common source of microphone power is 48v phantom power, though tube-powered capacitor mics require special power supplies. Most consoles provide 48v phantom power, so operating capacitor microphones is straightforward.

While capacitor mics have many obvious technical benefits, they tend to be less rugged than dynamic models, and they are significantly more expensive. Performance may also suffer if condensation is allowed to settle on the

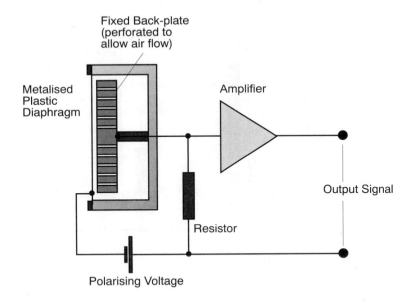

Figure 3.2: Capacitor mic schematic

diaphragm, so not all models are suitable for use in very humid environments. For this reason, capacitor mics tend only to be used in more specialised live performance situations, and where capacitor performance is required at a lower cost, the back-electret capacitor microphone is often used as an alternative.

electret mics

An electret mic is a type of capacitor microphone, but the diaphragm contains a permanent electrical charge sealed in an insulating material rather than relying on an external power source. Figure 3.3 shows an electret mic schematic.

A preamplifier is still required within the mic, but this may be battery-operated in some models, which is useful in situations where phantom power is not available. However, the majority of serious electret mics also operate from phantom power when required.

Originally, electret mics weren't particularly good performers, because a diaphragm that could hold a magnetic charge also tended to be much thicker and heavier than that on a true capacitor model. As with the dynamic mic,

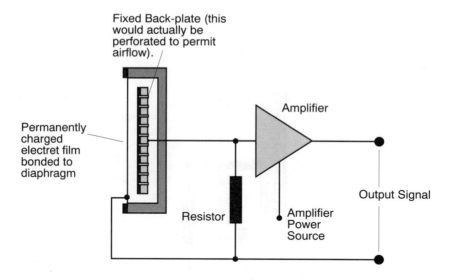

Fixed Back-plate (this would actually be perforated to permit airflow).

Permanently charged electret film bonded to diaphragm

Amplifier

Output Signal

Resistor

Amplifier Power Source

Figure 3.3: Electret mic schematic

increased mass results in limited sensitivity and a poor high-frequency response. Fortunately, a further refinement was destined to bring capacitor mic performance more into line with that of true capacitor models.

back-electret mics

Fixing the permanently charged material to the capsule's stationary back-plate rather than to the diaphragm was a simple concept that allowed electret mics to use the same lightweight diaphragms as conventional capacitor models – hence the term back-electret. The best of these can rival a conventional capacitor microphone in all aspects of performance, often at a much lower cost. In theory, the electrical charge on the capsule of an electret mic will leak away, which means the capsule will eventually need to be replaced, but the life expectancy is expected to be several decades. Figure 3.4 shows how a back-electret microphone works.

Back-electret mics are useful in live performance where sensitivity and high-frequency response are important. Dedicated hand-held vocal models can combine the ruggedness and punch of a dynamic model with the clearer top end of a capacitor model, though back-electrets are also suitable for use as drum overheads and for miking acoustic instruments.

polar patterns

The first microphones ever built were almost certainly omni-directional,

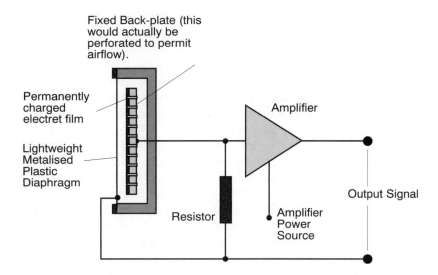

Figure 3.4: Back-electret mic schematic

which means that they pick up sound equally well from any direction. However, this isn't always ideal, and both live and in the studio, it's sometimes useful to have the microphone pick up sound more selectively. Nowadays, microphones are available with a wide range or directionality characteristics, the most common for live use being the cardioid or unidirectional polar pattern.

Dynamic and back-electret mics are available only with fixed pickup patterns, but some capacitor mics use a dual diaphragm capsule construction so that the polar pattern may be changed by means of a switch. These are most often found in studios, but some models are favoured for specific stage applications.

cardioid patterns

Unidirectional mics pick up sound from mainly one direction. The common name for this type of microphone is the "cardioid" because a graph of the microphone sensitivity at different angles is approximately heart-shaped. Because the cardioid microphone is most effective when picking up sounds from in front, it helps to exclude spill from back-line and stage monitors, and also helps reduce the risk of feedback. A very important fact to remember about cardioid mics is that they work by sensing the pressure difference or gradient between the front of the mic and a series of small holes or ports at the rear of the capsule. If you hold the mic too close to the basket, you risk obscuring these ports, which will affect the directional characteristics and increase the risk of feedback. Similarly, if a cardioid mic does start to feed back, don't try to cover the basket with your hands as this will usually make things worse.

Several versions of the cardioid pattern are available depending on whether the pickup angle needs to be narrow or wide. A wide cardioid pattern may be useful if the singer moves about relative to the mic, but the wider pattern inevitably means a little more spill from other sound sources. A narrower cardioid setting known as either "hypercardioid" or "supercardioid" can be produced for use in situations where spill from the sides is a potential problem, but the tradeoff here is that the mic is no longer most insensitive at the rear. If you refer to the polar pattern diagrams in Figure 4.5, you'll see that the hypercardioid mic has a significant area of rear sensitivity, and the least sensitive spot is around 45 degrees off the rear axis. It's important to know the characteristics of your microphones as stage monitors need to be placed in the microphone's "blind spot", which for a cardioid mic is directly behind, and for a hypercardioid mic, it's slightly to one side. This is discussed more fully in the chapter on monitoring.

proximity effect

All cardioid mics exhibit the so-called proximity effect, which results in a significant bass boost when the microphone is used with sound sources closer than a couple of inches. The closer you get to the mic, the more bass boost is created, and though the reason for this is rather complicated, it's essentially due to the relationship between the front of the mic and the rear ports that control directionality. Used creatively, the proximity effect can give the experienced vocalist a means to add tone and expression to a performance, but bad mic technique can result in a constantly changing tonality.

omni

Omni pattern mics pick up sound equally well in all directions, and because they don't rely on rear ports, their accuracy is generally better than on cardioid mics. On stage you run the risk of picking up unwanted sounds, and there may be a greater likelihood of feedback. However, the spill and feedback implications are not as different from those of a cardioid mic as you might imagine, so don't rule out omni mics for live work.

figure-of-eight

The figure-of-eight pattern mic is equally sensitive both front and back, but the sides are completely insensitive. The ribbon mic has a natural figure-of-eight pattern and they are particularly useful in certain stereo recording applications but are less used in live work. At one time, figure-of-eight mics

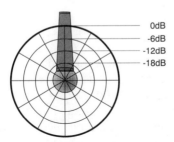

Omnidirectional:
Picks up sound
equally from all
directions. Used
mainly for recording or
for picking up multiple
sound sources at the
same time.

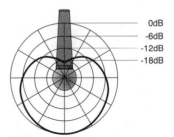

Cardioid:
Picks up sound
mainly from the front.
Least sensitive at the
rear, making it a
good choice for live
performance.

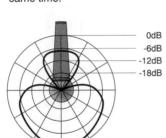

Hypercardioid:
Sometimes called a
Supercardioid, this is
a narrower pattern
than the cardioid,
but is more sensitive
to sounds coming
directly from behind.
Care should be
taken to place
monitors in the mic's
dead zone.

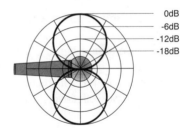

Figure-of-Eight:
This pattern picks up
sound both from the
front and rear of the
capsule, but not from
the sides. Note that
the capsule is
mounted sideways so
that the side of the
microphone, not the
end, must be aimed at
the sound source.

Figure 3.5: Main polar patterns

were popular for live backing vocalists because two singers could sing into opposite sides of the same mic – there's plenty of old Beatles footage to confirm this.

pzm or boundary mics

When a conventional microphone is placed within a room, it receives both direct and reflected sound, and because of phase differences caused by the longer path of the reflected sound, cancellation effects occur. The result is a so-called comb filtering effect where the frequency response of the combined direct and reflected sound shows a series of closely spaced peaks and troughs, rather like the teeth of a comb.

The "pressure zone" (PZM) or boundary microphone employs an omnidirectional capsule suspended in close proximity to a reflective back-plate or boundary so that the direct sound, and any sound reflected from the boundary, will arrive at the capsule at virtually the same instant, thus avoiding the phase differences that cause comb filtering. As a further benefit, because the reflected sound is essentially the same intensity as the direct sound, and in phase with it, a doubling of output level occurs.

Because sound is only picked up from one side of the boundary, the polar pattern is hemispherical rather than the usual spherical pattern of the conventional omni microphone. However, for the boundary to reflect low frequencies effectively (and to enable it to reject low frequencies from the rear), it must be at least three or four feet square. To achieve this, it is common practice to mount the microphone on either a rigid board, or to place it on a wall, floor or table. You'll often see a pair of PZMs fixed either side of a perspex sheet, suspended over the audience in concert halls, and these are used to provide a stereo pickup of nominally the same balance as the audience is hearing. Similar setups are also used to record audience sounds for inclusion on live albums. The edge of the perspex sheet is aimed towards the centre of the stage, and the main benefit of this type of microphone is its uncoloured sound due to the lack of undesirable comb filtering effects.

Though PZM mics aren't widely used at gigging band level, there are specific models designed to be used inside bass drums (where the drum shell works as the boundary), and fixing a pair to a wall provides a simple means of taping the gig in stereo if you're into doing post mortems afterwards!

frequency characteristics

A perfectly accurate mic would have a flat frequency response, but sometimes it's more helpful to use a mic with a deliberate degree of treble

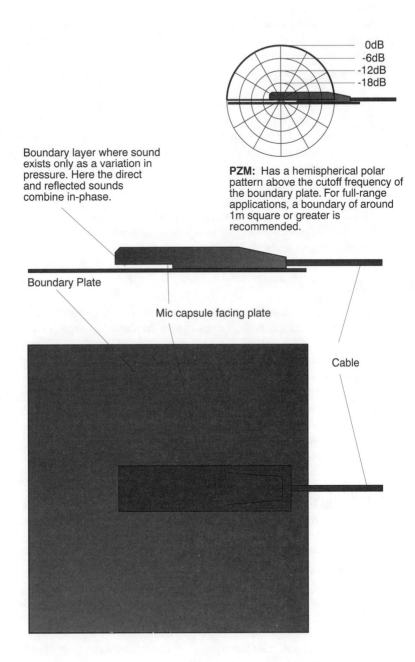

0dB
-6dB
-12dB
-18dB

Boundary layer where sound exists only as a variation in pressure. Here the direct and reflected sounds combine in-phase.

PZM: Has a hemispherical polar pattern above the cutoff frequency of the boundary plate. For full-range applications, a boundary of around 1m square or greater is recommended.

Boundary Plate

Mic capsule facing plate

Cable

Figure 3.6: PZM mic schematic

boost or presence to help vocals cut through a mix. This tailoring of the mic's response, often know as adding a "presence" peak, is one of the factors that accounts for why various models of mic sound different. Different voices benefit from mics with different characteristics, so it's best to pick a mic that works well with a specific vocalist, then stick to that mic.

Though dynamic mics don't have as good a frequency response as capacitor mics, they tend to deliver a punchier vocal sound that cuts through well in a live situation. They are also useful for drum miking, guitar amp miking and brass instruments. Dynamic mics with extended low frequency responses or pronounced bass boost characteristics are also made for kick drum and bass guitar amp miking.

Back-electret capacitor mics are good when you need a more open sound, and a lot of female cabaret singers find they work well. They're also good for acoustic instruments and drum overheads.

tube mics

All the early capacitor microphones had tube electronics, because semiconductors had not then been invented. Large external power supplies were needed to drive the tube circuitry, and the connecting cable was often thicker than a conventional mic lead. Nowadays, many studio engineers prefer the sound of tube microphones, claiming they provide a warmer, more natural sound. A number of microphone companies build modern equivalents of these classic microphones, though they tend to be costly and less rugged than their solid-state counterparts. Tube mics are rarely employed live other than by artists with big budgets and very specific requirements.

mic handling noise

Hand-held microphones invariably produce a degree of handling noise, and this varies from one model to another. The capsule within the microphone is invariably fixed via a resilient mount to try to isolate it from vibrations in the main body of the microphone, but low frequency noise still tends to get through to a greater or lesser extent. If you plug in a mic and rub your hands along the surface of the body, you'll probably hear a low rumbling noise, and the same is true if you tap the mic cable. A further source of noise is the cable itself, and with cheap or poorly designed mic leads, you may find that bending the cable produces audible crunching noises. If this is the case, change your cable for a better one.

A great deal of handling noise can be eliminated by good mic technique, which means gripping the mic firmly, and if cable-borne rumble is a problem, holding a loop of cable in the hand along with the microphone will help. Handling noise should not be confused with "popping", a problem that often occurs when B and P sounds are being pronounced. The severity of this problem varies from mic to mic and from singer to singer, but a useful tip for persistent poppers is to point the mic towards the chin and sing slightly over it rather than directly into it. In the recording studio, separate pop shields are placed between the singer and the mic, but on stage that isn't practical, so the solution is usually a combination of good mic technique, the right choice of microphone, and leaving the low-cut filter switched in on the desk's mic input.

To avoid mechanical noise being transmitted up the mic lead, stand-mounted mics can be "dressed" so that a loop of cable is taped to the stand just behind the mic. Low frequency noise can also be transmitted up the mic stand from the stage, so again, leaving the low-cut filter switched in is a good idea.

A further source of handling noise, which few people appreciate, is due to the inertia of the diaphragm when the mic is moved rapidly. Whenever you move a microphone, the diaphragm's inertia will make it try to stay where it is, so there will be a movement of the diaphragm relative to the magnetic assembly, resulting in a low frequency thump. This only happens when the mic is moved quickly and on the same axis as the diaphragm, but it pays to be aware of it.

direct injection

Whenever you use a microphone, the result is dependent on both the quality of the microphone and on the acoustic environment, which on stage is undesirably noisy. Most electronic musical instruments and electric guitars/basses can be recorded using a method known as DI or "direct injection". Direct inject involves plugging a signal from an electronic or electric musical instrument into a mixing system, often via some form of preamplifier or matching transformer. Because no microphone is used, there's no possibility of spill, and less risk of acoustic feedback, though acoustic guitars with pickups still tend to present some feedback problems.

DI is often used with bass and lead guitars (with suitable preamps or speaker simulators), synths, samplers, drum machines and so on, though in most cases, the performers will also have their own on-stage back-line amplification. Keyboards are nearly always DI'd into the main PA, even if the performer has a separate keyboard amplifier on stage. Guitarists, on the other hand, may either be miked or DI'd.

di box types

The DI box performs two important roles: it provides electrical ground isolation between input and output, and it matches the impedance of the source signal to that of the load. For example, a DI box with a high input impedance and a low output impedance may be used to match an electric guitar or bass to the input stage of a mixing console.

There are two main types of DI box – passive transformer and active electronics, though there are some active electronic electronic models that still include transformers. Transformer DI boxes require no power, while active DI boxes need either phantom power or batteries to operate.

transformer di boxes

The simple transformer DI box has the advantages of simplicity, excellent electrical isolation between the input and output, and lack of dependence on a power supply. Good quality transformers are expensive, which is why most low-cost DI boxes are active, but transformers used on their own are limited in what they can do by virtue of the fact that they are passive devices. If you discount any losses due to inefficiencies in the transformer, the total power going into a transformer equals the power coming out, and as power is equal to the current in amps multiplied by voltage, it's apparent that if you step up the voltage you end up with a lower current capability, whereas if you step up the current, the signal will be at a lower voltage. In the example where a transformer DI box is being used to match a guitar to a mixing desk, the output side of the transformer is required to deliver a higher current than the original signal source, which means a significant drop in signal voltage. To overcome this, the DI box needs to be plugged into a console mic input where sufficient gain is available to restore the signal level.

A transformer DI box usually comprises a single transformer with a centre-tapped secondary winding as shown in Figure 3.7. The centre tap provides the ground for the output signal, the ends of the winding providing the +ve and -ve balanced outputs. The unbalanced input is completely isolated from the output, but if it is necessary to connect the input ground to the output ground, this can be done by setting the ground lift switch to "off". Again, Figure 3.7 should make this clear. Note that the input connection has a "thru" socket so that the DI box can be used to take a feed from an

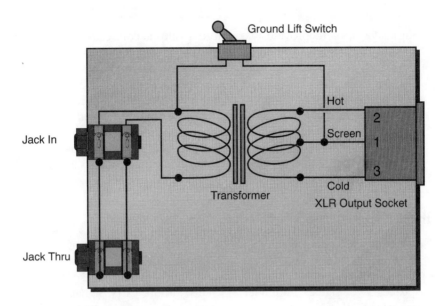

Figure 3.7: Transformer DI box

existing signal path without breaking the signal flow. A good example of this is keyboard amplification where the DI box can be inserted between the keyboard and its amplifier so as to permit an isolated feed to be sent to the FOH (front-of-house) mixing console. Note that a transformer DI box doesn't necessarily provide a foolproof safeguard against electric shock during fault conditions as it is possible that the connected cabling is grounded at some other point in the system.

active di boxes

Most active DI boxes dispense with transformers altogether, though as mentioned at the outset, some include both active components and a transformer output stage. A typical transformerless DI circuit uses a minimum of two op-amps to provide a "floating" output where the input and output signal grounds are independent, but unlike the transformer, there is no true galvanic isolation. As with transformer models, ground lift switches and thru sockets are generally fitted, but because active circuitry can produce power gain, the input to output voltage ratio can be made independent of the impedance ratio. To make the devices more flexible, it's not uncommon to include either switches, so the user can choose the output level, or to provide two different output connectors, one operating at line level and one at mic level.

Power for the active DI box can come from internal batteries, but most professional models can operate from phantom power, which means they must be plugged into a console mic input with the phantom power switched on. Many models can use either batteries or phantom power, and when phantom power is applied, it's usual for the internal battery to be automatically switched off so as to conserve power.

speaker di

Sometimes it is necessary to take a DI feed from the speaker output of an amplifier, and both active and transformer DI boxes can do this providing they are fitted with an input designed to accept speaker level signals. Amplifier speaker outputs carry signals of several tens of volts, while line level signals are usually only around a couple of volts, so it's evident that plugging a speaker signal into a line level input would overload it massively, probably to the point of causing damage. Mic inputs are designed to accept signals typically only a few thousandths of a volt in amplitude, so the effect of plugging in a speaker signal would be even more serious than in the case of the line input. DI boxes with speaker input jacks should also have thru connectors allowing the connection to the original speaker to be completed. The DI output signal will be at either mic or line level and can be fed down the stage multicore to the FOH mixing console in the usual way.

speaker simulators

Guitar amplifiers, and to some extent bass amplifiers, are special cases when it comes to DI as the final sound is dramatically affected by the character of the loudspeaker cabinet through which they are played. This is largely due to the restricted top end of a typical guitar or bass speaker, so when DI'ing from the speaker output of a guitar amplifier, some additional circuitry is necessary to emulate the frequency response of the speaker cabinet. This type of circuit is known as a speaker simulator, and both active and passive models are available. Passive models combine the elements of a DI box with those of a speaker simulator, but it must be stressed that unless the speaker simulator also contains a dummy loudspeaker load, it is necessary to connect a loudspeaker to the amplifier as well as the DI box. Failure to do so will leave the amplifier running into such a high

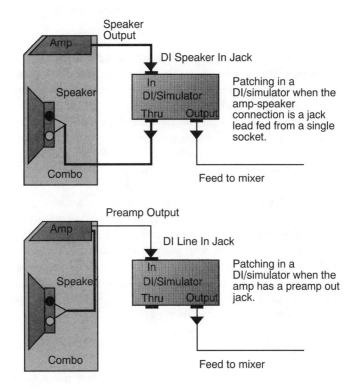

Figure 3.8: Guitar DI arrangement

impedance that it is effectively the same as having no load connected, and depending on the amplifier type, this could do serious damage to the output stage. Figure 3.8 shows a practical guitar DI arrangement.

di overview

DI boxes are essential pieces of equipment in live performance as they allow signals from either instruments, preamps or power amplifiers to be used as feeds to the FOH mixer, and because they have ground lift facilities, the risk of ground loop-induced hum is much reduced. In situations where an on-stage signal needs to be split to feed two amplifiers, for example within a stereo guitar rig, DI boxes can be very useful to provide isolation between the two amplifiers, again to prevent ground loop hum. Even relatively inexpensive DI boxes can work extremely well, so it's worth having at least one in your toolkit as they can solve problems that are very difficult to cure by other means.

radio mics

Just a few years ago, radio mics were either prohibitively expensive or they performed very poorly – and they were quite probably illegal too. But now you can buy a respectable VHF system for little more than the cost of a good wired mic. VHF radio mics comprise a mic with either an integrated transmitter, or a separate belt pack, and the signal is picked up by a remote receiver, the output of which feeds into the PA in the same way as a regular mic. Special transmitter packs are available for guitar use, and a separate receiver is needed for each radio mic used.

VHF (Very High Frequency) systems are relatively cheap, and in most countries they don't require a special licence, but the maximum number of VHF mics that can work together reliably is generally accepted to be no more than three. VHF systems are also more susceptible to interference from sources such as taxi radio systems. More VHF channels can be obtained by mixing regulated and deregulated frequencies, but then you have to pay for a licence to use the extra regulated channels, and you still have the problem of interference to worry about.

uhf systems

UHF (Ultra High Frequency) systems are rather more expensive than VHF, and they all have to be licensed, but you can run more channels at the same time and the immunity to radio frequency interference is significantly better than with VHF, especially in crowded suburban areas. A further benefit is that UHF antennae are very short so they don't interfere with clothing when body packs are being used.

If you only play the occasional weekend pub gig, then a VHF system is the more cost-effective solution, and the occasional taxi breakthrough probably isn't the end of the world. On the other hand, professionals need to be confident that taxis and radio hams won't be joining in on the choruses, and they often need more than three radio mics on the go at one time, in which case UHF is the best answer. UHF will enable you to use four or five mics maximum per band, and you can buy a licence for each of two available bands if you need to use both at once. Licensing regulations vary from country to country.

typical vhf system

A typical radio mic system will use battery-powered transmitters, though most will only accept conventional alkaline batteries, not rechargeables. Some models will work with rechargeables, but the unpredictable nature of nicad batteries means that you may run out mid show. Battery life is usually between one and two shows, though some systems claim up to 12 hours' use from a set of batteries.

If the mic has an integral transmitter, it will have a longer body than its wired counterpart, and the body will also include the battery compartment and a small stub aerial or antenna. Guitar versions have a guitar input jack on the body pack transmitter, generally accompanied by a sensitivity control. UHF systems are physically similar and are operated by the user in the same way.

receivers

VHF receivers come in either normal or diversity versions, and the diversity option is strongly recommended. Inside buildings, radio waves bounce off walls causing occasional dead spots where the signal from the mic doesn't reach the receiver with enough strength. A regular receiver has a single antenna, so if the signal fails, your sound is lost.

A true diversity system has two antennae and two receiver front ends, plus a circuit that constantly switches to the one with the stronger signal. Because the antennae are spaced apart, the chances are that one will always receive a viable signal, so the reliability of reception is much improved. Cheaper diversity systems use a switching matrix to select the stronger signal from one of two antennae, whereas a true diversity system has two separate receivers in the same box, each fed from its own antenna.

Most affordable radio systems now come as a half width, 1U package with removable antenna with power supplied via an external mains adaptor. I don't like external adaptors for live use, but sometimes you have no choice. Sometimes the antennae are removable and can be connected via cables to work up to several metres from the transmitter.

radio practicalities

Once the receiver is set to the same channel as the transmitter, it should be possible to switch on both the transmitter and receiver and test the system. LEDs or some other form of metering show the RF signal strength, and in the case of a diversity receiver , there should be LEDs to let you know which of the two receiver circuits is active. When setting up, don't put the receiver too close to walls, and try to arrange things so your normal playing position isn't less than around eight feet from the receiver, otherwise you may get problems caused by too much signal. A budget system should allow you to move 25 feet or more from the receiver in a typical venue, though metal framed buildings tend to reduce the useful range.

CORNWALL COLLEGE
LIBRARY

squelch

To prevent the signal from breaking up when you go out of range, there's usually a control known as "squelch", which sets a threshold so that the system will mute before the signal strength drops far enough to leave your audiences listening to amplified static. The best way to set up the squelch control is to switch off the transmitter so there's no signal, then increase the squelch level until the background hiss is just eliminated.

companders

All radio mics use some form of compander system to keep the background hiss to a minimum, and this works by compressing the signal at the mic end, then expanding it back to its original dynamic range at the receiver end. The use of a compander makes a huge difference to the perceived signal quality, but when the signal level is very low, you may occasionally hear the background noise increasing slightly during the signal, then falling back to silence during pauses. This is quite normal, and if the transmitter sensitivity controls are set so that you're getting as much level as possible without making the clip LED come on too often, you should rarely if ever hear it.

uk licensing

While VHF radio mics operating on deregulated frequencies don't need a licence, all UHF microphones must be licensed. To get yourself legal, you'll need to contact:

> Authority of Spectral Planning, ASP Frequency Management Ltd,
> Edgcott House,
> Lawn Hill,
> Edgcott,
> Aylesbury,
> Bucks HP12 0QW.

They'll send you a form RA 162 for general use or a form 161 for fixed installations. However, a multi-band licence only covers you for one of the two bands (low band or high band), so if you want to get more than four or five mics working together reliably, you'll need to spread your frequencies into both bands, which doubles the cost. A seven-day licence can be obtained for special events.

If you're touring the world, you're better off hiring systems locally, as the legal frequencies in one country may be illegal in another.

acoustic guitar amplification

Miking the acoustic guitar conventionally can be problematic because the high gains required invariably lead to feedback problems. A good pickup will often produce better results, but it won't eliminate the risk of feedback altogether. Sound picked up from the PA will cause the guitar body to vibrate, and these vibrations affect the strings, which in turn feed a signal back into the pickup. Above a certain level, the conditions for feedback reappear. You may have noticed that when an acoustic guitar feeds back, it does so at the resonant frequency of the wooden body whereas open vocal mics simply tend to squeal. Using a graphic equaliser to pull back the offending frequencies will allow you to work at a higher level, but the tone of the guitar is likely to be affected.

pickups and tone

Pickups will never give you quite the same sound as a microphone because the true sound of a guitar is a blend of the sound coming from the strings, from all parts of the body's surface, from the sound-hole and even from the neck. Magnetic pickups that clip across the sound-hole are convenient, but they tend to produce a sound that's more like a semi-acoustic electric guitar than a true acoustic. Piezo-electric transducers mounted in the bridge or stuck inside the body tend to produce a more authentic sound, but as they pick up vibrations from only one position, the sound won't be exactly the same as the guitar heard acoustically, so some additional EQ may be needed. The best of these systems mount beneath the bridge saddle and may be factory-fitted to certain new guitars.

piezo pickup matching

Piezo transducers have a very high impedance so a dedicated preamplifier is usually built into the guitar, sometimes with EQ controls as well as volume. Plugging a piezo pickup directly into a line input will produce a sub-standard sound because of both level and impedance mismatching.

Various manufacturers have developed dedicated acoustic guitar preamps that take the output from a guitar fitted with a pickup, then apply EQ specifically designed to suit the acoustic guitar. These can benefit guitars with inbuilt preamps, but most can also be used directly with a piezo pickup that doesn't have its own preamp. One control invariably adjusts the level of the body resonance sound, while another will balance the top and "zing" from the strings. With a little adjustment, it's usually possible to get close to the true acoustic sound of the instrument, though a lot will depend on the quality of the PA or guitar amplifier that's being used to amplify the instrument. Regular guitar amps don't have enough top end to reproduce the acoustic guitar sound with any accuracy. There may also be a variable frequency notch filter that can be used to pull back the most troublesome feedback frequency.

For performers where budgets allow, personal anti-feedback systems are very effective in controlling feedback when the guitar level needs to be relatively loud. These are covered in the chapter on effects and signal processing.

mixers

The main reason mixers can sometimes seem so complicated is that they're really a whole lot of different things parcelled up in one box, and the biggest mental leap comes when you move up from a simple mixer amp to a PA with a separate mixing console. Obviously a mixer has to mix signals together, but even a very basic live sound console will also include microphone preamps, line-level preamps, equalisers and probably some kind of routing system, not to mention systems for patching in external effects, processors and monitoring systems. Taken one at a time, these individual subsystems are really quite straightforward, so the best approach is to examine the various parts that make up a mixer, then see how they combine to form a typical live sound console.

mixing signals

Let's take the mixing part of the mixer first: you can't simply join audio cables together when you want to mix two or more signals, you need a special piece of circuitry called a mix amplifier; it's also necessary to be able to control the level of the individual inputs so that you can set a balance. The very simplest mixer that's of any practical use will comprise several inputs, each with their own level control, and one output, ideally with a master level control. Figure 4.1 shows this conceptually simple mixer as a block diagram. Each input, and the controls that follow it, is referred to as a channel. The outputs from each channel are simply mixed together and directed to the main console output.

On most consoles, the channels are set out as identical strips of controls arranged from left to right along the length of the mixer with channel 1 at the far left. The circuitry of the mixer will also need power, so there has to be some kind of power supply, and as you may have noticed already, some mixers have these built in whereas others have them in a separate rack unit or box. For live work, make sure that any external power supplies and their connecting cables are tough enough for the job.

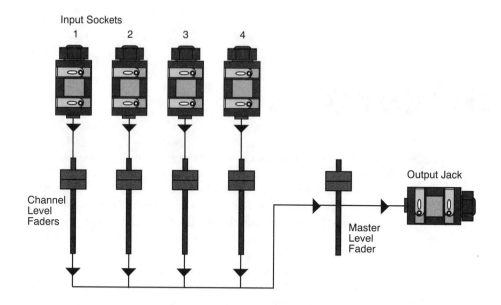

Figure 4.1: Simple four-channel, mono mixer

basic facilities

Few mixers are as simple as that illustrated in Figure 4.1 – even a budget mixer is likely to have stereo outputs, basic EQ on each channel, and possibly "aux" controls for sending signals to effects or for setting up a foldback mix. Move up a notch and you may find routing buttons that allow you to send channel signals to different outputs, not just a single mono out, but for the moment I'll stick with the basic mono mixer for simplicity.

Both mic and line signals can vary in level over quite a large range, which is why the input stage of a mixer includes a level or trim control. This often confuses newcomers to mixing as it isn't immediately obvious why a channel needs a level trim control at the input and another (the fader) at the end. The reason for this seeming extravagance is that the signal entering the mixer needs to be brought up to a level the channel circuitry can handle comfortably. Some professional mixers have separate gain controls for the mic and line level inputs, but most of the consoles found in small and medium-sized PA systems have a common level trim control and a switch to select between mic and line inputs. Correct adjustment of the input trim control is essential to produce the best signal-to-noise ratio without distortion, and this is known as optimising the gain structure.

gain structure

Like the human ear, all electronic circuitry has an optimum operating range – if the input is too quiet, we can't hear it properly above the background noise, and if it's too loud, it makes our ears hurt. If an electronic signal exceeds the level the mixer circuitry can accommodate, distortion will result, while if the signal falls too far below it, the amount of amplification required to bring it back up to a usable level will also make it noisy. Mixer circuitry is designed to work within a particular range of signal levels, usually between one and 10 volts or thereabouts. So-called line level signals are already within this range, such as the outputs from effects units, electronic instruments, tape machines and suchlike, but the signal produced by a microphone may measure only a few thousandths of a volt. Quite clearly, this is too small for the mixer circuitry to handle as it is, so we have to build in a mic preamp at the beginning of the channel, to get the signal up to strength before it is passed on to the rest of the channel circuitry. This microphone preamplifier may also be fitted with phantom power circuitry, which is necessary if you're using capacitor mics, non-battery back-electret mics, or DI boxes that require phantom powering. Gain structure is explained in greater depth in the chapter on technical stuff.

Because not all microphones produce the same level of output, and because the output level depends on how close and how loud the sound being recorded is, the microphone amplifier is equipped with a gain control to determine the amount of amplification applied to the signal. Usually the mic channel will have a mic/line switch to determine whether the input needs to go through the mic amp or not, and there'll also be two different types of input connector – an XLR for the mic, and a jack for the line. The simplest way to set the gain trim is to set the channel and output faders at their unity gain positions (the 0dB mark about three quarters of the way up), then feed in the loudest signal you're likely to encounter. Adjust the gain trim so the signal is just going into the red on the output meters and you're set. An alternative method using the console's PFL buttons (if fitted) will be described later in the chapter.

phantom power

All capacitor microphones need an electrical voltage to charge the capsule, while both capacitor and electret microphones use built-in preamplifiers which also need power. Because of their high current consumption, valve microphones require special power supply units, but the cost and fragility of these means they are seldom used live. The majority of capacitor and back-electret mics are designed to operate on phantom power as are many active DI boxes. Phantom power is a standardised microphone powering system which passes a DC current, from the mixer or mic preamp's phantom power supply, along the conductors of a balanced microphone cable. The standard phantom power supply voltage is 48v and is generated within the mixing console. If you're wondering about the name "phantom", it's because no additional wiring is needed to get the power from the console to the mic – it shares the same cables as the mic's output signal.

As long as a balanced microphone cable is used, it is necessary only to plug in the mic and turn on the phantom power supply. Dynamic mics do not require phantom power, but will still operate normally if phantom power is applied providing they are balanced and wired via a balanced cable. If you intend to use both dynamic and capacitor mics on the same gig with a console that has only global phantom power switching, it is vital to check that all cables are balanced and that all mics are internally wired for balanced operation. As a rule, if the mic body is fitted with a three-pin XLR socket, it is balanced.

WARNING Use of unbalanced cables or unbalanced mics with phantom power applied will compromise the sound and may damage the mics.

channel eq & fader

The next stage up from a mixer that has only level controls, is to add EQ or equalisation. This is simply a fancy name for tone controls, and at its simplest, there will be a high and a low knob, corresponding to the treble and bass knobs on a typical hi-fi. It's also as well to pick a mixer with an EQ bypass button, because if you don't need to use the EQ, the signal path will be a little cleaner if the EQ is switched right out of circuit. On more elaborate mixers, the EQ section may be a complex, multi-band affair offering sweep mid-range controls as well as high and low shelving filters. Equalisation is covered in depth towards the end of this chapter.

To make controlling the channel signal level easier, it's usual to fit a level fader rather than a rotary control, though some very small mixers still use knobs. Not only are faders nicer to use, they also provide an at-a-glance indication of which channels are turned up. You'll normally find the previously mentioned "unity gain" position about three quarters of the way up the slider, which signifies the signal leaving the channel is not being altered in level at all. If you pull the fader down from this point, the channel signal is attenuated (reduced in level), and above the unity gain point, more gain is being added. A typical desk will have around 10dB of extra gain available above the unity gain point.

on the buss

After leaving the fader, the channel signal is fed to the mix amplifier via a long piece of wire connecting all the channels. This is known as a mix buss, but because you might want to switch a channel off without having to change the fader setting, you'll usually find a switch called "on" or "mute", which isolates the channel from the mix buss when not required.

The mix buss carries the mixed signal from all active channels to the mix amplifier, but in order to control the overall level of the mixer's output, another level fader needs to be fitted after the mix amp. This "master level fader" sets the output level of the mixer, determining how much signal is sent to your power amplifiers or system processors.

stereo

For stereo, we need two signal paths, one to carry the left speaker signal and one to carry the right speaker signal. This is catered for by using two mix amplifiers fed by two mix busses, one mix amp feeding the left output and one the right. The channel signals are directed to these two outputs via a "pan" control, so moving the pan control from left to right changes the balance from being all on the left mix buss to being all on the right. In the centre position, both outputs receive the same amount of signal, so when the mixer is connected to a stereo amp and speaker system, the sound appears to be coming from directly between the two speakers. The pan control can be set at any position to make the sound appear to be coming from anywhere between the two speakers, but you have to remember that this is only true if the listener is right in the centre of the speakers, as you are when you listen to your hi-fi at home. The live sound world is a little less precise than the studio, so some stereo trickery make have to be foregone in order to give all members of the audience an acceptable mix. A point on terminology here; if you have a 12-input mixer with a stereo output, it is known as a "12 into two" configuration, sometimes seen on spec sheets as 12:2. That's because it has 12 inputs and two (left and right) outputs.

Figure 4.2 shows a basic stereo mixer schematic where the pan control is used to direct the channel signal between two mixing busses, often referred to in the singular as a stereo mix buss. Now we have two master faders, one for the left and one for the right signal, though some mixers

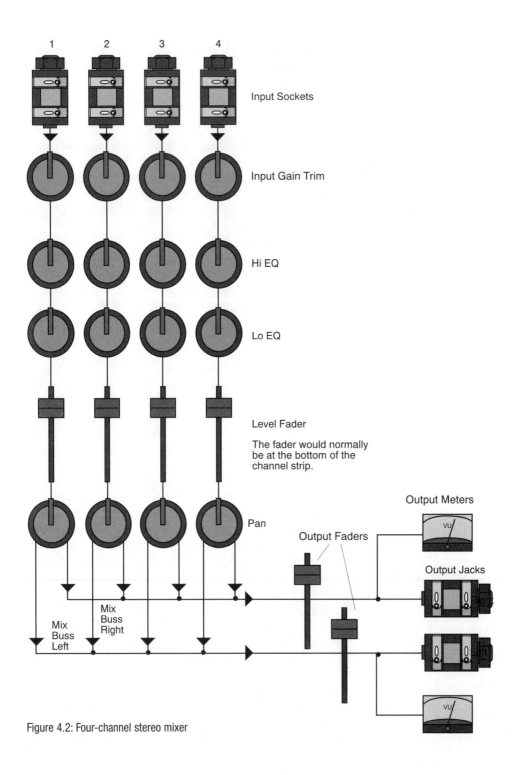

1   2   3   4

Input Sockets

Input Gain Trim

Hi EQ

Lo EQ

Level Fader

The fader would normally
be at the bottom of the
channel strip.

Output Meters

Pan

Output Faders

VU

Output Jacks

Right

Mix
Buss
Right

Mix
Buss
Left

Left

VU

Figure 4.2: Four-channel stereo mixer

use a ganged control with a single knob to save on cost and space. Figure 4.2 also shows a stereo level meter, which allows the user to monitor the output level of the mixer. This meter may be a moving-coil meter with a mechanical pointer or it could be a row of LEDs (Light Emitting Diodes) arranged in the form of a ladder.

So far I've described a very simple stereo mixer that allows several inputs to be mixed to stereo, but in most PA applications, we need to be able to add external effects, and to set up foldback mixes for the performers. That's where the "auxiliary" controls come in. Figure 4.3 shows a mixer with two aux controls fitted: aux 1 and aux 2.

pre-fade send

Aux 1 is effectively another level control feeding a mono mix buss feeding the aux 1 master level control and the aux 1 output socket. It is completely independent of the main mix, and as the signal feeding the aux 1 control is picked up before the channel fader, it is independent of any changes made to the channel fader setting. This type of aux is known as a pre-fade send, sometimes labelled "cue" or "foldback".

Any desired mono mix of all the channels can be set up using the aux 1 controls, and this will appear at the aux 1 master output under overall control of the aux 1 master level control. Because this mix is independent of the channel fader settings, it can be used to feed a stage monitor system with a mix that's quite different to the one being sent to the front-of-house PA system. Though only one pre-fade aux send is shown, larger consoles can have several of these, allowing a number of different foldback mixes to be set up. This way, different performers can have a monitor mix that is exactly to their liking without compromising the main stereo mix. For example, the drummer may want to hear more of the bass player, while the lead vocalists may prefer to hear more guitar and backing vocals.

effects sends

The second aux control, aux 2, picks up its signal after the channel fader (post-fader), so its level is affected by changes in the fader setting. This is what's required if aux 2 is being used to feed an effect, because, if the channel fader setting is changed, we want the balance of the effect and the original channel signal to remain the same. By using different settings of the aux 2 control on each channel, it is possible to send different amounts of each channel's signal to a single effects unit, such as a reverb processor, so all the channels can have different amounts of reverb

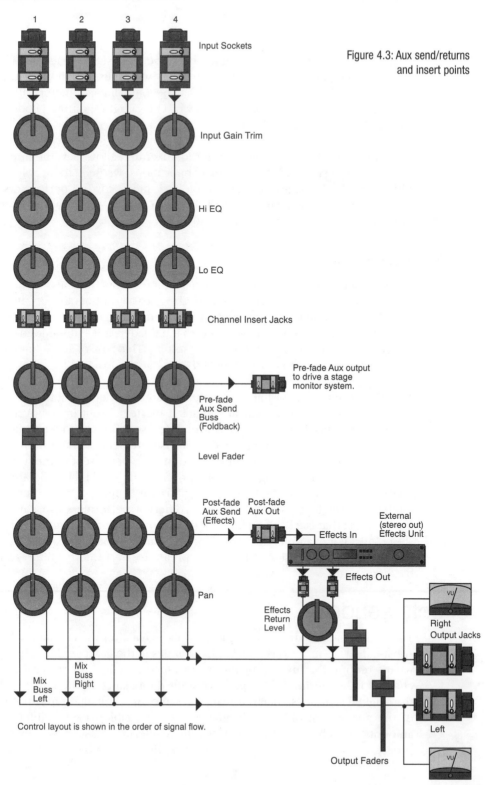

Figure 4.3: Aux send/returns
and insert points

Input Sockets

Input Gain Trim

Hi EQ

Lo EQ

Channel Insert Jacks

Pre-fade Aux output
to drive a stage
monitor system.

Pre-fade
Aux Send
Buss
(Foldback)

Level Fader

Post-fade   Post-fade
Aux Send   Aux Out
(Effects)

External
(stereo out)
Effects Unit

Effects In

Effects Out

Pan

Effects
Return
Level

Right
Output Jacks

Mix
Buss
Right

Mix
Buss
Left

Control layout is shown in the order of signal flow.

Left

Output Faders

86

added, even though only one reverb unit is connected. Post-fade aux sends are sometimes labelled "effect" or "FX". Again, a console can have any number of post-fade aux sends, enabling several different effects processors to be used at the same time.

Note: any effects unit connected via the aux system should be set up so that the effect balance is 100% effect, 0% original signal. All the original signal comes via the channel, so all we need to do is add pure effect.

effects returns

We have to get the output of the effects unit back into the mix somehow, which is where the console's returns come in. The outputs of the effect unit (they're nearly always stereo out) could be fed into the mixer via two spare input channels, but most mixers provide dedicated effects return inputs, also known as aux returns. These are basically input channels stripped down to their most basic form; they have no mic inputs, little or no EQ and few, if any, aux sends of their own. Normally they feed straight into the main stereo mix and are very often stereo, in which case you only need to tie up one aux return for each effect unit.

If you run out of dedicated returns, you can use spare pairs of input channels (panned hard left and right) as returns providing you ensure that the aux sends on these channels are turned down. If not, you may find that you're sending the signal round in a loop, which will cause an unpleasant howl or scream. The diagram in Figure 4.3 also shows an external effects unit connected to the stereo aux return; note the stereo return feeds the left and right stereo mix busses.

The controls shown in the schematic are arranged in order of signal flow, but for ergonomic reasons, manufacturers may not put them in the same physical positions on the mixer. On some models, the aux sends come before the EQ, while with others they come after the EQ section. Although the post-fade send is wired after the fader, the fader is invariably the bottom control on the channel strip.

insert points

What happens if you want to patch in a compressor to use on a single mixer channel? The answer is that you'd use a channel insert point, and again, even very basic mixers have insert jacks fitted, both on the channels and on the master stereo outputs. An insert point is really just a connector that allows the normal signal path to be interrupted and re-routed through an external device. On most mixers, the insert points are

TRS stereo jack sockets so that they can carry both the insert send and insert return signal down a single cable. You need a specially wired Y-lead or adaptor to be able to use them, and when no external device is plugged in, spring-loaded "normalising" contacts in the jack socket maintain the signal path through the channel. The stereo socket may be wired one of two ways, but the "ring send/tip return" system seems popular as it allows you to take a direct output from the channel without interrupting the signal flow simply by pushing a jack half way in.

Referring back to Figure 4.3 again, the insert points are depicted as jack sockets in the signal path. While it is permissible to connect any type of effect or signal processor via an insert point, only effects should be used via the aux system. In other words, delay, reverb, pitch shift, chorus and so on can all be connected either via inserts or aux sends, but processors such as EQ, compressors, gates and enhancers should only be connected via insert points unless you really know what you are doing and why.

multi-buss mixers

Simple "something into two" mixers are fine for small gigs and general purpose work and, if you have your own portable band PA, they're probably all you'll need, but more sophisticated consoles used for larger concerts, or as part of hire systems, tend to be much bigger and include multiple busses. The "bigger" part of the equation is usually down to more input channels, but additional facilities can also increase the size of the desk. A popular configuration for mid size systems is the eight-buss console, the term eight-buss meaning that the mixer has eight outputs in addition to the main stereo output. Bigger systems may have even more busses and more facilities, but for the sake of clarity, I'll stick with the eight-buss concept for the purposes of description.

Unlike the simple stereo console, any of the input channels of an eight-buss mixer may be routed to any of eight "group" outputs, or to the original stereo outputs, which still remain. In fact you could press down all the routing buttons and send your signal to all eight groups at the same time, but this wouldn't usually be a useful thing to do. If two or more channels are routed to the same output, they are mixed together under control of the channel faders, just as they are when you're routing to the main stereo outputs, and the pan control affects the balance of the signal between odd and even numbered busses. Each group has its own master fader to control the overall level of any signals routed to that particular group output, and the block diagram shown in Figure 4.4 should make this clear.

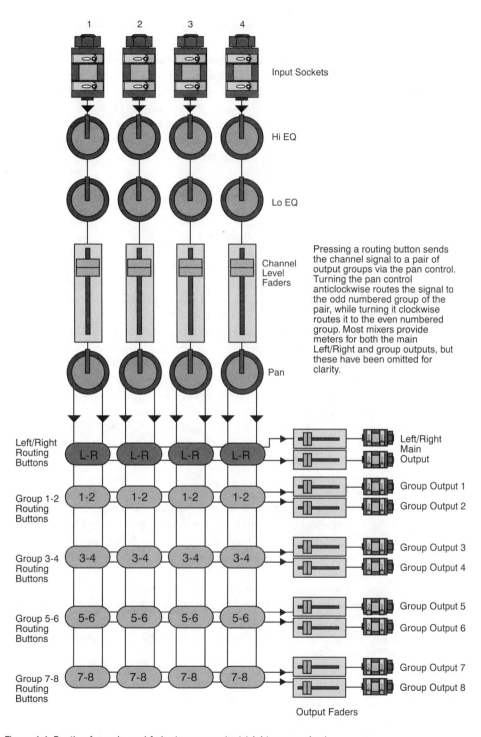

Pressing a routing button sends the channel signal to a pair of output groups via the pan control. Turning the pan control anticlockwise routes the signal to the odd numbered group of the pair, while turning it clockwise routes it to the even numbered group. Most mixers provide meters for both the main Left/Right and group outputs, but these have been omitted for clarity.

Figure 4.4: Routing from channel fader to group output (eight-group mixer)

In a live situation, these groups may be used to feed different sets of power amplifiers, and if you're really ambitious, you could set up speakers and power amps all around the room and use the busses to provide you with a surround sound mix. Group outputs are also often used to provide feeds to a multitrack tape recorder for the recording of live concerts. However, you're most likely to use the groups to provide control over submixes of logical groups of instruments, and this is possible because there's always a facility to let you route the group outputs into the main mix.

subgroups

A collection of input channels routed to the same group, or pair of groups, is said to form a "subgroup". Routing to one group would produce a mono subgroup while routing to an odd/even pair of groups and using the channel pan controls to position sounds would produce a stereo subgroup.

Creating subgroups in this way greatly simplifies mixing, as logical groups of instruments can be allocated their own subgroups, thus reducing the number of faders that need to be moved during the mix. Instead of moving lots of input channel faders, most of the mix can be carried out from a smaller number of group faders. Common examples are subgroups of drums, backing vocals and keyboards. If effects are to be added to these subgroups using the aux sends on the input channels, ensure that the effects returns are routed to the same subgroup, not to the stereo left-right mix, otherwise the effects level won't change as you adjust the group fader levels.

Subgrouping Example: imagine you have a drum kit that may have six or more mics on it – if you want to turn down the level of the whole kit from the input channels, that would mean adjusting six faders at the same time as well as trying to keep the balance between them consistent. However, if you route the drum mic channels not to the main left-right buss, but instead to busses 1-2, then route busses 1-2 into the main stereo mix, you'll find that the whole drum mix can be controlled using just the buss 1-2 faders. The reason for routing to two busses rather than one is to keep the mix in stereo, and the pan pot works as normal. Figure 4.5 shows the signal flow in this example.

routing

Routing input channels to specific groups or pairs of groups is accomplished by means of buttons located close to the fader of the

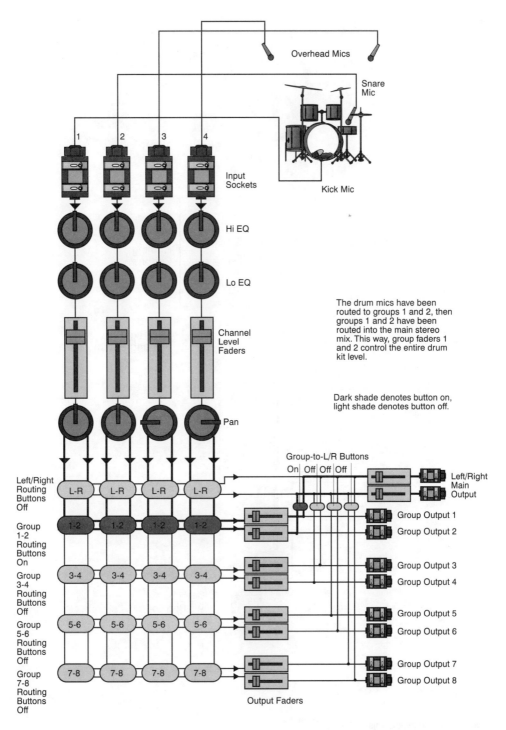

Overhead Mics

Snare Mic

1 2 3 4

Input Sockets

Kick Mic

Hi EQ

Lo EQ

Channel Level Faders

The drum mics have been routed to groups 1 and 2, then groups 1 and 2 have been routed into the main stereo mix. This way, group faders 1 and 2 control the entire drum kit level.

Dark shade denotes button on, light shade denotes button off.

Pan

Group-to-L/R Buttons
On Off Off Off

Left/Right Main Output

Left/Right Routing Buttons Off

L-R L-R L-R L-R

Group 1-2 Routing Buttons On

1-2 1-2 1-2 1-2

Group Output 1
Group Output 2

Group 3-4 Routing Buttons Off

3-4 3-4 3-4 3-4

Group Output 3
Group Output 4

Group 5-6 Routing Buttons Off

5-6 5-6 5-6 5-6

Group Output 5
Group Output 6

Group 7-8 Routing Buttons Off

7-8 7-8 7-8 7-8

Group Output 7
Group Output 8

Output Faders

Figure 4.5: Drum kit subgrouped via groups 1-2

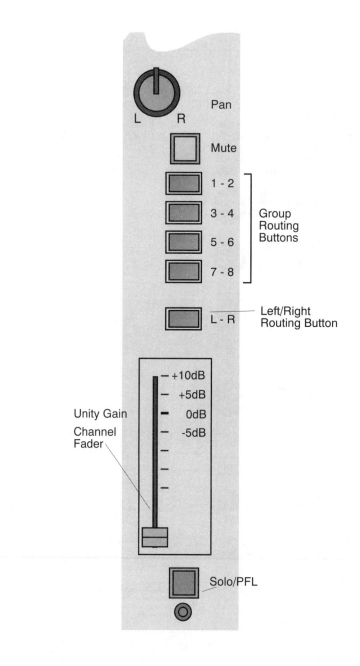

Figure 4.6: Routing buttons and busses

relevant input channel. On most desks, a single button handles the routing for a pair of groups, with the pan control being used to select between them. For example, if you want to route a channel to output group 2, you press the routing button marked 1-2, then turn the pan control fully clockwise. Turning it fully anticlockwise would send the signal to group 1, and leaving the pan in its centre position would send equal amounts of signal to both groups. On an eight-buss mixer, the layout would be: four routing buttons marked 1-2 3-4 5-6 7-8, with a further button marked L-R for routing the channel directly to the stereo mix. Figure 4.6 shows how the routing buttons are set out on a typical console.

mute, pfl and solo

Most mixers have "mute" buttons on their input channels so you can turn the channel off without having to pull the fader down and lose your settings. Operating mute also silences any post-fade aux (effects send) sends, though the pre-fade (foldback) sends are generally unaffected. On some consoles the Mute button is replaced by a channel "on" button, but the principle is the same. Because muting is an important feature, the majority of serious mixers have mute status LEDs or illuminated buttons.

Another feature that's especially valuable in a live situation is PFL, as it allows you to isolate certain channels, sends or returns in your headphone or monitor wedge mix without affecting the front-of-house mix or the performer's foldback mix. If you've lost a signal, or if there are strange buzzes or other noises in the mix, using the PFL button is usually the quickest way to track them down. The PFL button is usually found close to the mute button, though on some mixers, there may be a "solo" button instead. These two functions are similar, but not identical, and on larger consoles, there will be a global switch in the master section that allow the buttons to function either in PFL or solo mode. PFL/solo buttons may also be provided to monitor other important signal points in the mixer, such as group outputs, aux sends and returns. These switches are generally latching types, so there'll be a warning light by the switch and another master PFL lamp in the master section of the console.

PFL is short for "pre fade listen", a system that allows you to select any channel to be heard in isolation over the console's monitor outputs or headphone output. In PFL mode, the isolated signal is heard at a fixed level regardless of whether the channel fader is up, half up or completely off. That's because the signal is monitored in a part of the signal chain before the fader, hence the term pre fade listen – you're listening to the signal before it gets to the fader. When the PFL button is pressed, all the channels on which the PFL has not been pressed are excluded from the monitor mix and, at the same time, the signal level of the channel you are checking is displayed on one of the console's meters.

That brings us to a second and very important application of the PFL button – setting the channel input gain trims. By PFL'ing one channel at a time and adjusting the input gain trim, the signal can be monitored on the console's meter and the level optimised. By adjusting the input gain trim until the signal is just peaking at 0VU, the input signal is optimised for minimum noise – a good habit to get into.

solo

Solo also isolates the channel in the monitor mix but this time, the fader setting does affect what you hear because the signal is picked up post-fader. Such a solo system may also be known as "after fade listen" or AFL. In effect, when you press a solo button, all that really happens is that all un-solo'd channels disappear from the monitor mix. In mixers where the stereo placement and level of the original signal is retained while soloing, the term "solo in place" or SIP is also used.

master section

As with the smaller stereo mixers, the master section accommodates the master stereo faders, the aux send and aux return master controls, and all the other bits and pieces that don't belong anywhere else: test oscillators, talkback mics, monitor switching, headphones, solo/PFL switching and suchlike. An eight-buss console will also have eight group faders and routing buttons to patch the group signals into the main stereo mix.

Most consoles have at least a couple of dedicated auxiliary returns, and it has been known for these to confuse users, who often assume that aux return 1 must be used with aux send 1 and so on. This may well be appropriate, but it certainly isn't compulsory. An aux return is simply an additional line input channel but with fewer facilities than the main input channels. On smaller desks they will be permanently routed to the stereo mix buss while larger desks will provide the same routing arrangement as on the main input channels, and probably mute and solo switches as well.

There's nothing to stop you from feeding the outputs from your effects

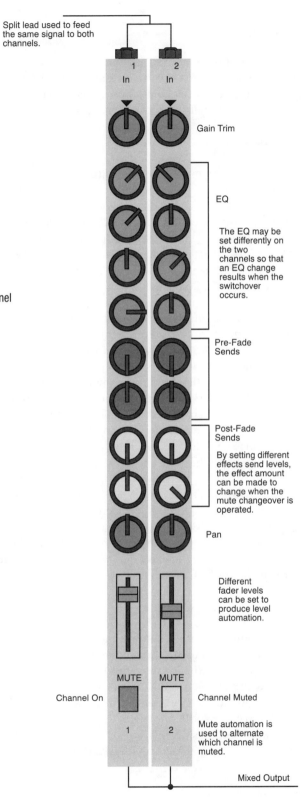

Split lead used to feed the same signal to both channels.

Figure 4.7: Mute automation for channel switching (for level changes etc)

Gain Trim

EQ

The EQ may be set differently on the two channels so that an EQ change results when the switchover occurs.

Pre-Fade Sends

Post-Fade Sends

By setting different effects send levels, the effect amount can be made to change when the mute changeover is operated.

Pan

Different fader levels can be set to produce level automation.

Channel On

Channel Muted

Mute automation is used to alternate which channel is muted.

Mixed Output

units into spare input channels, and equally, there's nothing to stop you from using your spare aux returns as additional line inputs for sequenced MIDI sound sources or backing tapes if you so wish. What's important is that you appreciate that the returns are just more input channels.

mute automation

Mute automation systems have been fitted to studio consoles for some years, but they can also be very handy live, especially if you're working in a venue with two or more bands and you need to change the setup of the desk during changeover. For example, you could set the desk up so all the channels are muted except those needed by the first band, then you store this setup for later recall. Do the same for the other bands and changing over becomes a matter of pressing one or two buttons rather than resetting the whole desk.

The simplest form of muting system remembers the mute switch settings for the whole desk in one go, and this memory setting is known as a "snapshot", because it represents a snapshot of the desk's mute settings for one moment in time. It's usually possible to store 99 or more snapshots, each identified by number, which can be called up later when needed. Most of the time, using the desk's own mute automation controls to call up snapshots is fine, but for situations where the snapshot changes need to be automated, you can often use MIDI program changes to do the job remotely. This can be useful if you're working with a band that syncs to a MIDI sequencer as snapshot changes can be made at strategic points during the song to mute unwanted channels, turn on effects and so on. You can even indulge in a crude form of level automation by feeding one signal into two mixer channels, then muting one of them. If the channels are set to different levels, swapping the muted and unmuted channel will result in a level change. With a bit of thought, this trick can be extended to changing EQ, effects level or pan positions. Figure 4.7 illustrates how this is done.

individual mutes

For more complex audio shows, individual channel mutes can be switched on or off using MIDI data, where MIDI note "numbers" usually correspond to individual mute buttons and MIDI "velocity" values determine whether the mute is on or off. You might imagine that simple "note on" and "off" messages would be simpler, but some MIDI sequencers won't handle the very long note lengths required. Using velocity values either side of 64 to denote on or off gets around this problem, and most manufacturers have adopted it.

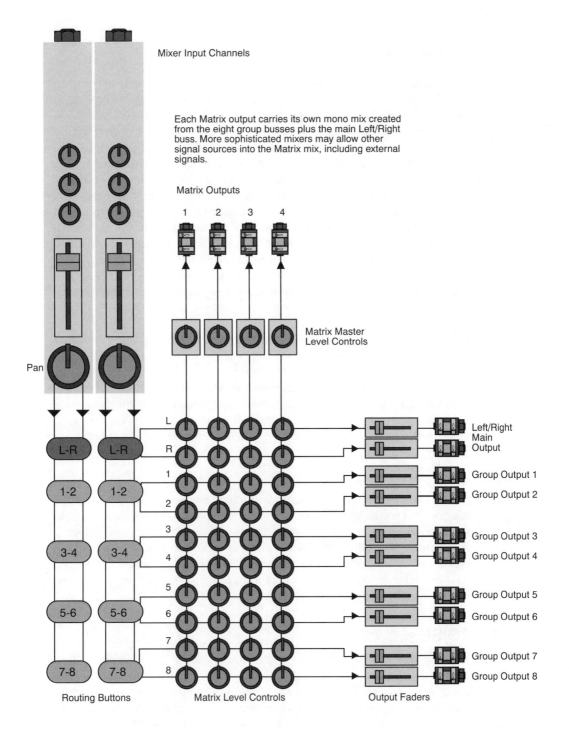

Mixer Input Channels

Each Matrix output carries its own mono mix created from the eight group busses plus the main Left/Right buss. More sophisticated mixers may allow other signal sources into the Matrix mix, including external signals.

Matrix Outputs

1 2 3 4

Matrix Master Level Controls

Pan

Left/Right Main Output

L-R   L-R   L   R

1-2   1-2   1   2   Group Output 1
                                    Group Output 2

3-4   3-4   3   4   Group Output 3
                                    Group Output 4

5-6   5-6   5   6   Group Output 5
                                    Group Output 6

7-8   7-8   7   8   Group Output 7
                                    Group Output 8

Routing Buttons   Matrix Level Controls   Output Faders

Figure 4.8: Matrix system

matrix outputs

Another feature found in larger consoles is the so-called "matrix" output, and Figure 4.8 makes this potentially confusing subject very clear. Essentially, the matrix system employs several rows of knobs that allow the user to set up several different mono mixes based on the group signals (busses one to eight in an eight-buss desk), the main left-right signals and possibly signals from an external source. The buss signals will usually be picked up pre-fader so that the matrix mix remains unaffected by adjustments to the group or master faders. Some mixers also have a mono master output in addition to the stereo outputs, and this too may be available on the matrix. In addition to the individual level knobs, each row of the matrix will have a master level control and probably a mute button and solo button as well. The mixes created using the matrix may be used to feed dressing room or foyer mixes in a theatre, multitrack recorder inputs for live recording, or even delay towers in a large concert system.

Delay towers are rather outside the scope of this book, but essentially they are separate PA systems set up at a distance from the stage and pointing towards the rear of the audience. Because sound travels at just over one foot per second, these remote speakers must be fed with a delayed signal so that the people nearby hear the sound at the same time as the sound from the main speakers at the front. Delay towers are often employed at outdoor festivals where the audience may be very large.

test oscillator

A test oscillator generates a steady mid-range tone, usually 400Hz, which may be sent to the main output busses to help calibrate levels or to help trace breaks in the signal chain. There may be a choice of different frequencies via a switching system and the oscillator will be fitted with an on/off switch and a level control. The way in which the oscillator is routed to the different mixer outputs varies from one model of mixer to another, but it's usually fairly self-explanatory.

pink noise

Because the majority of venues are acoustically imperfect, it is often desirable to equalise the PA feed so as to compensate for the worst of the room resonances. This is often achieved by feeding pink noise (a random signal with an equal amount of energy per octave) into the speaker system and then checking the frequency response shape using a spectrum analyser. A graphic equaliser can then be set up to "notch out"

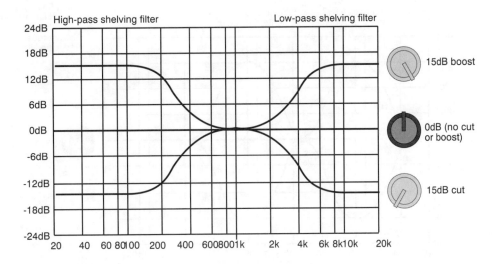

Figure 4.9: Shelving filter response

any serious room resonances. Several of the larger live mixing consoles have a pink noise generator built in for this purpose, and these tend to be located near the test oscillator.

talkback

Talkback is a means by which the engineer can plug a mic into the mixer (via a special "talkback" mic input), and then communicate with other members of the crew or the band via the mixer's various outputs. For example, the engineer could talk into the stage wedge monitor mix via the aux sends to communicate with the band, or there may be an external talkback output that enables the signal to be run to the monitor engineer who is operating a separate console by the side of the stage. On a typical mid-sized PA console, the talkback will be routable to the various aux outputs, the matrix section and an external talkback out socket. In most instances, a mic on a flexible gooseneck stand is plugged directly into the talkback mic XLR, and the talkback is operated by a non-latching button so you don't get caught out by leaving it on while you're insulting the drummer!

equalisation basics

The term equalisation came about because the very first equalisers were developed to help counteract or "equalise" shortcomings in telephone

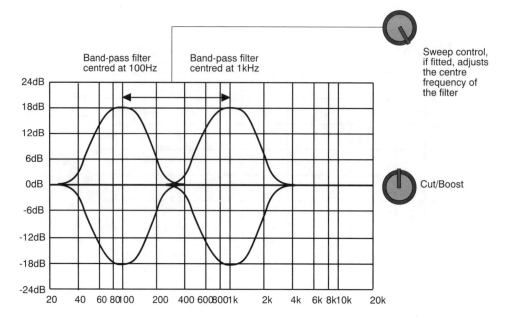

Figure 4.10: Band-pass filter response

systems, but today, equalisation is used creatively, as well as to fix problems. Equaliser circuits are based on electronic filters, hence the term filter, which crops up quite a lot when talking about EQ. Strictly speaking, a filter is a device that removes something, but in the context of active equaliser circuits, filters can boost as well as cut.

shelving equaliser

Though equalisers all do essentially the same job, there's a great deal of difference between a simple two-band treble/bass tone control and a multiband studio equaliser. The simplest equaliser is the shelving equaliser – a device that applies cut or boost, rather like a volume control, but only to the frequencies above or below the cutoff point of the equaliser, depending on whether the equaliser is based around a high-pass or a low-pass filter.

A low-pass shelving filter, as its name suggests, passes all frequencies below its cutoff frequency, but attenuates all frequencies above its cutoff frequency. Similarly, a high-pass filter passes all frequencies above its cutoff frequency, but affects all frequencies below its cutoff frequency. Figure 4.9 shows the frequency response graphs of a typical treble/bass EQ using high- and low-pass filters. Note that the filter graph shows a slope at the cutoff point – it isn't possible, or desirable to have a filter

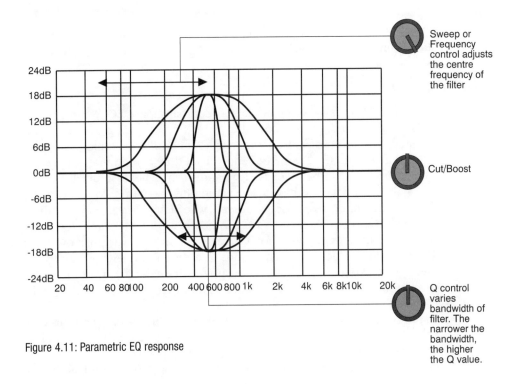

Figure 4.11: Parametric EQ response

that does nothing at one frequency, then, when you move up by just 1Hz, comes in with full effect. Simple shelving filters typically have a 6dB per octave slope so that their influence is felt more progressively, though it is possible to make much steeper slopes if required. The gentler the slope of the filter, the more frequencies outside of the range of the filter will be affected.

band-pass filters

A filter that passes frequencies between two limits is known as a band-pass filter, and on a mixer with a mid-range control, the mid knob controls a band-pass filter. On a typical mixer, the band-pass filter will have variable cut and boost, and on more flexible mixers, it will also be tunable so that its centre frequency can be varied. This is known as a sweep equaliser, because although the filter frequency can be changed, the width of the filter cannot be adjusted. Figure 4.10 shows a typical band-pass filter response, including sweep control function. In a typical mixer, the high and low shelving equalisers are used to control the high and low end with a band-pass filter controlling the mid range. However, some mixers use band-pass filters for EQ'ing the low end too. The argument for doing this is that a shelving high-pass filter will also boost all frequencies below the ones you want to work on, whereas a band-pass filter attenuates frequencies both below and above its cutoff points.

parametric eq

A parametric EQ is very similar to a sweep band-pass EQ, except that a third control is added to allow the width of the filter response to be adjusted. The width of a filter response is sometimes described as its "Q" value, where Q is the filter frequency divided by the number of Hz the filter affects – in other words, its bandwidth. The formula for Q is: $Q = F$ (centre)/bandwidth, where F is the filter's centre frequency in Hz. Because the filter response is curved, the actual frequency width is measured between the points on the graph where the signal level has fallen by 3dB. A high value for Q corresponds to a very narrow filter whereas a low value of Q corresponds to a wide filter. High Q values are useful for picking out sounds that occupy a very narrow part of the audio spectrum, whereas lower Qs produce a smoother, more musical sound.

A studio parametric EQ may have several filter sections enabling three or four parts of the frequency spectrum to be treated simultaneously. Parametric EQs can be time-consuming to set up properly, but they are the most powerful and most flexible of the conventional EQ types. Figure 4.11 shows a typical parametric equaliser response.

graphic equaliser

A graphic equaliser can be recognised by the row of faders across the front panel, each fader controlling its own narrow section of the audio spectrum. For example, a 30-band graphic equaliser provides independent control over 30 different bands spaced one third of an octave apart.

Other than the highest and lowest faders, which control shelving filters, each of the filters in a graphic equaliser is a fixed frequency band-pass filter where boost is applied by moving the fader up from its centre position, and where cut is achieved by moving the fader down. Graphic equalisers have the advantage of being very easy to set up, but unless they are very well designed, they can have an adverse effect on the sound unless used sparingly. They are also less flexible than the parametric EQ, which can be exactly tuned to specific frequencies. With the graphic equaliser, the range covered by each fader is fixed, and the width of each individual band of a third octave equaliser is actually rather wider than a third of an octave so as to allow a smooth overlap between bands. Figure 4.12 shows the response of a typical graphic equaliser.

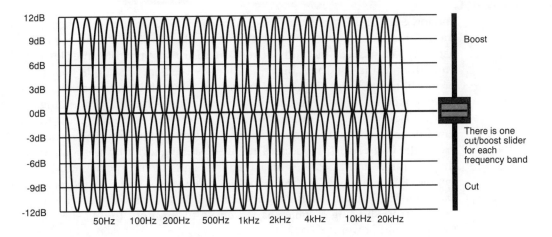

Figure 4.12: Graphic equaliser response

Graphic equalisers are used extensively in live sound to tame wayward room acoustics by cutting frequencies that aggravate room resonances, and they're also used to pull back the frequency bands in which feedback or ringing are occurring. Separate graphic equalisers are generally employed on the monitor system where feedback is a particular problem. For details on how these are used, see the chapter on monitoring.

the sound of eq

No matter how complicated the EQ, it is still really just a frequency selective volume control, but its subjective effect on the sound is often more profound than this description might leave you to expect. It's well known to circuit designers that EQ doesn't only change the level of specific parts of the spectrum, it also changes the phase of the affected frequencies relative to those that aren't being cut or boosted. Every design of EQ affects the audio spectrum and phase response in a different way, and leaving aside technical criteria such as noise and distortion, this might explain why some EQs have a more natural, musical sound than others.

eq and loudness

The human hearing frequency curve isn't flat, but instead is more sensitive to mid-range sounds than to frequencies at the extreme high and low ends of the spectrum. We don't notice this, because we've heard things this way all our lives. However, as the level of sound we're listening to increases, the mid boost of the hearing system becomes less, and the result is that high and low frequency sounds seem proportionally louder. This is an interesting physiological fact that can be exploited by fooling the ear into believing it's perceiving something that isn't entirely true. For example, if we know that extreme high and low frequencies stand out more when we listen to loud music, we can create the impression of loudness at lower listening levels by attenuating the mid-range and boosting the HF and LF ends of the spectrum. The loudness button on a stereo system does exactly this, and if you look at the graphic EQs used in a night club or band PA system, you'll often see them set up showing a smile-shaped curve to promote the illusion of loudness and power.

to cut or boost?

In general, the less EQ boost you use, the more natural the final sound will be – the human ear is far more tolerant of EQ cut than it is of boost, so rather than adding lots of top to vulnerable sounds such as vocals in order to get them to sit at the front of the mix, try applying high end cut to other sounds in the mix that are conflicting with the vocal. Furthermore, EQ boost increases the risk of feedback at the boosted frequency.

As a general rule, console equalisation should be employed only after all efforts have been made to obtain the best sound at source, though it is worth using low-cut filters to remove low-frequency spill from channels that aren't carrying bass instruments. Sometimes, a combination of cut and boost is required, but always use the bypass switch to flip back and forth between the equalised and unequalised sounds, to make sure you really have improved matters.

multicores

Unless the mixer is on stage with you for self operation, you are likely to need a multicore to feed the mic signals from the stage to the console. A multicore is simply a bunch of small-diameter mic cables inside a common protective outer sheath, and it is important that you use the type containing individually screened pairs rather than the type that only provides a single outer screen for all the cables. At the stage end, the multicore (or snake as it is sometimes known) terminates in a metal box upon which XLR sockets are mounted. A good strain relief system is necessary to prevent stress on the cable ends and soldered joints when the cable is packed and unpacked. Depending on the type of cable, there will be a limit to the cable's flexibility, so always follow the manufacturer's recommendations regarding minimum winding diameter when stowing the cable or winding it onto a drum.

At the mixer end, a small multicore may simply terminate in a bunch of flying jack leads, but for larger systems, it is common practice to fit a multi-pin connector to the end of the cable and the mating half of the connector onto the mixer flight case bottom. In this case, the mixer would be permanently fixed to the flight case bottom and a series of short cables used to connect the mixer inputs to the multi-pin connector. This greatly simplifies setting up as the individual mixer input connections never need to be disturbed – all that's needed is to connect one large multi-pin connector.

Power amplifiers should always be set up as close to the speakers as possible to minimise speaker cable length, which means quite long signal cables may be required.

mixer terms

buss

Piece of circuitry or wiring connecting several parts of a system. A mixer may have several busses carrying the main stereo mix, the aux sends and – on more sophisticated recording mixers – sub-mixes of different groups of channels.

dry signal

A sound source which has no added effect. Conversely, a sound treated with an effect such as reverberation or echo is often referred to as wet.

equalisation

Tone control. Usually comprises treble, mid and bass where the mid (or mids) may be fitted with variable frequency controls.

gain

Adjusts the amount by which a signal is amplified.

insert point

A connector that allows the normal signal path to be interrupted and re-routed through an external device, such as a compressor.

line level

Mixers and signal processors tend to work at a standard signal level known as line level. In practice, there are several different standard line levels, but all are in the order of a few volts. Microphones produce a much lower signal, in the order of tens of millivolts.

pan

Alters the balance of the signal fed to the left and right mix busses.

chapter 5

effects, processors and power amps

I n addition to mixers, loudspeakers and microphones, PA systems usually
incorporate external devices for signal processing or for adding effects,
such as reverb or echo. This chapter examines the principles and
applications of all the common processor and effect types before concluding
with a section on power amplifiers and crossovers.

compressors

Compressors and limiters are vital components of the live sound audio
chain, but there's a lot of confusion as to what they actually do. As far as I'm
aware, compressors were first developed for the film industry to help keep
location dialogue at a more or less even level, but it wasn't long before they
made their move into the music recording studio and onto the stage. In an
ideal world, sound balance would simply be a matter of setting the faders
and leaving them alone – promoters would always pay on time, the roadie's
armpits would smell of violets and circling pigs would be heard asking for
landing clearance in perfect three-part harmony!

Unfortunately, balance is at the mercy of untrained singers with less than
perfect mic technique, so even if the back-line is behaving, you could find
the vocal level is going all over the place. The poor man's cure is to keep one
hand on the fader and ride the gain, but you'll always respond too late
because you can't start to move the fader until you hear the problem, by
which time your audience will have heard it too. This is better than having
no control at all, and understanding "gain riding" provides a valuable insight
into how compressors go about their business. Figure 5.1 shows manual
gain riding in block diagram form.

compression basics

A compressor does essentially the same job as manual gain riding, but of
course it's much faster and far more precise. Every compressor includes

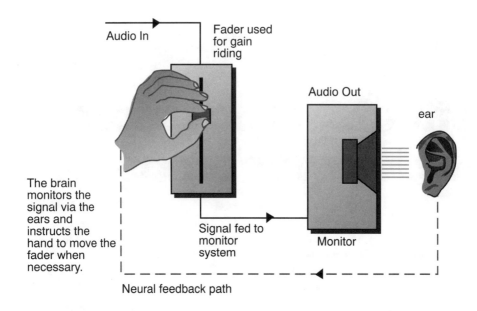

Audio In

Fader used for gain riding

Audio Out

ear

The brain monitors the signal via the ears and instructs the hand to move the fader when necessary.

Signal fed to monitor system

Monitor

Neural feedback path

Figure 5.1: Manual gain riding

some form of gain control element, usually a VCA (Voltage Controlled Amplifier), and this replaces the manual fader. The advantage of the VCA is that its gain can be controlled electronically rather than needing moving parts, which allows the human ear and mental judgement to be replaced by more circuitry. To find out what the levels are doing, the compressor monitors its own output level by electronic means (though some designs monitor the input level). The part of the circuit that monitors the signal level is called the "side-chain", and this follows the envelope of the audio signal. The envelope's level is then compared to a fixed threshold level set by the user, and when the signal exceeds the threshold, the side-chain generates a control signal to reduce the gain of the VCA. Figure 5.2 shows a simplified block diagram of a typical compressor, and I'm sure you'll see the resemblance between this process and manual gain riding.

compressor controls

The level above which the compressor decides to turn the gain down is known as the "threshold", and if the side-chain signal level doesn't reach the threshold, then no gain change occurs. The threshold is set by a front panel control and is fully variable by the user. How much the gain is reduced depends on the compressor's "ratio" control, and the value is expressed as a mathematical ratio in the format, X:1. Typically, the ratio control is variable from 1:1 (no effect at all) to infinity:1 (where the output level is never

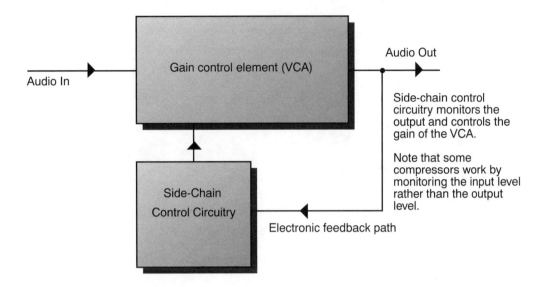

Figure 5.2: Basic compressor block diagram

allowed to rise above the threshold). High compression ratios result in limiting because, in this instance, the threshold level sets the limit beyond which the signal cannot rise further. The figures around the ratio control relate to dBs in that for a 6:1 compression setting, a 6dB increase in the input signal will result in the output level rising by only 1dB for as long as the input exceeds the threshold value. Below the threshold of course, no change occurs, so a 6dB rise in the input will result in an equal 6dB rise in the output. The higher the ratio, the more gain reduction is applied to signals exceeding the threshold, and once you get up to ratios of 10:1, the result is so close to true limiting that it makes virtually no difference. Figure 5.3 shows a graph of the input versus the output of a compressor for different ratio settings.

soft knee

What I've described so far is a very conventional compressor, but in some applications, straightforward compression can be a little unsubtle, because as soon as the signal reaches the threshold, gain reduction comes in straight away. This is known as hard-knee compression, and it is useful where you need firm control, or where the side-effects of the compression can be used creatively to make the music seem more punchy.

For applications where less obtrusive compression is required, the soft-knee

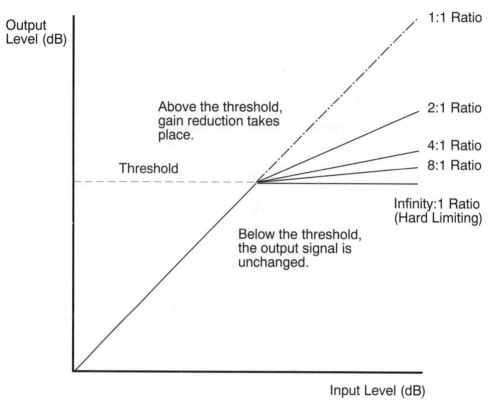

Figure 5.3: Graph of compressor action

compressor may be more useful. The main difference between a soft- and a hard-knee compressor is that in the case of a soft-knee device, instead of everything happening as soon as the signal hits the threshold, the gain reduction comes in more progressively, starting a few dBs below the threshold. In effect, the compression ratio increases as the threshold is approached, then continues to increase up to a maximum of the value set by the front panel ratio control. Typically, this soft knee occurs over a region of 10dB or so. Figure 5.4 shows a graph of input versus output for a soft-knee compressor with a ratio setting of 8:1.

Note that not all soft-knee compressors have a ratio control – some are completely automatic, which means the degree of compression can be controlled by a single knob. Though soft-knee compressors don't apply such assertive gain control as hard-knee models, they are more forgiving of casual setting up, and they're useful for controlling vocal levels when you don't want the end result to sound processed.

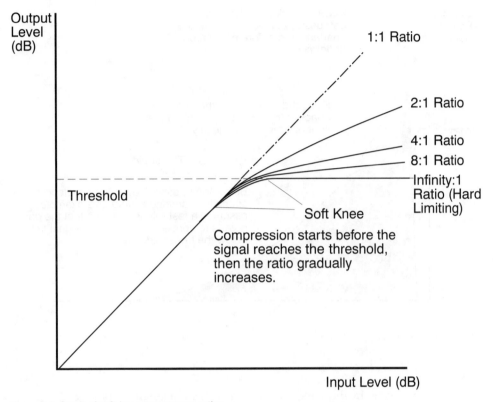

Figure 5.4: Graph of soft-knee compressor action

attack and release

Unless the compressor is fitted with an auto attack and release function, it will probably be fitted with both attack and release time controls. Attack sets the reaction time of the gain reduction circuitry, rather as the amount of beer consumed sets the reaction time of a human sound engineer! A good compressor can react so fast that it seems instantaneous, but that's not always the best thing to do. By slowing down the reaction time of the compressor to 10mS or so, it's possible to allow the attack transient of a percussive sound to get through unchecked, and this has the effect of giving the sound a stronger kick. If this attack is only a few milliseconds in duration, the momentary increase in energy won't overheat your speakers, yet it can make the sound appear to be much bigger, especially when used on drums and bass guitar. For sounds such as vocals, where we don't want a percussive attack at the start, a short attack time is more appropriate. Figure 5.5 shows a percussive sound being treated by a compressor with a fast attack time,

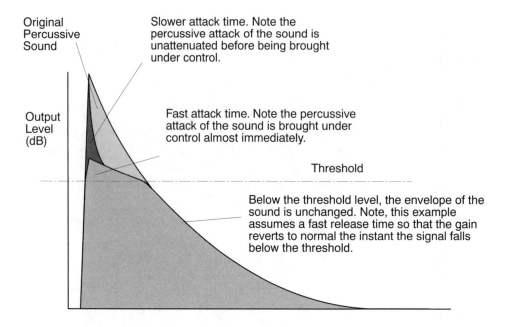

Original Percussive Sound

Slower attack time. Note the percussive attack of the sound is unattenuated before being brought under control.

Output Level (dB)

Fast attack time. Note the percussive attack of the sound is brought under control almost immediately.

Threshold

Below the threshold level, the envelope of the sound is unchanged. Note, this example assumes a fast release time so that the gain reverts to normal the instant the signal falls below the threshold.

Figure 5.5: Effect of compressor attack

then again by the same compressor with a longer attack time set.

The "release" control sets the recovery time once the input signal has dropped back below the threshold – it determines how long the compressor's gain takes to return to normal once the peak has passed. The reason a release time control is necessary is that if the gain is brought back up too quickly, the gain change is audible – many engineers refer to this effect as gain pumping. If, however, the release time is too long, the gain may not have returned to normal by the time the next peak comes along, so it will be reduced in level unnecessarily. Usually, you try to find the shortest release setting without obvious pumping occurring, and for most pop music applications, around a quarter of a second is about right.

auto compressors

Some compressors dispense with physical attack and release controls (or some may just leave out the release control), and an additional piece of circuitry monitors the dynamics of the input signal and varies the time constants accordingly. Auto settings are particularly useful for material that is constantly changing its dynamic characteristics, but they're especially useful in live situations as they're very quick to set up, and will often give better results than a manual compressor with fixed settings.

compressor sound

Though all compressors do much the same job, different models produce a different sound. One difference between models is the way the compressor evaluates the signal level – some react to average (RMS) signal levels while others monitor the signal peaks. RMS probably comes closest to the way human ears respond to sound, but a peak compressor will react to short transients that an RMS compressor might miss. Compressors may also introduce distortion, and though the amount is relatively small, it can be enough to create a subjectively pleasant sonic signature, and that's why some purists prefer valve compressors, or those that work using photocells and lamps instead of VCAs. Though contrary to instinctive reasoning, a slightly distorted signal can actually sound brighter and punchier than a perfectly clean signal. Photocell compressors are characterised by a relatively slow attack and a fairly fast release time, usually combined with a high ratio.

stereo linking

If a two-channel compressor is to be used on a whole stereo mix or stereo subgroup, it's important that the unit has a stereo link switch, and that this is set to "link". That's because the same gain reduction must be applied to both channels at all times, otherwise the louder channel will receive the most compression, and this can cause the stereo image to appear to shift from side to side. When linked for stereo operation, both channels of the compressor react to the average of the sound passing through the two channels, so both channels always apply exactly the same amount of gain reduction. Both channels must be set up exactly the same for this to work properly, though most compressors automate this task by making both channels respond to just one set of channel controls, usually the left one, when in linked mode. However, there may still be some controls that aren't linked, so check your manual for details.

side-chain access

In live sound, compressors are used mainly to keep signal levels from wandering too far, or to prevent certain parts of the mix from getting too loud, but they can also be used to allow one signal to control the gain of another. Though this isn't used much in live music, it can be useful in other areas of live sound, for example, where background music needs to "duck" automatically whenever a speaker's microphone is used. This is only possible on compressors that have side-chain access jacks on the back panel, and it works as follows:

Assume the music is being played through the main compressor input, but that the side-chain input is being fed with a voice signal from a mixer send or some other convenient point. Figure 5.6 shows how this is set up in practice. Now the compressor is no longer responding to the main signal but to the voice signal at the side-chain input. When the voice exceeds the threshold, the compressor turns down the music, and when the voice stops, the gain will return to normal. In this context, the rate at which the music level ducks and then rises back up is determined by the attack and release settings, so an auto compressor isn't really appropriate for this kind of work. How much the music will be turned down depends on the threshold and ratio settings and some experimentation is necessary to get the desired result. As a rule, a fairly fast attack is combined with a medium to slow release, so that the music doesn't come back in too abruptly when the speaker stops.

limiting

As described earlier, a limiter is basically a compressor with a very high ratio, but there's no point in having a high ratio if the compressor can't respond quickly enough to catch any transients before they overshoot. Limiting is a vitally important function in PA work, because very often it's only the limiter that stands between the drivers and a smoky death! If a general purpose compressor is used as a limiter, it must be set to its fastest attack time, but a dedicated limiter is a better option if you don't already have limiters built into your crossovers or system processors. A dedicated limiter will have a very fast response time, and it will normally have a fast release time so that gain reduction ceases the moment the clipping danger is over. If the limiter threshold is set just below the level where the PA power amps clip, drivers will be protected from peak damage while enabling you to get the greatest perceived level out of the system.

Some compressors come with a separate limiter section designed to catch any peaks that the compressor may let through, and these can be very helpful in ensuring you don't run out of headroom.

implications of compression

Compressors are wonderful allies, but there are things you need to be careful of. If you're using a compressor to even out vocal levels, you're effectively reducing the peak signal level, so to get back to the same peak signal level you had before, you're going to have to turn either the compressor output or the mic channel fader up. More gain means a greater

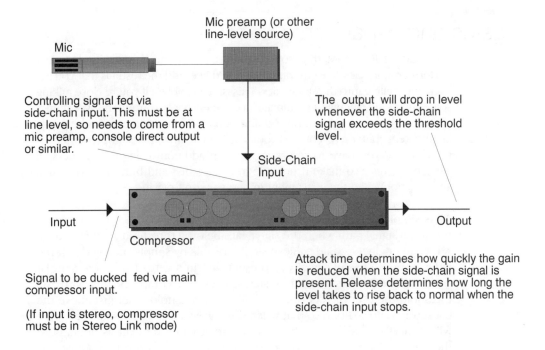

Mic preamp (or other line-level source)

Mic

Controlling signal fed via side-chain input. This must be at line level, so needs to come from a mic preamp, console direct output or similar.

The output will drop in level whenever the side-chain signal exceeds the threshold level.

Side-Chain Input

Input

Output

Compressor

Signal to be ducked fed via main compressor input.

(If input is stereo, compressor must be in Stereo Link mode)

Attack time determines how quickly the gain is reduced when the side-chain signal is present. Release determines how long the level takes to rise back to normal when the side-chain input stops.

Figure 5.6: Compressor set up for ducking

likelihood of feedback problems, so rather than expecting too much of the compressor, it's probably best to set the threshold high with a fairly high ratio and use it just to tame the singer's worst excesses of level. In large concert situations where the PA is further away from the mics, this may be less of a problem, but if your setup is more "Claire's brother" than Claire Brothers, it's something to keep in mind. By the same token, using compression to increase the average signal level means that low level noise and unwanted spill will also be increased in level, so a compressor with a built-in gate or expander can help.

Compression increases the average signal level, so if you apply a lot of compression to bass instruments, your PA speakers are going to be handling a higher average power level. Though using limiters will protect the drivers from the results of clipping, a high average power means a lot of heat to dissipate. Loudspeaker power compression is more likely to occur if your speakers aren't adequately rated, and in extreme circumstances, running highly compressed signals at high levels for extended periods can cause thermal failure of components. The moral here is that if you like a dense, compressed sound, make sure your speaker system can handle it.

gates and expanders

It's a fact of live work that you can never put as much distance between performers and back-line equipment as you'd like, and the result is that you get back-line spilling into the stage mics. This isn't a problem if you're close miking something loud, such as a guitar stack or the end of a trumpet, but vocal mics are another matter. Careful positioning of back-line equipment can help to a large extent, but there comes a point at which no further improvement is possible and you have to resort to gates. In addition to improving the spill situation, gates also make it possible to silence hiss and hum from back-line amplification when the instrument in question isn't playing.

At its simplest, a gate is little more than an automatic switch that turns off the audio signal path when the signal falls below a threshold set by the user. A human engineer could achieve similar results by simply pulling down the fader when no useful signal was present, but in a gate, a side-chain circuit continually monitors the input signal level and compares this with the threshold the user has set up. Normally, this threshold is set just above the background noise floor, so that when there are pauses in the signal, the gate will mute, shutting out any background spill. When the gate is open, both the wanted sound and the background noise will pass through. Obviously this is much faster than the manual "hand-on-fader" technique, and leaves you free to concentrate on other aspects of the mix.

If you think this sounds similar to the way a compressor works, you're not wrong. The difference is that a compressor turns down signals that exceed the threshold, while gates and expanders turn down the gain of signals that fall below the threshold.

gate attack and release

Though it is possible to build a gate that functions as a straightforward on/off switch, it wouldn't sound too good on most material. By opening too fast, the gate could cause clicks on some non-percussive material, and if it closed instantaneously between sounds, the effect of the background noise being switched on and off would be more obtrusive than the noise itself. Furthermore, the ends of decaying sounds might be cut off prematurely.

Like compressors, most commercial gates have attack and release parameters that determine how quickly the gate opens and closes. This is the equivalent of the human engineer moving the fader up and down more slowly. On simpler models, these attack and release times may be preset or automatic, while on a more comprehensive model, they will be fully accessible to the user via front panel knobs.

The fastest attack settings allow percussive transients to pass through cleanly, while a slow attack forces the gate to open more gradually. By slowing the gate attack down to a few milliseconds, unwanted clicking should be avoided when gating non-percussive sounds. Percussive sounds usually require the fastest attack time possible so as to maintain their transient impact.

Having a variable release time enables the gate to close gradually when sounds with a slow decay are being processed. If the gate were to close abruptly, the tail end of naturally decaying sounds, such as reverb tails or decaying plucked guitars, would be cut off. Setting a gate decay time to match that of the signal being processed allows sounds that have a long reverberant "tail" to be cleaned up without their natural decay characteristics being affected too significantly. Figure 5.7 shows the attack and release phases of a typical gate.

side-chain filtering

More elaborate gates include side-chain filtering, usually comprising a pair of shelving equalisers, one high-pass and one low-pass, connected in series with the gate's side-chain. By adjusting the upper and lower limits of the filters, it is possible to make the gate open only when it "hears" the band of frequencies between the two filter settings. This can help enormously in situations where spill from other instruments is likely to cause false triggering.

Filtering is often used when miking drum kits to prevent a crash cymbal from opening a tom gate. To achieve this, the upper filter frequency would need to be lowered so as to exclude the high frequencies from the cymbals, but still allow the sound of the tom to trigger the gate. Similarly, it is possible to prevent a kick drum from accidentally triggering a gate on the snare mic by increasing the low filter setting. Because the filters are only in the side-chain, they have no effect on the actual sound of the signal being processed, only on how the gate opens and closes in response to certain sounds.

hold

There are a couple more controls that you might come across depending on which gate you use, the first being "hold time". Hold time delays the closing of the gate slightly once the input signal has fallen below the threshold. To understand why this might be necessary, imagine a sound with level modulation, such as a guitar played through a tremolo effect, being passed through a gate. If the gate were set with a very fast attack and release time, it might try to open and close each time the tremolo effect pulsates. Usually, setting a longer release time will prevent this, but in a situation where a faster release time is required, hold may be used to force the gate to remain open long

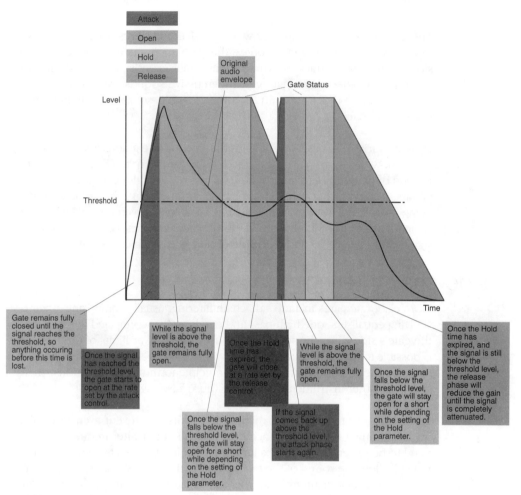

Figure 5.7: Gate action

enough to prevent it "chattering" in response to level modulation. Even if the gate has no hold control, it probably has a preset hold time built in, because without it, low bass sounds could open and close the gate on each cycle of the sound. The hold parameter is also shown in the graph of Figure 5.7.

range

The other control sets the amount of attenuation that occurs when the gate is closed, and this may be called "range", "floor" or "attenuation". In situations where the background spill is relatively high in level, even a well set up gate can sound a little odd as the background noise will alternate between being quite noticeable and completely silent as the gate opens and closes. Sometimes it is more natural sounding simply to have the background noise fall in level by a few dBs rather than shut off altogether. If you have a unit with a range control, you can set the signal to drop by any amount you like, from just a dB or two to complete silence.

expanders

Expanders differ from gates insomuch as they are really more like compressors in reverse, though in most applications, they can be used to do the same jobs as gates. Gates are like the opposite of limiters, because signals falling below the threshold are silenced. Expanders also act on signals falling below the threshold, but instead of muting the signal, an expander simply makes quiet sounds even quieter, depending on how far the signal level falls below the threshold. A gate starts its release phase when the signal falls below threshold and keeps going until the gain has fallen to zero.

To go back to the engineer and fader analogy, in the case of a gate, as soon as the signal falls below the threshold, the engineer starts to pull the fader down towards zero. With an expander the more the signal falls below the threshold, the further the fader is pulled down. As with a compressor, an expander has a ratio, and an expansion ratio of 2:1 means that for every 1dB the signal falls below the threshold, the output level will fall by 2dB. An expander with an infinitely high ratio would function exactly like a gate. Figure 5.8 shows a graph of how an expander behaves.

In practice, the main difference between the expander and the gate is that the switching action around the threshold is less abrupt in the case of an expander, which can make them a little more forgiving to set up, especially where fast attack and release times are involved. At longer release time, there's little to choose between the two as the effect of the release time masks the subtle differences.

Expanders are often built into into compressors because it is possible to build an expander that can be controlled using only a single threshold control and a slow/fast release switch. Compressors tend to be used in conjunction with gates, because in trying to make quiet sounds louder, they also bring up the level of any background noise and spill present in the original signal. When combining compressors and gates, it helps to put the gate before the compressor where the dynamic range of the signal is greatest.

gate applications

Gates and expanders are valuable in keeping drum sounds separate and for shutting down vocal mics when not in use. Because gates can only clean up

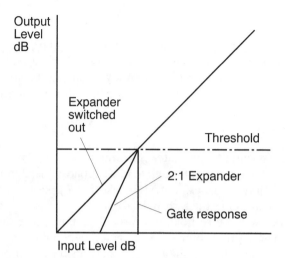

Figure 5.8: Expander action

the pauses between sounds, they shouldn't be considered as a substitute for careful setting up, and in cases where the spill is really bad, they can make things sound even worse rather than better. Under really adverse conditions, it may be impossible to set the gate so as to trigger only on those sounds it's supposed to pass through, so you really do have to take all possible precautions to minimise spill first. However, used with a little care, gates can be used to make a significant improvement to sound separation, and to cut out noise from instrument amplifiers during pauses between phrases.

gate connections

Gates and expanders should always be connected "in-line" with a signal, usually via the console's channel or group insert points. They will not work in the aux send/return system in the same way as effects, such as reverb or delay. It is good practice to try to ensure, where possible, that devices connected via insert points operate at the same nominal level as the mixing console. For example, if the console is designed to operate at a nominal +4dBu, then if level switching is provided, the outboard gear should be set to the same sensitivity. Also be aware that on many pieces of balanced equipment, using balanced-to-unbalanced leads to patch into unbalanced insert points can result in a 6dB level loss.

Guitar versions of gates in the form of pedals may be used to help clean up the noise caused by overdrive pedals or the hum from single-coil pickups in electrically noisy environments. These should always be placed after any overdrive devices, though putting any echo or reverb pedals after the gate will help ensure the effects die away naturally rather than being gated prematurely.

Back-line amplification being DI'd or miked via the main PA may also be gated in the same way as microphones so as to ensure perfect silence between musical phrases, or when the instruments are not playing. As a general rule, the more percussive the sound being gated, the easier it is to set the gate up to sound unobtrusive.

stereo linking

Dual channel gates often have a stereo link switch, and this is included so that the gate can be used to treat a stereo signal, such as the output from a stereo keyboard rig or guitar setup. Without a stereo link switch, each gate would operate independently, and if the stereo image were not symmetrical, then one gate would close before another, giving rise to apparent image shifts. The stereo link switch simply forces both channels of the gate to open and close at exactly the same time, thereby maintaining the stereo image of the signal being processed. As with compressors, many gates hand over control to a single channel when in link mode.

external gate keying

Some gates have an external key or side-chain input so as to allow the gate to be triggered from an external source. This facility is often used in the studio for creating special effects but is less often employed in live situations. As a rule, percussive sounds are the easiest to use for external keying.

Some gates are fitted with a ducking function, enabling the key input to be used to reduce the level of the signal being passed through the gate's main input. This is often used in voice-over work to reduce the level of background music while a speaker is talking (exactly like compressor ducking), and the decay control setting determines how quickly the music fades back in after the speaker's voice has fallen below the threshold level. Again, this is less often used in live music applications, though in difficult small venues, ducking may be used to pull down the volume of a console subgroup carrying back-line instruments whenever the vocalist sings. Stereo ducking can be accomplished using the stereo link switch. Providing the amount of ducking is kept to just 1 or 2dB, the process should not interfere with the perceived overall sound quality, yet the vocalist will be heard more clearly. The degree of ducking is usually set using the gate's range control.

exciters and enhancers

If the sound out front isn't quite the way you want it, the easiest thing to do is reach for the EQ controls, but adding significant amounts of EQ boost to a mic channel can eat into your feedback headroom, and in any event, if the instrument isn't producing frequencies in the range where you want to hear them, no amount of EQ is going to do any good. Equalisers work by cutting or boosting the level of a specific part of the audio spectrum, and careful use of EQ can help brighten dull sounds, bring up the bass, bring down the mid-range or whatever, but an equaliser can only affect frequencies that are already there. If you turn up the treble control in an attempt to brighten a sound that contains absolutely no high in the first place, you'll just get more hiss, and again if it's a mic signal you're dealing with, you run the risk of feedback at the frequency you've boosted. This type of problem can arise when you're miking bass amps, acoustic guitars with old strings, or even vocalists who have very little natural high end in their voices.

EQ is also a blanket treatment, so if you apply it to a drum kit submix, for example, the whole sound will change. However, it might sound better if the EQ was only applied on the main beats. Dynamic equalisers can do this to some extent by linking EQ change to signal level – the louder the beat, the more EQ is applied for the duration of that beat, but dedicated dynamic equalisers are expensive and usually quite difficult to set up. They may also be too sophisticated for the job in hand, because in such situations, the area that needs boosting is nearly always at the high end of the spectrum, an area that exciters and enhancers are specifically designed to deal with.

Most exciters or enhancers combine elements of dynamic EQ with other processes including harmonic synthesis and phase manipulation. Not all manufacturers use the same combination of principles, the outcome of which is that each type of enhancer has its own characteristic sound. However, most produce a sense of increased clarity and projection.

exciter principles

The first exciter was developed by Aphex (TM), and the story goes that the exciter principle was discovered by accident when an engineer wrongly assembled a valve amplifier kit! One channel worked normally, but the other produced only a thin, distorted sound which, in isolation, sounded awful. However, mixing the two channels produced an unexpected result. The combined signal sounded somehow clearer and more detailed than the original. Wisely, they investigated the effect further and eventually produced a box to do the job in a predictable and controllable manner.

Why does adding distortion to a signal make it seem clearer? As it turns out, the process emphasises transient details, and these details provide important psychoacoustic clues as to the nature of what we're hearing. In video terms, it's rather like enhancing a slightly out-of-focus picture by drawing a line around the edge of the object. In fact some TV sets have a sharpness circuit that does almost exactly that by hardening up the edges within the picture, and that's pretty much what the exciter does for audio. Okay, that's what it does, but how does it do it?

the aphex process

The Aphex Aural Exciter involves a side-chain which processes high frequencies, then adds them back to the original signal in quite small amounts. Inside the side-chain is a variable frequency high-pass filter feeding into a harmonics generating circuit. The high-pass filter ensures that only high frequencies are processed, then the filtered signal drives a circuit that both compresses and adds harmonic distortion, which is musically related to the frequencies passed by the filter. A small amount of this processed signal is then added back into the original signal, which has the effect of emphasising transient detail and adding brightness, but without significantly increasing the signal level. This latter point is most important, because if the perceived sound can be changed significantly without actually increasing the level by more than a few per cent, feedback is far less likely than if you attempt to use EQ boost to achieve the same ends. Figure 5.9 shows the block diagram of a harmonic exciter working on the Aphex principle.

The "drive" control comes before the "tune" control, so after setting the tune by ear, it is often necessary to readjust the drive control for optimum results. Current Aphex units have dispensed with the drive control making them easier to use. Because the process only emphasises the high-frequency end, some low-frequency EQ may be required to maintain a proper bass/treble balance, and some current models include bass EQ or other forms of low-frequency processing. However, in a live situation, it's usually the high end that needs to be given more clarity and definition.

Aphex obviously patented their principle, but there are many competing designs working in different ways, including the use of dynamic equalisation and phase manipulation. A properly designed enhancer is effective for pulling vocals forward in a mix, and also for adding life to dull acoustic guitar or cymbal sounds.

psychoacoustic principles

The reason enhancers work is to do with the psychological perception of hearing, or "psychoacoustics". There is still much work to be done in this area, but one of the simpler psychoacoustic principles is based on the way our perception of the audio spectrum changes as sounds become louder. At high levels, we tend to hear the high and low frequencies more

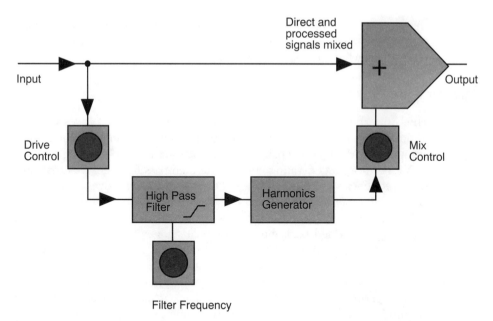

Figure 5.9: Harmonic Exciter

strongly while the mid-range doesn't seem to increase by the same amount, so using an equaliser to cut the mid-range can produce a louder sounding mix. This is the familiar "smile" curve described earlier in the book. Most engineers know this trick, but why does an enhancer make sounds appear louder?

I'll look at harmonic synthesis first. When an audio signal is distorted, high-frequency harmonics are produced. Normally distortion sounds pretty bad, but by using filters to confine the distortion to the top end of the spectrum, the human hearing system is fooled into thinking these new harmonics are a legitimate part of the original signal. That means that sounds originally lacking in high-frequency content can be processed to synthesise a new and musically believable top end. By including a dynamic element, most harmonic enhancement is added to percussive or transient sounds, which is why the sound appears more detailed than before.

Of course you can have too much of a good thing, and over-enhancing a signal can produce a harsh, fatiguing result that sounds particularly bad through PA horns. Enhancers work, but you have to use them with restraint. Used sensibly, enhancers of whatever type can be used to make the sound coming over your PA appear more detailed, brighter and louder, without actually increasing the overall signal level by more than a small amount. You could patch the whole mix through an enhancer, but that might not be the best thing to do – it's usually more effective to enhance only those parts of the mix you want to stand out, such as the lead vocals, acoustic guitars and maybe the drum overheads. You can do this by patching the enhancer into a subgroup, then routing the signals you need to treat via that subgroup. Note that most enhancers have to be connected in-line with a signal in the same way as an equaliser or compressor, so you can't use the effects send and return loop (though there are one or two exceptions). Enhancers aren't a universal panacea for poor sound, but they're valuable tools for putting a slight gloss on your mixes, for getting the vocals over in difficult situations, or even for making the front-of-house sound seem louder in situations where the maximum SPL you are permitted to produce is limited.

effects

In the early days of live sound, effects were confined to tape echo, spring reverb, and guitar amp tremolo, but the digital age changed all that. Now we have low-cost multieffects units that can generate anything from rotary speaker simulations and chorus effects to delay and reverb, often in quite complex combinations. Along with multieffects boxes come presets and easy edit options, which on the whole is a good thing, but it does mean that those users who missed out on the early manually-settable effects may not know how all the effects work. For that reason, I'm going to start by examining the main effects types.

digital delay

Digital delay is the successor to the tape echo unit, a special type of recorder using one record head and between one and four replay heads. A continuous loop of tape was used on most machines to prevent the tape running out part way through a performance, and the principle was simply that any input signal was recorded, then played back a short time later via the replay heads. An erase head then cleaned the tape before returning it to the record head. The delay time was set by the tape speed and the head spacing, and by incorporating a variable speed control, and on/off switching for the replay heads, various delay effects were possible. Repeat echoes were achieved by feeding some of the output signal back to the input as shown in Figure 5.10.

Digital delay or DDL is one of the key elements of a modern multieffects unit, and performs essentially the same task as the tape loop echo machine, but there are no tapes to wear out and the range of adjustment is far greater. It's also possible to modulate the delay time to create effects such as chorus, vibrato, flanging and phasing. Whereas most tape echo units were mono,

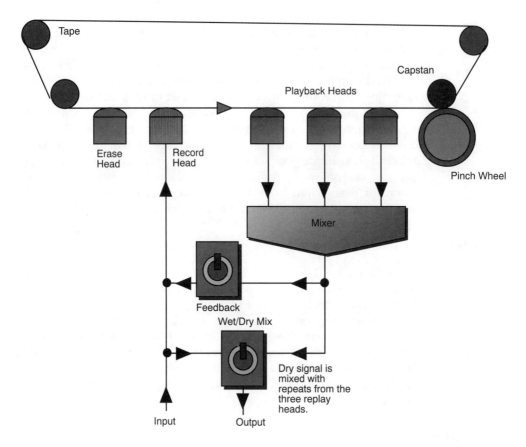

Figure 5.10: Tape loop echo unit

today's digital effects are invariably stereo. A typical DDL effects block offers variable feedback, to produce multiple decaying repeats, and some offer multi-tap delay where several repeats at different delay times can be created. This is directly analogous to the multiple heads of the tape loop echo, and by feeding back some signal from all the taps, the density of the repeats builds up very quickly into a kind of pseudo reverb. Figure 5.11 shows how a multi-tap delay operates.

Further variety can be created by arranging for the repeats to come from alternating sides, or by feeding some of the left channel's output back into the right input and vice versa. These options are usually presented in the form of "algorithms", where the routing is set, but the user has control over the values of various parameters, including delay time and feedback. There's also a mix parameter or control allowing the original and delayed sounds to be balanced.

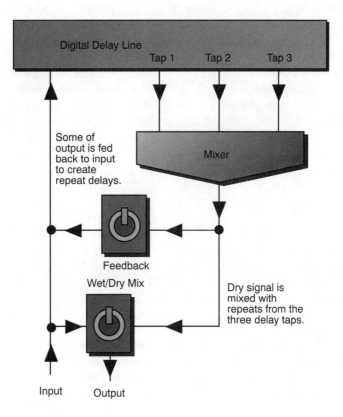

Figure 5.11: How a multi-tap DDL operates

delay effects

The DDL is the basis of a number of familiar effects, some of which are produced by modulating the delay time, but the simplest DDL effect is a single repeat using no modulation and no feedback. Short delays of between 30 and 100mS are used to create slap-back echo effects or pre-delays for reverb effects, while longer delays produce a distinct single echo. Echoes timed to coincide with the tempo of the song can occasionally be effective.

Multiple, equally spaced delays are obtained by increasing the feedback value. At longer delay times, you'll hear the familiar repeat echo effect, but as the delay time is shortened, you'll notice that the echo effect disappears, and is replaced by a metallic resonance, sometimes called tunnel echo. The frequency of resonance depends on the delay time; for example, a 5mS delay time will resonate at 1000/5 = 200Hz. Increasing the feedback will maximise this resonant effect, and several good examples can be found on the more adventurous dance records or dance loop sample CDs.

Using a multi-tapped delay enables a less rhythmic echo effect to be created, and for the best effect, the delay times of the various tapes should not be set to exact multiples of each other. This simulates the multi-head tape echo where the heads were often spaced at irregular intervals. Adding feedback causes the echo decay to become quite complex, and this effect is popular on electric guitar, on vocals and on instruments such as synth lead lines, sax or flute. Combining delay with reverb is a useful way to make vocals sound more interesting.

tap tempo

Delay effects used on instruments often sound best when the delay time is set to match the tempo of the music, but live bands have a habit of playing at different speeds depending on how the night is going. One way of making tempo setting easier is to use a DDL with a tap tempo facility, a feature that's best controlled by footswitch when you're performing. When you're in tap tempo mode, you simply tap your foot on the switch at the tempo of the song and the delay time will be set to the time interval between your taps. You only need to tap twice, but if your song speeds up (either by accident or by intent!), you simply tap again to bring the delay back in time with the new tempo. Obviously the maximum delay time can't exceed the maximum delay time of your DDL, no matter how long you leave it between taps!

delay modulation

By modulating the delay time using an LFO, the pitch of the delayed signal wavers both sharp and flat at the rate set by the LFO speed. The depth of modulation determines how far sharp or flat the sound goes. The simplest modulation effect is pitch vibrato, where only the delayed sound is used. The original sound is turned off using the mix parameter. The sound we hear from the output will be delayed slightly, but if the delay time is set to less than 10mS, it will be too short to notice. If you set a modulation rate of say 4Hz, then turn the depth control up slowly, you should hear the sound being processed take on a wavering effect, not unlike that produced by the mod wheel on a synth.

phasing

To convert vibrato to phasing, set the mix parameter to give equal amounts of dry and delayed sound and experiment with delay times between 1 and 10mS. As you adjust the modulation speed and depth, you'll hear the individual harmonics that make up your sound moving in and out of phase with each other, which has the effect of filtering the sound in a very dynamic and complex way. This is known as comb filtering, because a frequency graph would show a series of narrow spikes and troughs, rather like the teeth of a comb. As the delay is modulated, these "teeth" move up and down the audio spectrum, and you'll probably recognise the effect as being similar to what you get from guitar phaser pedals. You can vary which harmonics are affected by changing the delay time; the shorter the delay time, the higher the frequencies that are affected and vice versa. If your unit has a feedback invert function, try switching this in, as it too affects the harmonic structure of the effect.

flanging

Flanging dates back to the sixties and was first created by simultaneously running two tape machines carrying copies of the same music, then mixing the two outputs with precisely equal levels. If the two machines are perfectly in time (sync), with each other, the two signals add normally, but if the timing between the machines drifts for any reason, you hear a phasing effect due to comb filtering. By deliberately slowing down one machine and then the other by using hand friction on the supply reel, the phasing effect can be controlled, though it takes some practice to get it right.

Flanging can be approximated digitally by adding a delayed signal to the original sound, then modulating the delay time of the delayed signal. The settings for flanging are similar to those used for phasing, except longer delay times of typically 10 to 50mS are used, and the feedback value increased to make the effect more resonant. On more sophisticated units, it may be possible to modulate the delay using some source other than the LFO, for example, the input signal's envelope. This can help make the effect less obviously repetitive, and hence more like its tape counterpart.

As with phasing, inverting the phase of the signal fed back to the input allows different harmonics to be accentuated by the filtering process. Try both options and see which you prefer.

chorus

The chorus effect is essentially the same as vibrato, but with an equal proportion of the dry sound mixed in. The idea is to produce the illusion of two instruments playing together by simulating the slight timing and pitching differences that occur between two or more performers playing the same part on the same instrument. By setting a longer delay time than for vibrato, say between 30 and 150mS, the effect of the timing differences between instruments is made more pronounced. You can also use very gentle modulation on even longer delays to create a combined chorus and echo effect. The modulation speed is usually set in the range 2Hz to 6Hz and the depth set by ear so as not to sound too out-of-tune. The longer the delay time, the less depth will be needed. More sophisticated chorus effects blocks may include a multi-tapped algorithm, which produces the effect of multiple chorus devices operating at the same time.

Chorus was first developed for use on electric guitars and synth string machines, but it can be used on virtually anything, from fretless bass to synth pads. However, it never seems entirely successful on vocals as the effect is too regular to sound entirely natural. Though most chorus effects now come as stereo, you can fatten up a mono chorus by panning the original, untreated sound to one side and the modulated delay to the other. The result is a moving, wide sound source that appears to hang between the speakers.

rotary speakers

All organ players are familiar with the Leslie speaker sound, and many multieffects units include an algorithm to simulate their rotary speaker cabinets. A real rotating speaker works by means of a rotating baffle around the bass speaker, plus a rotating horn to carry the high end. A motor and pulley system provides two operating speeds, and because of mechanical inertia, the system takes a finite time to switch between these two speeds. In a multieffects unit, the effect is usually created by a combination of modulated delay and filtering, but as far as the user is concerned, there may only be fast, slow and off speed options to select from. The inertia effect is simulated by using a special LFO that changes speed over a period of a second or so rather than instantly, and the skill of using a rotating speaker (or emulation) is to operate the speed change at appropriate points during the performance to provide the right feel. This effect also works well on guitar, synth pads, and sometimes even on voice. Because this is a performance effect, it is likely to be controlled by the musician on stage.

algorithms

In the context of a multieffects unit, modulation effects are likely to have their own algorithms, rather than relying on the user to create the effect from scratch using a general purpose DDL block. Irrelevant parameters will normally be excluded and the delay time range restricted to that relevant to the particular modulation effect being created. This helps guide the inexperienced user in the right direction, and may allow the manufacturer to introduce further parameters to increase the flexibility of the effect.

reverberation

Reverberation is a very familiar effect, and in nature, it's created when sound reflects around inside a confined space such as a building. Though the concept is simple, the resulting reflection patterns are immensely complex. For example, a single handclap in a cathedral can generate thousands of reflections within the first second, and as the reverb decays, the complexity continues to increase as each reflection is re-reflected from multiple surfaces. The first set of reflections from the walls and ceilings are known as "early reflections", and their pattern provides strong psychoacoustic clues as to the nature of a space, even when we can't see it. In a large hall, the first few echoes may well be quite distinct before they build up into a dense reverberation, whereas in a smaller room, the distances are much shorter, so the reverb density builds up far more quickly.

Though technically quite complicated, the low cost of DSP chips (Digital Signal Processors) has brought us a whole range of affordable reverb and multieffects devices. These invariably have stereo outputs which create a wide, spacious effect, even when the input signal is in mono.

The most obvious parameter is the time reverb takes to die away after a percussive sound such as a handclap or drum beat. For contemporary music production, decay times of between one and three seconds are the most useful, though most units have a far wider range to allow for the creation of special effects. Reverb settings with strong early reflections and a fairly fast decay are an effective way of creating a wide stereo effect from a mono source such as a voice or instrument recorded with a single microphone.

In a large space, there is a delay between the original sound and the first reflections being heard. It takes around a tenth of a second for a sound to travel to a wall 50 feet away and then bounce back to the listener. Most reverb units have a pre-delay parameter, and the effect of adjusting this is to vary the apparent size of the room without changing the overall decay time. It also helps give the mix more clarity by leaving a breathing space between the original sound and the reverb that follows it. Reverb treatments are based on algorithms (in this case, a mathematic model simulating the reflective properties of a room), and a typical unit will include algorithms for halls, rooms, chambers and plates (mechanical studio reverb device based on a large metal plate), as well as non-natural reverbs, such as gated and reversed versions. Figure 5.12 shows how reverb develops from a percussive sound.

Soft furnishings in a room will absorb more high-frequency energy, hence reducing the high-frequency decay time, but a tiled room or stone cavern will reflect well at high frequencies, resulting in a very bright reverb. To

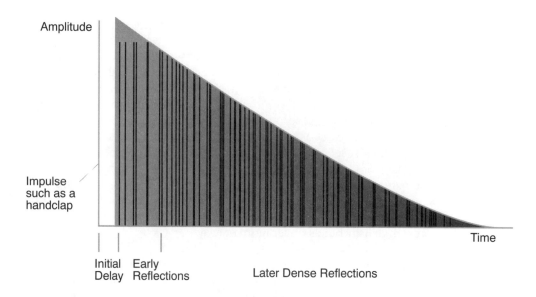

Figure 5.12: Reverb development from a percussive sound

emulate these environments, the basic algorithms include parameters for adjusting the relative HF and LF decay times. Brighter sounds work well with drums, electric guitars, acoustic guitars and pop vocals, while more classical acoustic instruments often work better with a more natural-sounding reverb. Though having hundreds of parameters to play with can be worthwhile in the studio, the fact that some natural room reverberation is always present at a typical venue means that subtle differences between reverb programs can easily be lost. Most live sound engineers prefer a reverb unit with a handful of good sounds to one that requires days to program.

gated reverb

Gated reverb was probably one of the first multieffect treatments as it was first achieved by miking a drum kit in an extremely live room, then using a noise gate to cut the reverb off abruptly at the end of each beat. Though the effect is less fashionable in this context today, most multieffects devices and reverb boxes provide gated reverb capability. Sometimes this is as a single algorithm, while on other units you have to create it from separate reverb and gate "blocks".

Reverse reverb is a burst of early reflections starting off at a low level and gradually increasing before ending abruptly. This reverse envelope is responsible for the reversed illusion the effect creates. Figure 5.13 shows the envelopes of gated and reverse reverb.

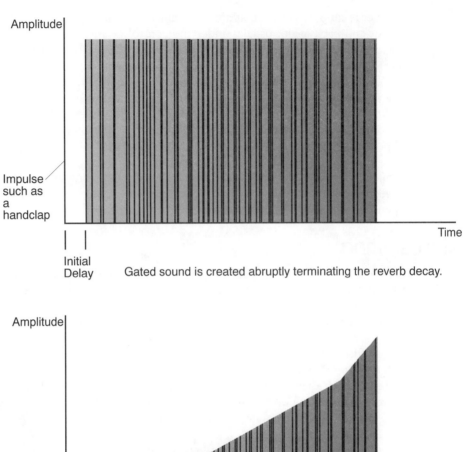

Gated sound is created abruptly terminating the reverb decay.

Reverse sound is created by applying a reverse envelope to conventional reverb reflections.

Figure 5.13: Envelopes of gated and reverse reverb

panner

A panner is simply a device that automatically pans a mono signal from left to right and back again, usually under the control of an LFO. It is closely related to tremolo, an effect created by modulating the level of a signal using an LFO, except in the case of the panner, there are two modulating circuits, one of which is at maximum gain while the other is at minimum – as shown in Figure 5.14. Some effects units incorporate options for triggering the pan to MIDI notes or sync'ing it to tempo via MIDI Clock, in which case it's possible to synchronise the panning to the tempo of the music, providing the performance is being sync'ed to a MIDI sequencer.

Panning can work well with a stereo instrument rig, but wholesale panning between the PA speakers isn't always effective as the subjective result will depend on where the listener is relative to the two speaker stacks.

pitch shifting

Pitch shifting is a process for changing the pitch of a sound without changing its duration, unlike the effect you get from speeding up a tape machine. The range is usually one or two octaves up or down with fine tuning as well as semitone step adjustment.

Pitch shifting works rather like a type of sampler that samples very short sections of the sound, loops these sections, then plays them back at a different speed. Clever algorithms are used to hide the splicing between subsequent loops, but on all but the most sophisticated devices, the splicing shows up as a warble when large amounts of pitch shift are used.

Most multieffects devices include a pitch shifting section, which may allow simultaneous shifting up and down in pitch. If small shifts of between five and 10 cents, both positive and negative, are applied to a signal, you get a nice alternative to chorusing without any obvious cyclic sweeping. This is good for thickening vocals, especially when combined with delay and reverb. It's also common to find an option for adding delay to shifted sounds, and the facility to feed the shifted output back to the input so that it will be shifted again. This can be useful as a special effect to create spiralling arpeggios, but it gets very tedious if you overuse it.

Larger pitch shifts over whole semitones usually sound too "warbly" to be useful in musically discriminating applications, but they may still be used for special effects, or mixed in with a high percentage of the unshifted sound.

A basic pitch shifter is of little use in creating true musical harmonies as it

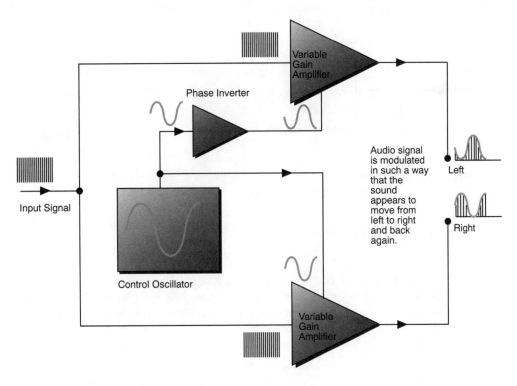

Figure 5.14 Panner block diagram

produces only parallel musical intervals, and the only useful fixed intervals tend to be octaves and fifths. However, some models now include intelligent pitch shifting, where the user defines a musical scale, and the device automatically picks the correct harmony interval. This is done by tracking the pitch of the input signal (which must be monophonic for clean tracking), then applying the correct amount of shift to produce the desired harmony note. The harmony scales may either be presets or user programmable.

formant correction

Though not yet available in typical multieffects units, it can only be a matter of time before "formant-corrected" pitch shifting becomes standard issue. With a conventional pitch shifter, moving the pitch up creates a Micky Mouse effect, because not only does the musical note change, the timbre of the sound also changes, just as though you were speeding up a tape. In real life, when a singer sings a new note, certain components of the sound stay the same, such as the throat and chest cavity resonances.

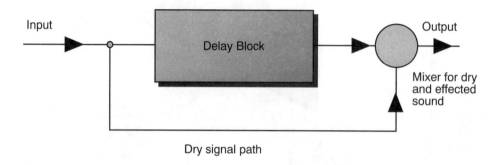

Figure 5.15: Delay block with wet/dry mixer

Using formant-corrected pitch shifting, it should be possible to move notes to any pitch, but still leave the fixed resonances in place to produce a much more natural sound. Alternatively, you could deliberately move the formants to make a male voice appear female or vice versa. I predict that this is going to be a hugely important area in the not too distant future.

vocoder

A vocoder is a special type of multi-band filter that automatically mimics the frequency spectrum characteristics of a signal being fed into its control input. You can visualise it as a graphic EQ that's able to listen to any signal, and constantly adjust its fader settings to match the spectral content of that signal. Now, when a signal is passed through the vocoder's filters, it takes on the same spectral characteristics as the control input. The most famous effect is probably the singing keyboard where a harmonically rich keyboard sound is articulated using the human voice. Vocoding would normally be handled by the individual instrumentalist on stage rather than by the FOH mix engineer.

combining effects

Every time two effects block outputs have to be mixed together, or when a dry signal has to be mixed with the output of an effects block, a mixing element is needed, and these are provided within multieffects units as part of the effect algorithm. As far as the user is concerned, it's usually only necessary to adjust levels – the routing within the algorithm takes care of the mixing. When the output of one effects block is fed into the input of another, there will be no need for a mixer (series connection), but when the outputs from two parallel effects blocks need to be combined, a mixer will be required. Blocks may also incorporate mixing elements – for example, a delay block requires a mixer to balance the dry and delayed sound, as shown in Figure 5.15.

Simpler multieffects units may be limited to connecting the blocks in a series chain, and the simplest of these place the blocks in a preset order, leaving the user with choice of which blocks to use and which to turn off. More sophisticated systems allow the user to rearrange the blocks into a different order, and it's quite common for both series and parallel connections to be permitted. Figure 5.16 shows both series and parallel routing options.

equalisation

Equalisation is covered in the chapter on mixing, and any type of EQ may be included in a multieffect, from a simple top-cut filter to a multi-band parametric or graphic equaliser. Graphic equalisers have the advantage of simplicity, though you obviously lose the physical fader control once you get into multieffects box territory. Even so, some units provide a graphic style readout on the display so that you can still see the shape of the curve you have set up.

swept filter

The filter used in a typical analogue synthesiser is closely related to the parametric equaliser, the main difference being that the frequency of the filter can be controlled electronically rather being left to the user. For example, an LFO could be used to sweep the frequency up and down, or an envelope could be generated to provide a filter sweep. You'll probably also find the filter can be set to a higher Q. Some of the more sophisticated multieffects processors include not only resonant synth-type filters, but also a variety of possible control sources, including envelopes derived from the input signal level, MIDI triggered envelopes, LFOs and so on.

gating

Gates are normally found in dedicated units, but they may also be incorporated into multieffects boxes to tame the background noise from sources such as electric guitars or noisy keyboards. By setting the threshold at just about the background noise level, any pauses or gaps in the programme material can be silenced. While the gate is open, both the wanted signal and the noise pass through, but unless something is seriously wrong with your source material, the wanted sound will be loud enough to hide the noise.

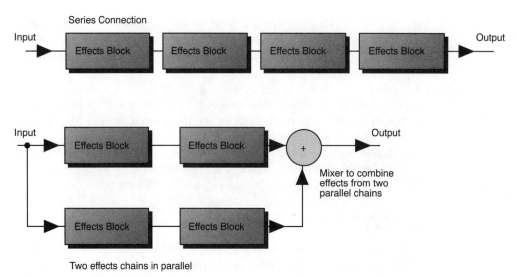

Figure 5.16: Series and parallel routing options

Though not a complete solution to noise, gates can be useful when working with electric guitars, which often generate a lot of hiss and hum, especially when overdrive is being used.

amp/speaker simulator

While keyboards tend to work best through a hi-fi type of system with a flat frequency response and minimal distortion, guitar and bass amplifiers are "voiced", which means their frequency response is shaped to suit the instrument rather than being left flat. Furthermore, the loudspeakers and enclosures used in guitar and bass amplification tend to have a very limited frequency response, which enables them to filter out the rougher sounding components of amplifier distortion. This is explained more fully in the chapter on microphones and DI.

If you were to DI a distorted guitar without EQ, the result would be very thin and harsh compared to what you would hear from an amplifier. One solution is to use a DI box with an integral speaker simulator, but now speaker simulation is often included as part of a multieffects box's repertoire.

overdrive

The overdrive sound of electric guitar amplifiers is so complicated that some designers are now resorting to physical modelling as a means of replicating it digitally. However, even without physical modelling, it is possible to produce a digital equivalent of an overdrive pedal, and that's what many multieffects boxes give you. Serious guitarists may still want to use their own analogue distortion pedals, but the quality of the overdrive included in multieffects units is improving all the time.

fx connections

The different things you can do to an audio signal break down neatly into two areas: Effects and Processors. Effects add something to the original sound whereas a processor takes the original sound and changes it in some way.

Effects invariably involve some form of delay circuitry and include reverb, delay, echo, chorus, flanging, vibrato and pitch shift. Not all these effects require the original signal to be mixed with the treated signal, but all use delays, even if these are very short.

Effects such as those mentioned may be connected either via the (post-fade) aux send/return system or they may be used at the console insert points. When used in the aux send system, the dry signal level should be turned off on the effects unit, but when used via insert points, the dry/effects balance must be set on the effects unit itself.

Using too much in the way of effects invariably sounds worse than using too little, so always err on the side of restraint, especially when it comes to reverb. If you have two spare mixer channels (panned hard left and right for stereo) to bring your effects back into line rather than the usual aux returns, you can use the desk EQ to take some bottom end out of the effects signal which might help clean up a messy sounding room. If you're picking a unit that can be operated from on stage, don't forget to ensure the model you're considering has a bypass footswitch socket – surprisingly, some don't.

Processors, as distinct from effects, include equalisers, enhancers, compressors, limiters, gates, expanders and panners. These process the whole of the incoming signal, and with the exception of enhancers, the dry signal isn't used at all. For this reason, processors may only be used via console insert points or connected directly "in-line" with a signal; they can't be used in the aux/send system.

anti-feedback systems

Acoustic feedback is the enemy of every live performer, especially in small venues where the positioning of your equipment is dictated more by the layout of the room than by optimum acoustic practice. A number of different systems have been used to try to reduce the amount of feedback, ranging from pairs of out-of-phase microphones held together by gaffer tape, to frequency shifters that make everything you play and sing sound slightly out of tune, but none offered a complete solution. Today, the most popular form of feedback control is the graphic equaliser, though as we shall see, it isn't ideally suited to the task

Anti-feedback devices tend to work on the principle that once your system is set up in any given room, the geometry and acoustic properties of the space, combined with the characteristics of your sound system, will cause feedback to occur at some frequencies before others. During setup using conventional graphic equalisers, the system gain is increased until the ringing that announces the onset of feedback appears, then the appropriate graphic slider is pulled down slightly to restore stability. This 'ringing out' procedure is repeated for all the most serious feedback frequencies, and in the hands of an experienced engineer, the system stability can be increased significantly, but the solution is far from perfect for two important reasons. Firstly, the operator needs a lot of skill to know which faders to pull down and by how much. Even a skilled operator can take up a lot of time ringing out a system, because not only do they have the main PA to worry about, there are probably several sets of graphic equalisers in the monitor system that also need setting up.

Another problem is the resolution of the graphic equalisers themselves. Even a third-octave (30-band), graphic equaliser is a fairly coarse tool, and moving a single fader will affect a region of the audio spectrum almost one octave wide. Feedback, on the other hand, tends to occur at spot frequencies, so pulling down a fader to cure a feedback problem will take out a far wider portion of the frequency spectrum than is necessary. Things get worse if the feedback frequency falls between two of the slider frequencies, because then you'll have to pull down both sliders to kill the feedback, and that in turn means an even more significant change in the sound of the PA. By the time the graphic equaliser has been set up to keep the feedback under control, the overall sound of the PA can be severely compromised. Figure 5.17 shows the effect of moving one and two adjacent graphic equaliser sliders.

auto anti-feedback devices

During the mid-nineties, a new generation of processor was developed to simplify the control of feedback while having less of an audible effect on the sound of the PA. A little thought tells us exactly what is needed – an equaliser where the bands are very narrow, and where they can be precisely tuned to match the feedback frequencies. The problem is that the narrower the bands,

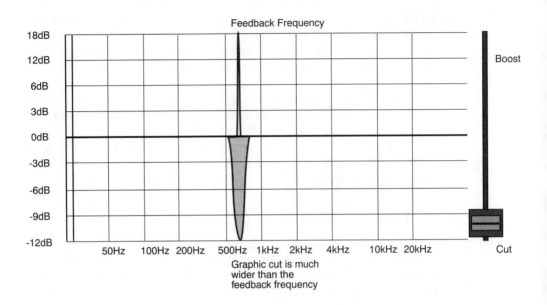

Graphic cut is much
wider than the
feedback frequency

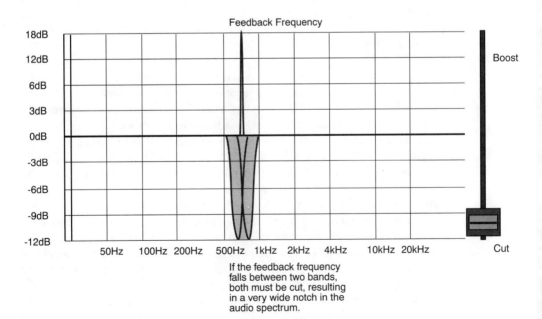

If the feedback frequency
falls between two bands,
both must be cut, resulting
in a very wide notch in the
audio spectrum.

Figure 5.17: Feedback suppression using a graphic EQ

the harder it is for an operator to set the right frequency, so some degree of automation is vital. To perform all the necessary tasks with the required degree of precision requires the use of digital electronics, and now several manufacturers offer automatic systems that work on broadly similar principles. These new systems all include filters that can automatically lock onto feedback frequencies without any intervention on behalf of the operator.

Once the system gain has been increased to the point where ringing occurs, the ring frequency is automatically measured, then a very narrow notch filter is positioned at exactly that frequency to kill it. Increasing the gain further will cause the system to ring at a new frequency, and again a filter moves in to kill it. This is repeated until a number of filters are in place to suppress the strongest feedback modes.

assigned and floating filters

During a performance, feedback may occur at new frequencies as the singer moves the microphone, so a typical system will leave some filters unassigned, deploying them only if a new feedback frequency is detected. This can be very effective, but it still isn't perfect as audible feedback must occur for a second or so before the system can kill it. However, the response time is usually faster than a human engineer can manage, and because the filters are only a few Hz wide, the effect on the overall audio quality is insignificant compared with the damage done by a conventional graphic equaliser.

A typical unit may be either mono or stereo and will include 10 or more separate filters, each of which can lock onto feedback anywhere in the audio spectrum. The filter width may be as narrow as a twentieth of an octave or so wide, though some units have a switchable filter width so that you can choose to accept slightly more audio degradation in exchange for more robust feedback suppression in difficult situations. A number of the filters are set up and locked during the initial ringing out process, with the remaining filters left floating to stand guard against new feedback frequencies. What tends to happen is that each time a new feedback frequency is detected, one of the floating filters locks onto it and then remains fixed at that frequency. When all the floating filters have been used up, the next time feedback occurs, the first is reset to the new feedback frequency. Depending on the make and model of anti-feedback device, the user may be able to choose how many filters remain fixed after setup and how many remain free to deal with new feedback problems.

A typical setup procedure involves switching the unit into its auto setup mode, then you slowly bring up the system gain so that ringing occurs. As each ring is dealt with, you increase the gain further until all the fixed filters have been set. Note that some units actually handle the gain increase for you as well, in which case you only need to press the "go" button and then sit back.

personal systems

With any automatic anti-feedback system, it is necessary to allow the system to feed back in order to allow the circuitry to track the feedback frequency, so ringing out the system can be pretty antisocial. A stereo device would normally be patched via the console's master insert points, but personal models are also available. Personal anti-feedback systems are fitted with integral microphone preamplifiers and connect between the mic and the console's mic input. Setting up is similar to the procedure already described.

A limiter is a good idea in any PA system, and some of the personal anti-feedback devices have one built in, which prevents loud sounds from overloading the unit. Other facilities may also be included, such as switchable phantom power, equalisation or enhancement.

realistic expectations

Having tried a number of anti-feedback devices working on the tracking filter principle, I have to admit that they work surprisingly well, though exactly how much extra gain you can get before feedback depends on the room you're in and on the quality of the other components in your system. Under typical conditions, it isn't unreasonable to expect an additional 5 or 6dB of feedback-free gain, and as a bonus, you'll probably find that your system sounds a lot clearer when it isn't ringing on the verge of feedback.

Stereo systems that work on the whole PA are obviously good value, but they won't deal with monitor system feedback at the same time. For this you'll need either to buy more units for the monitor system, or use personal anti-feedback boxes for the stage mics most likely to give feedback problems. The great benefit of a personal system is that because it comes first in the signal chain, it can deal with feedback due to either the main PA or the monitor system, and in a situation that includes a complex monitoring system, personal anti-feedback devices probably provide the most cost-effective and easy to set up solution. What's more, if you're working with a hired system, it's relatively easy to patch in a personal unit, whereas the engineer may be less keen to let you connect a stereo unit to his main mixer outputs or insert points.

spectrum analysers

The spectrum analyser is a device that shows the sound level in a number of frequency bands, and on a professional model, these frequency bands are one third of an octave wide, corresponding to the bands on a graphic equaliser. Indeed, the spectrum analyser has much in common with the graphic equaliser insomuch as it uses the same type of filters, but instead of having a row of faders to change the sound, it has a row of bar graph meters to monitor the sound energy in each frequency band.

If a sound system is fed with pink noise (random noise with an equal amount of energy per octave), and an accurate microphone is used to pick up the sound, the spectrum analyser can be used to interpret the output from the microphone so as to identify peaks or troughs in the combined response of the system plus the room in which it is operating. To analyse a room properly, it is necessary to take measurements at different positions and then average them, as position in the room will affect results, but an experienced user can move the mic while watching the display to identify genuine problems that don't change with mic position. The important thing is to identify significant peaks so that they can be tamed by pulling down the graphic EQ faders at these frequencies. It is less important to add boost where there are dips in the response, and in some cases, this will actually have an adverse effect. Adjusting the graphic EQ until all major peaks are flattened is usually the best you can do.

power amplifiers

Power amplifiers are rarely the most glamorous components of a PA rig, but their correct function is vital to the performance of the system as a whole. The job of the power amplifier is simply to take a line-level signal from a mixer output or active crossover, then increase it to a power where it can drive the system's loudspeakers. Depending on the type and size of system, there may be only one power amplifier or there may be many, but the task is the same – to take an input signal and amplify it without changing it in any other way. Inevitably some changes between input and output do occur, and these changes are what we know as distortion, but a well designed amplifier run within its operating limits can produce extremely low levels of distortion.

While hi-fi amplifiers may be fitted with tone controls, source switching and preamp stages, professional power amplifiers tend to come as two-channel rack-mount devices with no controls other than a power switch and volume controls. They may also be fan-cooled. Some have meters, others have only "signal present" LEDs, and some have clip indicating LEDs. Whatever other metering is present, I feel that choosing an amplifier with a clip indicator is important as this will warn of potential speaker-damaging situations. The power amplifiers fitted to powered mixers are technically similar to stand-alone power amplifiers.

power rating

Perhaps the most important parameter of a power amplifier is its power rating, which also takes into account the impedance of the loudspeaker load connected to it. For example, an amplifier might be specified as providing 200 watts of continuous power into a four ohm load. Using a load with a lower impedance may well draw excessive output current causing the amplifier to overheat, while driving a load with a higher impedance will result in less power being available. As a rule of thumb, doubling the load impedance will halve the available power, so our amplifier rated at 200 watts of continuous power into a four ohm load will only deliver around 100 watts into eight ohms or 50 watts into 16 ohms. This relationship isn't always exact as other factors come into play, such as how much heat the amplifier can dissipate or how much current the power supply can deliver on a continuous basis.

The significance of the term "continuous" is exactly as it suggests – the amplifier can deliver this level of power over long periods of time. However, music isn't generally continuous in nature but instead contains peaks, such as drum hits, so most well designed amplifiers are constructed to handle brief peaks several dB in excess of their continuous rating. Many amplifiers are power supply current limited to some extent so that music with a high average-to-peak ratio has more headroom than something like highly compressed music. Short peaks don't cause the power supply voltage to fall, but when a lot of power is drawn continuously, the power supply voltage sags, limiting the amount of power to a safe level. Without power limiting of some kind, the output devices may overheat and fail.

It may seem counter intuitive, but by running an amplifier at a lower average level, the available peak power may actually be greater than when running it flat out, simply because the power supply isn't constantly putting the brakes on by applying current limiting. The important thing is to keep an eye on the clip LEDs to make sure the amplifier isn't being driven into clipping, and if you need to amplify heavily compressed music that has a low average-to-peak ratio, choose an amplifier with an adequate continuous power rating – don't rely on peak figures.

protection racket

Without some form of protection, power amplifiers are very vulnerable to abuse, and even though most large amplifiers are fan-cooled, it's still possible to generate more heat than can be safely dissipated, by constantly driving the amplifier into clipping, by running into too low a load impedance, or by obstructing the ventilation in some way. Fortunately, most amplifiers include several forms of protection that will either reduce the available power, or switch the amplifier off altogether if a dangerous condition arises.

Virtually all designs include thermal protection, so that if the heatsinks containing the output devices get too hot, the amplifier will shut down until a safe operating temperature is restored. Some models even link the heat sensors to the fan, so that the fan increases in speed when the amp is working hard.

Protection is also provided against short circuits at the speaker terminals so that a faulty lead doesn't destroy your amplifier. Without this protection, a short circuit would cause the amplifier to attempt to deliver huge currents, blowing the output devices in an instant. A less well known, but equally vital form of protection is designed to guard the loudspeakers against damage in the event of an amplifier failure. A typical power amplifier runs from a dual rail power supply so that the output voltage can swing both positive and negative, but in the event of an output stage failure, you could find one of these power supply rails effectively feeding straight into your speaker! Such a high DC voltage on the amplifier output almost always causes serious speaker damage, so the more considerate designers include protection against DC offset.

When amplifiers are mounted in racks, it is vital that proper ventilation is provided, otherwise the protection circuitry will operate earlier than it would under normal conditions, reducing the amount of power you can safely draw from the amplifiers. As you might expect, overheating is more of a problem in hot environments, and in some situations, additional fans may be required inside the amplifier rack to help carry away the hot air.

bridge mode

Some stereo power amplifiers include a specification for a "bridged" mono mode power rating, and a rear panel switch is generally used to select bridged operation. Essentially, bridged mode uses both power amplifiers to drive a single load in a differential mode by connecting the loudspeaker between the positive terminal of both amplifies, then feeding one of the amplifiers with an out-of-phase signal. This is shown in Figure 5.18.

The advantage of bridged mode is that higher powers are available than with just a single amplifier, though it should be noted that the minimum load impedance is also doubled, so an amplifier normally rated into four ohms should not be run into loads of less than eight ohms when bridged. This is because the voltage available at the output terminals in bridged mode is roughly double that available from a single amplifier, and as power is proportional to the square of the voltage ($P = V$ squared$/R$ watts), running into the original four-ohm load would cause the two amplifiers to try to produce four times the

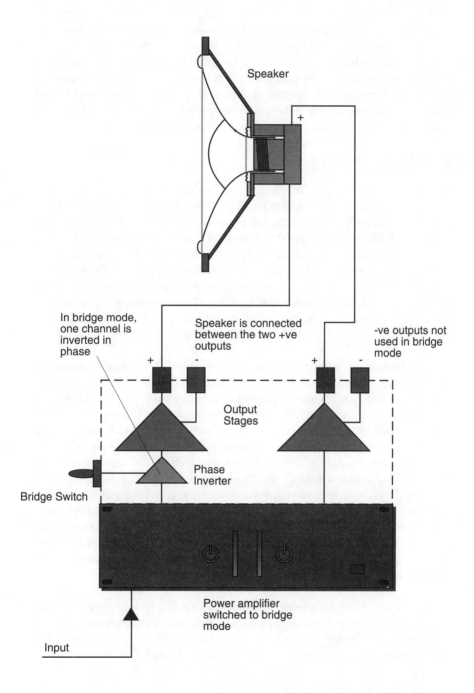

Speaker

In bridge mode, one channel is inverted in phase

Speaker is connected between the two +ve outputs

-ve outputs not used in bridge mode

+ −

+ −

Output Stages

Phase Inverter

Bridge Switch

Power amplifier switched to bridge mode

Input

Figure 5.18: Bridged power amp operation

power of a single amplifier. This would obviously cause overloading problems, so by doubling the load to eight ohms, the power from the bridged amplifiers is about double what you'd get from a single amplifier. This keeps the amplifiers running within their rated parameters and provides an effective means of delivering a large amount of power to a single load. Note that you should never switch to bridge mode when the amplifier outputs are connected conventionally as this would put the two speakers out-of-phase with each other.

power amplifier distortion

As stated earlier, no power amplifier is perfect, and all produce some degree of distortion. Good design can keep this distortion to very low levels, but if any amplifier is driven too hard, there will eventually come a point where no more voltage is available, so the signal will be clipped as shown in Figure 5.19. Here you can see a sine wave that has had its top flattened or clipped when the amplifier has run out of headroom. The flat top represents the maximum voltage the amplifier can deliver, so no matter what shape the signal is above this point, the output will always be a flat line. The same thing happens when the amplifier voltage reaches its negative extreme, so both the top and bottom of the waveform are clipped when the amplifier is overdriven.

The result of heavy clipping is a very audible and very unpleasant distortion that generates a large proportion of high-frequency harmonics that weren't present in the original signal. A guitarist's fuzz box clips the signal deliberately to produce a rasping sound, but as you can imagine, that doesn't sound too good on a PA. What's worse is that these newly generated harmonics can damage drivers, particularly tweeters in systems that use passive crossovers. In active systems, clipping at the bass end won't affect the signal fed to the tweeters, but heavy clipping can damage even a large bass speaker by increasing the average power the speaker receives, thus overheating the voice coil. A square wave contains approximately 100% more power than a sine wave of the same peak level, so whenever an amplifier is clipping, the loudspeaker is receiving twice as much power as usual. Clipping also causes the speaker cone to slam against the extremes of its excursion, which in combination with an overheated voice coil, can cause the driver to shake itself apart.

Clipping can be detected using the clip LEDs on the power amplifier, but a safer option is to use a limiter before the power amplifier to prevent clipping altogether. The limiter threshold should be adjusted until the amplifier clip LEDs just come on, then it should be backed off by half a dB or so.

choosing and using amplifiers

It's apparent from the above facts that clipped signals pose a far greater threat

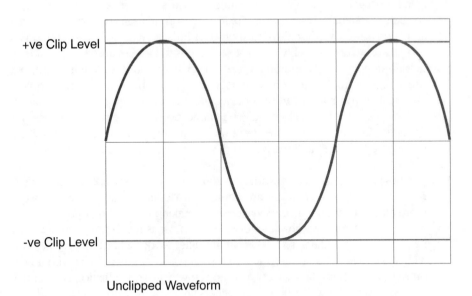

+ve Clip Level

-ve Clip Level

Unclipped Waveform

When the gain is increased so that the signal reaches the clip point, it can go no further and so becomes flattened or clipped.

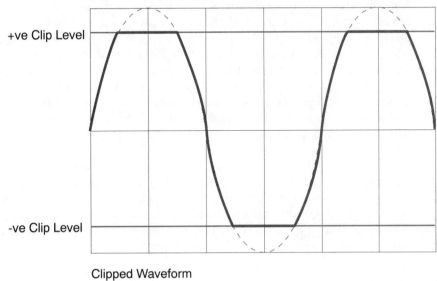

+ve Clip Level

-ve Clip Level

Clipped Waveform

Figure 5.19: Clipping distortion

to a loudspeaker than short term, undistorted signal peaks that exceed the speaker's nominal power rating. For this reason, it's safer to have too much amplifier power at your disposal than too little as there's less likelihood of clipping distortion. Possibly the best scenario is to have an amplifier capable of delivering between 25 and 50% more power than your speakers require, but use a limiter to ensure the amplifier can never be driven into clipping. Obviously, if you have an amplifier rated at a higher power than your speakers and you still drive it into clipping, you're almost certainly going to damage your speakers, so you need to have some way to prevent clipping. Some amplifiers now come with built-in limiting, and this seems to me like a good idea.

For powers of greater than around 200 watts per channel, fan cooling is recommended, though there are some new designs of amplifier that work more efficiently than conventional designs, making fan cooling unnecessary. A regular class A/B power amplifier dissipates almost as much power in heat as it delivers to the speakers, so a 600 watt amplifier working hard might leave you with 400 to 500 watts of waste heat to dispose of. That's around half the power output of an electric fire bar, so you can see why good ventilation is essential. Leaving spaces between power amplifiers in racks is a good idea, and you should be careful not to put any heat sensitive equipment directly above a power amplifier.

Most power amplifiers have big power supplies, which in turn makes them heavy, so when rack-mounting them, it's vital to support them from the rear as well as from the front panel. As with any electronic equipment, they don't like physical shocks, so a flight case with some form of resilient mounting is better than a solid box. If several amplifiers are mounted in the same flight case, it is advisable to fan cool the rear of the case, and if the amplifiers are going to be used in a position where you can't see the clip LEDs, a limiter provides a high degree of speaker protection. In an active system, it is possible to buy active crossovers with integral limiters, and these should be set up so that a maximum peak signal is just short of power amp clipping.

Finally, don't skimp on speaker cable as in a high power system you can lose a lot of your power in poor cable. For small systems, such as those based around a powered mixer, high current mains cable is okay to use as speaker cable, but for larger systems, you should choose a commercial speaker cable from a pro audio supplier. The main requirement is a low electrical resistance, so the shorter you can keep your speaker cables, the better.

crossovers

Any loudspeaker system using separate drivers to handle different parts of the audio spectrum requires a crossover of some kind to ensure that each speaker receives only the range of frequencies that it is designed to reproduce. Crossovers are available in two main types: high-level passive and low-level active. A high-level passive crossover comprises resistors, inductors and capacitors and is designed to filter the signal from the output of a power amplifier – hence the term high level. A simple two-way portable PA cabinet will almost certainly include an internal passive crossover so as to ensure that the bass/mid speaker receives only bass/mid frequencies and the tweeter receives only high frequencies. Passive crossovers have the advantage of simplicity – only one power amplifier is needed per cabinet, and only one speaker cable is required. However, in high-power systems, capacitors with a higher voltage rating are necessary, which adds to the weight and expense. For this reason, passive crossovers tend to be used mainly in smaller systems, though some pro concert systems use a mixture of active and passive crossovers where the passive crossover usually handles the mid/high transition and the active the bass/mid filtering. Figure 5.20 shows a typical two-way passive crossover.

Passive crossovers also suffer the disadvantage that some of the power passed through them is lost, and even using the most efficient design, it is sometimes necessary to deliberately "waste" power to make the sensitivity of one driver match up with that of the others. For example, if the tweeter is 6dB more sensitive than the bass/mid driver in a two-way system, the power fed to the tweeter must be reduced in order to maintain an even sensitivity across the audio spectrum. Furthermore, because every loudspeaker and cabinet combination has a unique impedance/frequency plot, passive crossovers must be individually designed for specific systems.

Because a passive crossover comes between the speakers and the power amplifier, any power amplifier clipping will produce harmonics that pass through the high-pass filter section feeding the tweeter, increasing the risk of driver damage. For this reason, it is recommended that systems using passive crossovers be protected by limiters, or at the very least, the power amp clip LEDs should be monitored during performance.

active crossover facilities

Active crossovers are connected before the power amplifier, so regardless of how powerful the system is, they handle only line level signals. This enables conventional active circuitry to be used, and because such electronic components are relatively cheap, it is possible to build many more features into the crossover. For example, it may be possible to adjust the crossover frequencies, select different crossover slopes and adjust the gain of the various bands as well as providing integral limiting. Other common features include a mono sub-bass output, individual band delays for time alignment and equalisation for constant directivity horns. A typical three-way active crossover setup is shown in Figure 5.21.

Because the crossover performance is independent of the load's impedance characteristics, the same active crossover device can be used with a number of different loudspeaker types. What's more, any power amp clipping will affect only the speaker connected to that power amplifier, so a distorting bass end won't put the tweeters in jeopardy.

So far it sounds as though active crossovers have all the advantages, and in most respects they have, but whereas a passive system can feed a full-range speaker system from a single power amplifier, an active crossover needs a separate power amplifier for each frequency band. What's more, because the amplifiers are generally located away from the speaker cabinets, more speaker cabling is needed.

A typical active crossover comes as a 1U rack processor providing two channels of processing where each channel is switchable to cover two or three frequency bands. The crossover slopes may be fixed or they may be adjustable – the steeper the crossover slope, the less overlap there is between drivers at the crossover point. As a rule, active crossovers can be built with steeper slopes than their passive counterparts. Different speaker systems require different crossover points, so these again tend to be variable, either via a rotary pot or via stepped switches.

time alignment

In a system where separate speaker cabinets are being used for the bass, mid and high end, it is quite possible that the acoustic sources of the various cabinets won't be precisely aligned with each other when the cabinets are stacked. If the acoustic sources aren't aligned, any frequency overlap at the crossover points will compromise both the sound of the system and the dispersion pattern of the sound. For example, a tweeter at the end of a long horn may well produce a sound at the front of the cabinet a fraction of a second after a cone driver that's mounted directly on the front baffle. You could move individual speakers backwards or forwards to compensate for this, but doing that could make the stack unstable. Instead, crossovers often have an inbuilt facility to add a very slight delay to the various frequency bands so as to restore time alignment without physically moving the cabinets. In our example where the sound from the long horn was emerging last, the other bands would need to be delayed to put all the drivers back in sync with each other, as shown in Figure 5.22. To get an idea of how little delay is actually needed to restore time alignment, sound travels at around one foot per millisecond. In other words, delaying the signal fed to one cabinet by 1mS makes it behave as though it has been physically moved backwards by one foot.

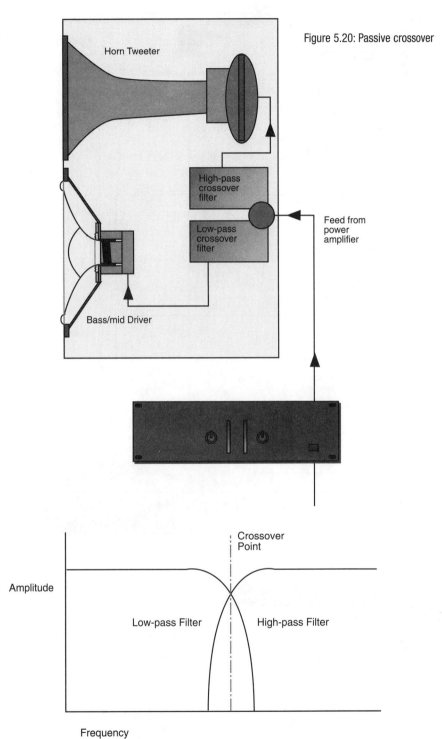

Figure 5.20: Passive crossover

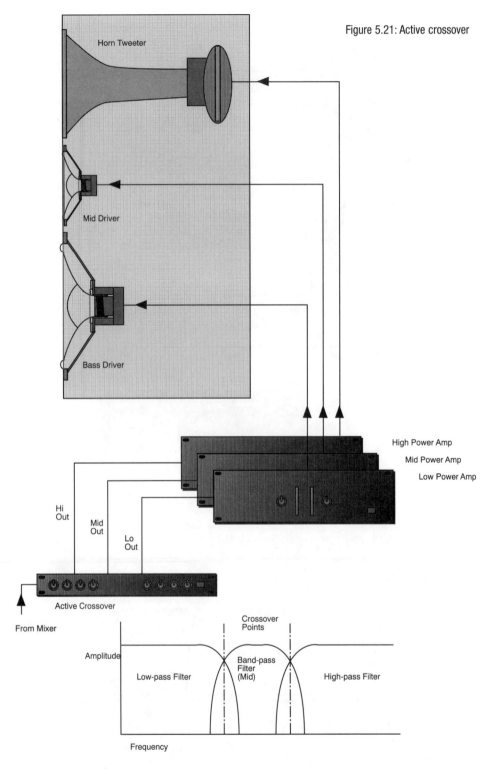

Figure 5.21: Active crossover

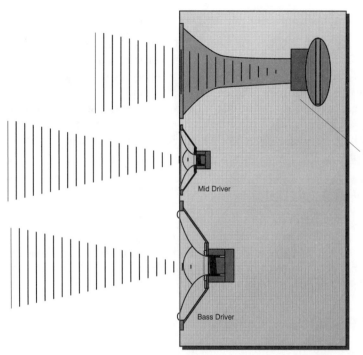

Figure 5.22: Time alignment

Tweeter output is
delayed compared to
the mid and bass
units because the
acoustic centre of the
driver is further back.

Mid Driver

Bass Driver

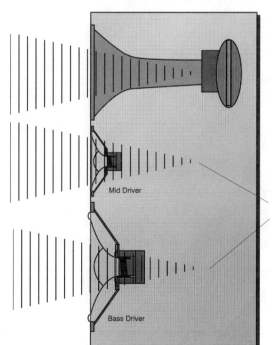

Delaying the bass and
mid outputs brings
them back into
alignment with the
output from the
tweeter.

Mid Driver

Bass Driver

band level controls

Having separate level controls for each band means that power no longer has to be wasted to make the most efficient driver match the output of the least efficient driver. Instead, more amplifier power can be fed to the less sensitive drivers, resulting in a flatter system frequency response with less power wastage. Limiters can be fitted to the various outputs so as to prevent power amp clipping, and for use with constant directivity horns, the appropriate high-frequency filter profile can be included to maintain a flat on-axis response.

mono sub-bass output

For smaller systems with mono sub-bass speakers, it is useful to be able to derive a mono sub-bass feed based on the two input channels while keeping the higher bass, mid and treble in stereo. Such a mono sub-bass feed allows a single sub-bass enclosure to be used with a stereo PA system, and several crossover designers now include a mono sub output as standard.

system processors

System processors may be either analogue or digital, and tend to combine the functions of crossover, limiting, and system frequency correction. If a designer is removed from the constraints of producing a loudspeaker enclosure with a perfectly flat frequency response, it may be possible to make the enclosure smaller than would otherwise be the case, then specific EQ correction built into the processor can be used to restore a flat response. Furthermore, it is possible to deliberately design bass cabinets to have a hump in their natural frequency response, then remove this hump via EQ in the processor to provide additional low frequency headroom.

The simplest form of processor is the type supplied with compact loudspeaker systems, such as Bose 802s, where analogue filters are used to compensate for the falling high and low frequency response of the enclosure. At the other end of the scale, a digital processor could bring together very complex system EQ, crossover, time alignment delay, limiting, and even an intelligent protection system that rolls off some of the low bass when the system is being driven dangerously hard. At the moment, sophisticated processors are commonly used only with fairly large concert systems, but some of the technology is certain to spin off into the portable PA market.

chapter 6

stage miking

For all but the smallest gigs, you'll almost certainly get a more professional sound if you mic up the drums and back-line as well as the vocals, but you need to know what mics to use and where to put them if you're to get the best results. Mixing a full band is also a lot more complicated than simply balancing vocals against an existing back-line, but providing you approach the task logically, it shouldn't be too much of a problem.

electric guitar

In the recording studio, you have the luxury of time to experiment, and if you're doing overdubs, you can place mics anywhere in the room without the fear of spill ruining things. On stage you don't have quite so much flexibility, so if you decide to mic your amp, the mic has to go pretty close to the speaker. However, you don't have to mic up your guitar amp – you could DI it if you prefer, and both approaches are discussed here.

choice of amplifier

Though there are some very good solid state guitar amps on the market, most serious players still prefer the sound of valve amplifiers, but whichever type you use, the overdrive characteristic also depends heavily on the choice of speakers and the enclosure they're mounted in. I mention this because it's necessary to capture not just the sound of the guitar amp electronics, but also of the speaker cab, and that's very important if you choose to DI. It's also important to realise that if you're expecting your amplifier to be heard without help from the PA, a 2x12 cabinet or stack will project better than a 1x12 combo. While a 1x12 combo may sound impressive close up, the sound tends to become thin, or even nasal-sounding with distance, and with some models, the sound also takes on a boxy character at higher playing levels. Of course this doesn't matter if you're miking up the amp or DI'ing it as you can set the amp to whatever level it sounds best at, but if you aim to work mainly without PA support, then the choice of amplifier is very important.

amp miking

If you've ever put a mic in front of a guitar amp, you'll probably have noticed that the sound changes quite a lot depending on the position of the mic relative to the speaker. In live work, the mic needs to be as near as possible to the speaker grille so as to exclude unwanted spill, and you'll find that the brightest sound occurs when the mic is pointing directly towards the centre of the speaker cone. As you move the mic towards the edge of the cone, or if you angle the microphone, the sound tends to become more mellow.

Most sound reinforcement companies use dynamic mics for guitar work, though certain players prefer the extra top end you get from a capacitor microphone. However, it can be argued that a typical guitar cab doesn't have a lot of inherent high end due to the limited frequency response of the speaker, so there's relatively little to be gained from using a capacitor mic. In any event, dynamic mics are both cheaper and tougher than capacitor models, and they have the further advantage that they don't require phantom power to operate.

polar pattern

Most of the time you'll find cardioid or hypercardioid mics used for guitar miking, but don't discount omni models. Omni mics pick up sound from all around, so you'd expect them to be worse as far as spill problems are concerned, but when the mic is only an inch or two from the grille of a loud guitar amplifier, it really doesn't make a great deal of difference! Omnis tend to sound more open than cardioid models, and they don't suffer from the proximity bass boost of cardioids, but historically, cardioids and hypercardioids are used on most occasions. Shure's SM57 is a popular choice for guitar cab miking, but most good quality, general purpose dynamic mics will work fine. Different models of microphone sound slightly different depending on their presence characteristics and other anomalies, so if you have a few mics to choose from, try them all and compare results. The best paper specification doesn't necessarily produce the best guitar sound.

mic position

You sometimes see a mic hanging down by its lead in front of the guitar amp, but while that may be fine for an omni model, it's not usually the best method when using a cardioid mic, as its most sensitive axis will be pointing directly at the floor. There'll probably be plenty of level even so, but the off-axis sound of a mic is different to the on-axis sound (usually duller), so unless you've hit on a lucky combination that just happens to sound brilliant, it's better to put the mic on a short stand and point it directly at the speaker as shown in Figure 6.1. However, be aware that stage vibrations can

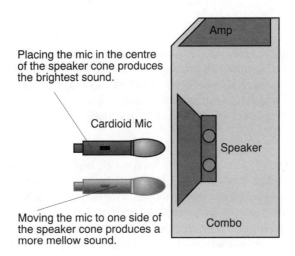

Placing the mic in the centre of the speaker cone produces the brightest sound.

Cardioid Mic

Moving the mic to one side of the speaker cone produces a more mellow sound.

Amp

Speaker

Combo

Figure 6.1: Miking a guitar combo

enter the mic via the stand, so it may be prudent to switch in the low-cut filter on the mixing desk.

where to mic

Where there's more than one speaker in a cabinet, try to determine if one is better-sounding than the others, then always mic that one. If the miked sound is too bright, you can get the out-front sound to more closely match your onstage sound by moving the mic slightly away from the centre of the speaker cone rather than using the desk EQ from the outset. Once you've got the best match you can then use EQ to fine tune it, and possibly to roll off a little bass end if the proximity effect has kicked in too hard. You should also bear in mind that a typical guitar combo sounds a lot brighter when you're directly in front of it than it does when it's standing on the floor or a low stand, and you're playing guitar close to it.

The best way to hear what you really sound like is to run some of the miked or DI'd sound through a wedge monitor in front of you. Alternatively, if you're using a small combo, you could prop it up in front of you so that it is angled towards you in the same way as a stage monitor would be. The audience will then hear mainly the guitar sound via the PA, whereas you hear the amplifier exactly as it sounds. To give the guitar more of a sense of space, it may be useful to reduce the amount of spring reverb used on the amp, then add a little stereo digital reverb at the mixing desk.

di'ing guitar

DI'ing a guitar amp via its preamp output jack tends to produce a thin, raspy sound, because the preamp output bypasses the tonal contribution of the speakers and speaker cab. You also lose the effect of power amp distortion, which is important in valve amps. A few amps are starting to appear with speaker simulators built into the preamp output, but these are still in the minority.

A practical solution is to use a combined DI box and speaker simulator – a speaker simulator is simply an electronic filter that shapes the sound in the same way as a speaker cabinet would. The better models sound very close to what you'd expect from miking the amp, and you can get both active models (which need batteries or phantom power), or passive models that need no batteries and produce a balanced, mic level output. Speaker simulators are particularly important for overdriven guitar sounds, though for very clean rhythm sounds or bugged acoustics, you can go into the desk via a conventional DI box.

speaker simulators

Most speaker simulators intended for live use can be fed either from a preamp output jack or from the loudspeaker outlet of the amp, but they usually provide different sockets for this purpose as speaker level signals are much bigger than line-level signals. NEVER feed the speaker output of an amplifier into a conventional line-level DI box or speaker simulator designed for instrument or line level-signals as you'll almost certainly damage the DI box and you may damage your amplifier. Most models that accept speaker level signals have an input jack (which you connect to the guitar amp's speaker output) and another thru jack where you plug the speaker. In other words, the DI box/simulator sits in-line between the amp and the speaker. As most combos use jacks to plug the speaker into the power amp, that isn't a problem.

If the amp has two speaker jacks (wired in parallel), and only one has a speaker plugged in, you could simply plug the free speaker out jack into the speaker level in socket of the simulator. If neither of these options is open to you, it's probably best to get a spare jack socket soldered across your speaker terminals so you have somewhere to plug your speaker simulator. Figure 6.2 shows the main options.

The output from a combined speaker simulator/DI box will either be at mic or line level depending on the model, and for serious work, it should be balanced. Most have a balanced mic output on an XLR connector, which is

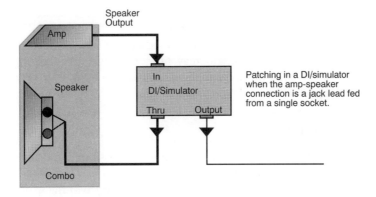

Patching in a DI/simulator
when the amp-speaker
connection is a jack lead fed
from a single socket.

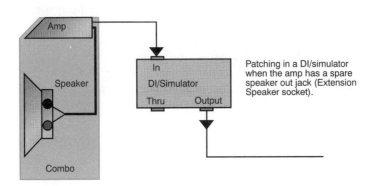

Patching in a DI/simulator
when the amp has a spare
speaker out jack (Extension
Speaker socket).

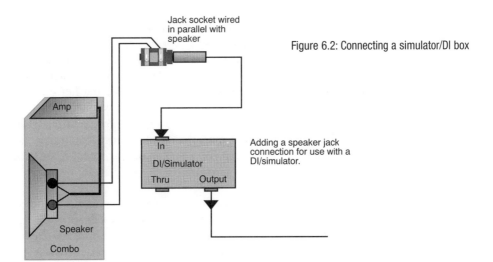

Figure 6.2: Connecting a simulator/DI box

Adding a speaker jack
connection for use with a
DI/simulator.

simply connected to the stage box like any other mic. Controls on these boxes tend to be minimal, but you may find some way of adjusting or switching the level, and there's usually a switchable option to provide brighter or warmer voicings.

stereo guitar setups

It's possible to either mic or DI a guitar amp relatively simply, and the end results should be comparable if you discount the total lack of spill when you DI. However, if you have a stereo rig, you'll either need two mics, or two speaker simulator DI boxes of some kind. Whether you choose to mic or DI is a matter of personal choice, but in my view, if you can get the sound you want using a DI system, the results are more repeatable from one gig to another. On the other hand, if your guitar amplifier has a distinctive sound that DI'ing can't capture, simply use a mic.

some useful desk eq settings

Boost at 120Hz to add punch to the sound of rock guitars.
Cut below 100Hz or switch in the high-pass (low-cut) filter to reduce low frequency spill or stage vibration.
Boost at 2-3kHz to add bite.
Boost at 5-7kHz to add zing to clean rhythm sounds.
Cut at 200-300Hz if the sound seems boxy.
Cut above 5kHz to reduce edginess.

using guitar effects

While the traditional rock or blues player can probably get by with an amp that distorts nicely, and includes a spring reverb, a great many contemporary guitar sounds rely on the use of effects. Most guitar effects come as individual pedals, multieffect pedal systems or rack effects, though there are now a number of amplifiers on the market with their own integral effects. Lack of choice is not a problem we face, but it's not always clear what is the best way to connect effects. For example, should you put them between the guitar and the amplifier, or should they go in the amplifier's effects loop? And, if you're using pedals, what order should they be connected in?

There is no definitive answer that will be right for everyone, because not all equipment offers the same facilities, but there are a few basic rules that'll help you find the best solution for your particular setup. There are really just three main factors you have to take into account: the order in which the effects are connected, signal levels, and impedance.

order of effects

What I'm going to describe is the connection order which delivers the kind of sounds most people consider typical, but there are no unbreakable rules, so once you've tried the traditional methods, I encourage you to experiment.

Overdrive or distortion normally comes first in the effects chain, and that's true whether the distortion comes from a pedal, a multieffects box or from the amp itself. This can be a problem when you're using the amplifier's own overdrive, because this effectively precludes you from using any effects pedals at the same time. For example, if you have a delay or chorus pedal and put that between the guitar and the amplifier, when you hit overdrive, you'll have the effects connected in the wrong order. This won't stop the effects from working, but by overdriving the output from a delay box rather than vice versa, the delay sound will get pretty messed up by the overdrive. If the amount of overdrive isn't too high, and if you have no other way to connect the effects, then you will probably get away with it, but putting the delay, chorus or flanger after the overdrive does give a better defined sound. If you want to use pedal effects in front of the amplifier, then it's probably wise to consider putting a good overdrive pedal at the front of the chain, and use this instead of the built-in amp distortion, at least for any highly overdriven sounds.

noise gates

If you need to use a noise gate, this should come after the overdrive but before delay or reverb. It's okay to put a gate after chorus or flanging, but if you were to put it after reverb or delay, there's a strong chance that the decaying repeats, or the reverb tail would be cut off short by the gate. Figure 6.3 shows the optimum connection order of effects.

guitar pickup impedance

Guitars with conventional magnetic pickups need to be plugged into a high-impedance input – if you plug them into a low- or medium- impedance input, you are likely to suffer a loss of level, a loss of tone and even a loss of sustain. Guitar amplifiers have an input impedance of around 1 Mohm (one million ohms), and the same is true of most guitar pedals, which are designed to be connected between the guitar and the amplifier input.

Rack-mount effects boxes designed for studio use quite often have input impedances of around 50 kohms, which is too low for use with guitars, though some high impedance units built with guitarists in mind are available. If you want to use a studio effects box on the input to your amp (which you may want to do if you've no effects loop), the easy way to do it is to put one conventional

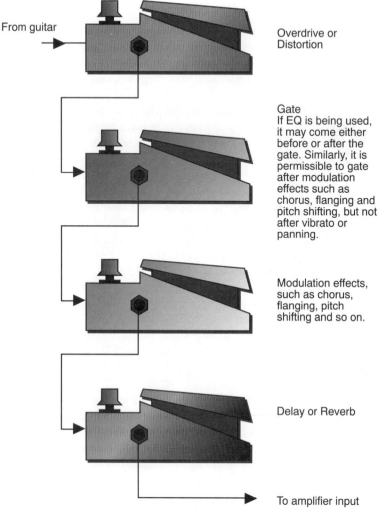

From guitar

Overdrive or
Distortion

Gate
If EQ is being used,
it may come either
before or after the
gate. Similarly, it is
permissible to gate
after modulation
effects such as
chorus, flanging and
pitch shifting, but not
after vibrato or
panning.

Modulation effects,
such as chorus,
flanging, pitch
shifting and so on.

Delay or Reverb

To amplifier input

Figure 6.3: Optimum order of effects

guitar pedal first, as shown in Figure 6.4. This way the pedal will act as an impedance matcher, but make sure you get the type of pedal that still acts as an impedance matcher when it's in bypass mode. If in doubt, phone the manufacturer's product support line and ask – that's what they're there for.

loops and levels

If you want to use your amp's own preamp distortion, then you're probably better off connecting your effects via the send and return loop on the amp's back panel, but this isn't always as straightforward as it seems. These loops

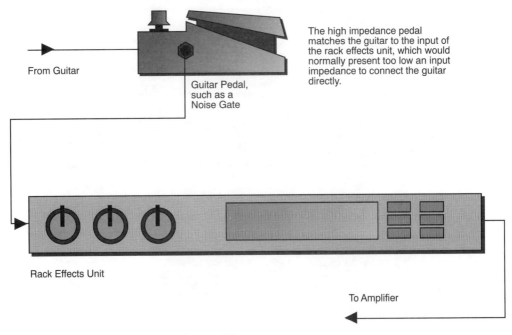

From Guitar

Guitar Pedal,
such as a
Noise Gate

The high impedance pedal
matches the guitar to the input of
the rack effects unit, which would
normally present too low an input
impedance to connect the guitar
directly.

Rack Effects Unit

To Amplifier

Figure 6.4: Using a pedal as an impedance matcher

are usually designed to accept studio processors operating at so-called line level, which is around 10 times higher than the signal you get directly out of a guitar. Pedals are designed for guitar level signals, not line levels, so if you put a pedal in the effects loop, the chances are that the pedal will overload and sound less than great. Some amplifiers try to help you out by giving you a level control on the effects send socket, but if you turn this down far enough so that the pedal doesn't distort, you'll probably find that the level coming out of the pedal is now too low to drive your power amp hard enough, and you won't be able to get your amplifier to go loud enough. The more considerate manufacturers provide a further gain control on the effects loop return to compensate for this, but they are in the minority.

setting levels

If you're lucky enough to have send and return level controls on your amp, the right way to set them up for use with pedals is to play the amp at gigging volume, then plug in the effects pedal. Turn up the send level to the effects device until you can hear distortion, then back it off a little to leave yourself some safety margin. Now, adjust the return level control so that the amp volume is roughly the same as it was before the pedal was connected.

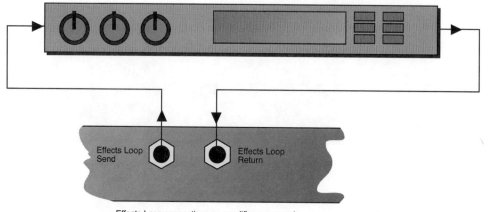

In a conventional effects loop, the whole of the preamp signal passes through the effects unit, so the dry/effect balance must be set using the mix control on the effects unit.

Set the input gain control on the effects unit to produce an optimum meter reading, but leave a little safety margin, just in case you turn up your preamp levels. Set the effects output level so that the amp sounds as loud as it did before the effects box was plugged in.

Rack Effects Unit

Effects Loop Send

Effects Loop Return

Effects Loop connections on amplifier rear panel

Figure 6.5: External processor connected via effects loop

If you're working with a studio effects box, this will probably have its own input and output level controls, so you don't need to worry if your effects loop doesn't have controls of its own. Proceed as with the pedal, but this time adjust the effects box input control until the level meter or level LEDs register a healthy signal level, with some safety margin left over. Then, simply turn up the effects output level control until you get the same level you have before you connected the effect. Figure 6.5 shows an external processor connected via the effects loop.

effects preamps

Effects units with built-in guitar preamps are usually best connected at the input of the amplifier, because that automatically keeps all the different effects in the right order. However, this does assume that you'll be using the overdrive in the effects box, not the overdrive channel of your amplifier. You may also need to change the tone control settings on your amp, because the preamp will probably already EQ the signal to some extent. If you prefer the overdrive in your amplifier, then you're probably best off putting the effects preamp in the amp's send/return loop and bypassing the effects overdrive section.

Some of the units that combine analogue overdrive with digital effects allow you to split the overdrive and effects sections so that each can be connected separately. This provides you with a means to put only the digital effects in your send/return loop, and if you want to, you can wire the overdrive section between your guitar and amp input, giving you a choice of using both internal and external overdrive for different songs without compromising the effects order.

As a rule, a good effects preamp will work best with an amplifier that has a relatively neutral tone, and the obvious advantage of a preamp over conventional pedals is that you can program your effect combinations for instant recall. My own preference is for guitar effects preamps that are built into floor pedal units as these are easy to control live.

stereo effects

The majority of rack-mount effects and effects preamps have stereo outputs, though they'll also have a mono output option for those who want to use them conventionally. For small gigs where little or none of the guitar goes through the PA, a stereo guitar rig can help to fill out the sound, and here stereo effects can make a big contribution. The setup needn't be anything too elaborate, and if you're using the effects unit in the send/return loop, you could simply take one of the effect outputs to a second small combo as shown in Figure 6.6.

wet and dry

Some guitar players will tell you that digital effects are all very well, but they tend to change your basic guitar sound, even when the effects are off, and guitar players can get pretty obsessive about their sound. The reason for this happening is straightforward, but the solution may be more difficult. A digital effects unit converts the whole of the input signal into the digital domain, adds the necessary effects, then combines the treated digital signal with the untreated or dry digital signal before passing it to the output via digital-to-analogue converters. In other words, even your basic dry guitar sound has passed through the digital converters, and this can have an effect on the sound. There are two possible solutions, both of which rely on buying the right equipment.

The first option is to use a guitar amp with a so-called additive effects loop. Here the dry part of the signal is sent directly from the loop send to the loop return just as if no effects had been plugged in. The loop send still feeds a signal to the effects box, and the loop return adds it back to the dry sound, so in effect, the dry sound goes through the amp as normal and the effects loop only contributes the effected part of the sound. Figure 6.7 should make

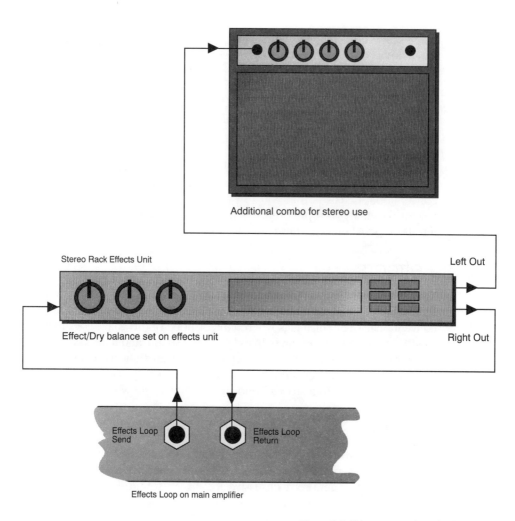

Additional combo for stereo use

Stereo Rack Effects Unit

Left Out

Effect/Dry balance set on effects unit

Right Out

Effects Loop Send

Effects Loop Return

Effects Loop on main amplifier

Figure 6.6: Using a second combo for stereo

this clear. For this to work properly, the effects unit must be set up for 100% effect, no dry sound (normally the mix is set to give the desired amount of effect), and a control on the amplifier's front panel sets the amount of effect added. Obviously this is only going to work for effects that are added to the dry sound – it's not going to work for overdrive, so you'll either need to use the amp's own overdrive or use a pedal.

The second option is in some ways nicer, and that is to choose one of the relatively few effects units that keep the dry part of the signal in the analogue domain all the way through, and only digitises the effect part of the signal. In my view, this should be the standard way to build guitar effects, but

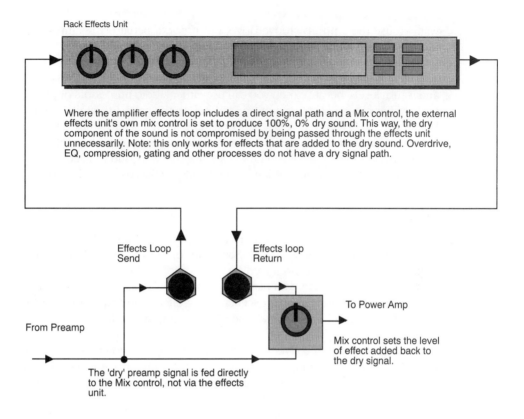

Rack Effects Unit

Where the amplifier effects loop includes a direct signal path and a Mix control, the external effects unit's own mix control is set to produce 100%, 0% dry sound. This way, the dry component of the sound is not compromised by being passed through the effects unit unnecessarily. Note: this only works for effects that are added to the dry sound. Overdrive, EQ, compression, gating and other processes do not have a dry signal path.

Effects Loop Send

Effects loop Return

To Power Amp

From Preamp

Mix control sets the level of effect added back to the dry signal.

The 'dry' preamp signal is fed directly to the Mix control, not via the effects unit.

Figure 6.7: Effects loop with wet/dry mix

manufacturers are all too often worried about keeping the price right down rather than doing the job properly.

effect overview

Being able to hook up your effects in the best possible way relies on you having the right effects boxes and the right amplifier. If you have an amplifier with no effects loop, then you've either to go for pedals or for an all-in-one guitar effects preamp, which you connect between the guitar and the amplifier. The restriction here is that you can't really make the best use of your amp's own overdrive as it comes after the other effects, so you'll need to choose something that gives you the overdrive sound you want at source.

If you have an effects loop with no controls or no switchable sensitivity, then the chances are it won't be much good with pedals, so you'll need a studio type processor that works at line level. This is the best option if you want to use the amp's own overdrive, but if not, a pedal or preamp setup might still appeal.

The most flexible option is if you have an amplifier with variable effects send and return levels, because then you can use either studio processors or pedals in the effects loop, or you can put pedals before the amp. In fact you can do both if you like! However, very few people have all the facilities they'd like, so some compromise is often inevitable. At least now you're in a position to know what combinations of equipment are likely to work and what aren't, and hopefully you'll be able to get better results out of what you already have.

bass guitar

At one time, pretty much everything was miked up, including the bass guitar and the keyboard amps. Nowadays, bass is more likely to be DI'd, though miking is still an option preferred by some people. Part of this change is down to the evolution in bass playing styles, with cleaner sounds becoming more popular. There are also excellent bass effects preamps available for those who want to DI with the sound of a real amp plus effects.

Bass guitars fitted with conventional, non-active pickups don't interface well directly with mixer line inputs because the mixer impedance is too low for proper matching. The result is a dull and unresponsive tone. One option is to use a DI box between the bass guitar and the amplifier so that a low impedance, balanced feed can be fed to the mixer via the stage multicore. Active basses and guitars can be plugged directly into a desk, though it may still be beneficial to use a DI box in order to provide ground lifting as an insurance against hum. This simple setup will provide clean feed from the bass guitar into the PA, but it won't help capture the character of the amplifier.

A bass guitar amplifier doesn't have a flat frequency response – it is "voiced" to suit the instrument, and as a consequence, you may find that you need to apply a degree of EQ to the DI'd sound to make it approximate the sound coming from the back-line bass amp. A console with a four-band EQ section helps, but graphic or parametric equalisers are much more flexible. With bass guitar, there's little point in boosting much above 5kHz as this will only bring up noise, so some experimentation is called for.

miking the bass

If it is preferred to mic up a bass amplification system, the procedure is similar to that used for regular guitar amplifiers, the main difference being that the mic is usually set up a few inches from the speaker grille rather than being pressed right up against it. It is also useful to choose a mic that has a good bass response rather than a general purpose mic where the bass has been rolled off to avoid the proximity effect making vocals sound too bass heavy. As with guitar amp miking, there may be a difference of quality between the speakers in the enclosure, so it can help to listen to each one in turn and pick the best sounding one – or at least one that doesn't rattle. As with guitar amp miking, moving the microphone off axis will produce a more mellow tone.

bass compression

Modern bass styles also cry out for compression, because the different techniques of plucking, slapping and pulling produce notes with widely differing volume levels. A compressor set with a 5mS attack time and a 0.5S release time will even things out a lot; a ratio of around 4:1, or a soft-knee compressor will work well in most cases, but if you don't feel comfortable adjusting compressors, use one of the models with an auto setting. Higher ratios may be used to create a more tightly limited sound, and of course using a compressor to limit peak levels can also help save loudspeakers from stress.

preamps

For those demanding a more distinctive bass sound, there are several bass preamps on the market that include integral effects. These devices may be plugged directly into a power amp on stage and a split feed can be taken directly to the mixing desk, ideally via a DI box so as to avoid ground loops. Most conventional bass sounds can be achieved simply by using EQ and compression, but a subtle overdrive effect can help recreate those nostalgic rock bass sounds of the late sixties and early seventies, while delay is essential for dub and reggae.

Chorus treatments work well on fretless basses, but they can also be used to good effect on conventional fretted basses, in moderation. Flanging is also viable, but because it is such an obvious effect, it really should be used sparingly.

As with any other element of live mixing, getting a good bass sound in isolation doesn't necessarily mean the sound will be right when everyone else is playing. For this reason, it's important to make the final adjustments during the soundcheck when everyone else is playing.

There's no magic to getting a good bass sound – even a simple DI box with whatever EQ you have on the desk will produce usable results if the instrument is of good quality and played well. Most serious problems tend to stem from badly set up instruments or poor playing technique, so if you find you have problems, examine those areas first. If you want a bright bass sound for example, don't expect to get it from very old strings, and if you

want a powerful, punchy sound, the instrument has to be played that way –
you can't add "attitude" in the mix.

working with drums

To study drum miking in depth could take up a whole book, but just a few
simple rules and guidelines will help you get a good sound from the outset. On
the positive side, drums are generally so loud that you never need to use
enough mic gain to get into trouble with feedback. On the other hand, so many
factors go to make up a good drum sound that without a little knowledge, it's
very easy to end up with a sound that's not as good as it could be.

Whether on stage or in the studio, a good drum sound starts with a good-
sounding drum kit, and providing the kit is fitted with heads that are in decent
condition, it should be possible to coax any reasonable kit into sounding half-
way decent fairly quickly. On the other hand, a kit with worn heads and
stretched snares is unlikely to sound great no matter what you do with it.

miking the kit

Once the drum kit has been tuned and the drummer has finished fine tuning
the positions of cymbal stands and so on, you can go ahead and put up the
microphones. The simplest way to get a natural drum sound is simply to use
a stereo microphone pair (usually spaced a few feet apart) a few feet in front
of the kit. Though using the mics at this distance makes them a little
susceptible to spill from other instruments and back-line, the volume
produced by a typical drum kit should mean the spill is kept to acceptable
levels. This technique works well for styles such as jazz where a natural
acoustic kit sound is needed.

For pop work, simple stereo miking often produces a result lacking in the power
and immediacy that you can get by close-miking individual drums, but if you
don't want to mic up every drum in the kit, a good compromise is to keep the
stereo pair and use additional close mikes on the kick drum and snare.

The snare mic should be placed a couple of inches above and from the edge
of the top head as shown in Figure 6.8. A cardioid dynamic mic is the usual
choice, and you should ensure that the cable doesn't foul any of the
cymbals, and that the mic stand isn't touching any of the drum rims. If the
stand does touch a drum rim, you run the risk of picking up thumps from
the stand whenever the drum is struck.

The kick drum should also be miked using a dynamic cardioid microphone,
ideally one with an extended bass response specifically designed for use with

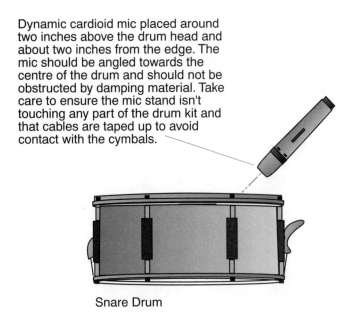

Dynamic cardioid mic placed around two inches above the drum head and about two inches from the edge. The mic should be angled towards the centre of the drum and should not be obstructed by damping material. Take care to ensure the mic stand isn't touching any part of the drum kit and that cables are taped up to avoid contact with the cymbals.

Snare Drum

Figure 6.8: Snare mic position

bass drums. This should be positioned inside the drum shell, pointing towards the spot where the beater hits. Most kick drums used for pop work have a hole cut in the front head, and the boom stand can be used to position the mic through this hole. If you don't have a suitable stand, you can generally get acceptable results simply by laying the mic on top of the damping blanket.

close-miking drums

Close-miking is the accepted way of getting a pop drum sound, and though it doesn't sound much like a natural acoustic kit, it's the sound we now associate with pop and rock music. If you have enough mics and mixer channels, then it's probably best to mic each tom as well as the kick and snare.

Snare drums are the brightest drums in the kit so a dynamic mic with a good high-end response is probably the best choice. Toms also produce bright attack transients so use good quality dynamic microphones. Cardioid pattern mics give the greatest immunity from spill and the usual mic position for the toms is a couple of inches above the drum head, a couple of inches in from the edge and angled towards the centre of the head. This is more or less the same as for the snare drum. Any damping should be placed out of the way of the mic.

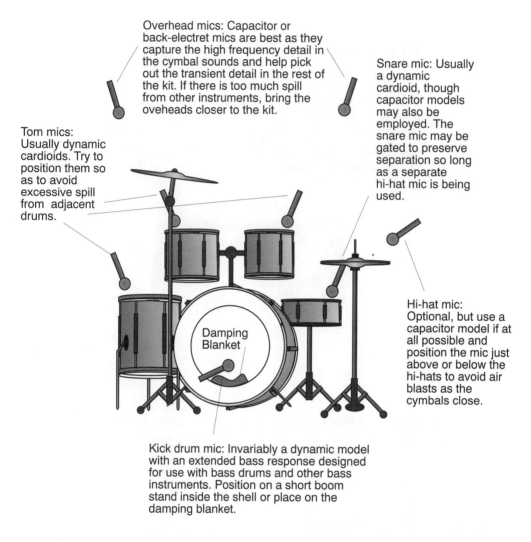

Overhead mics: Capacitor or back-electret mics are best as they capture the high frequency detail in the cymbal sounds and help pick out the transient detail in the rest of the kit. If there is too much spill from other instruments, bring the oveheads closer to the kit.

Snare mic: Usually a dynamic cardioid, though capacitor models may also be employed. The snare mic may be gated to preserve separation so long as a separate hi-hat mic is being used.

Tom mics: Usually dynamic cardioids. Try to position them so as to avoid excessive spill from adjacent drums.

Damping Blanket

Hi-hat mic: Optional, but use a capacitor model if at all possible and position the mic just above or below the hi-hats to avoid air blasts as the cymbals close.

Kick drum mic: Invariably a dynamic model with an extended bass response designed for use with bass drums and other bass instruments. Position on a short boom stand inside the shell or place on the damping blanket.

Figure 6.9: Close-miking the whole kit (with overheads)

To capture the cymbals, and to bind the overall sound of the kit together, we still need a pair of stereo mics, often called overheads because in the case of a close-miked kit, they tend to be placed above the kit rather than in front of it. Capacitor or back electret mics are best in this role because of their ability to handle high frequency sounds, and in most cases, you'll find you pick up enough hi-hat without needing a separate mic. Figure 6.9 shows a fully-miked drum kit, though some of the stands have been omitted for clarity. If a separate hi-hat mic is needed, as may be the case if you decide to gate the snare drum, a suitable arrangement is shown in Figure 6.10.

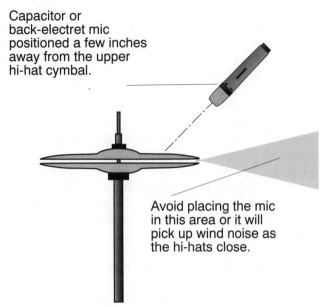

Capacitor or back-electret mic positioned a few inches away from the upper hi-hat cymbal.

Avoid placing the mic in this area or it will pick up wind noise as the hi-hats close.

Figure 6.10: Hi-hat miking

Ethnic percussion or congas are best miked in stereo from above at a mic distance of between one and two feet depending on the instrument and the spill situation. Bringing the mic closer to the instrument will reduce the effect of both room acoustics and spill, but moving too close may result in an unnatural sound. Using a capacitor mic will produce a more accurate, detailed sound on bright-sounding percussion, but a good quality dynamic mic will work well enough in most situations.

drum tuning

Inexperienced engineers often worry unnecessarily about drum miking because such a mystique has been built up around the subject, but as with most aspects of PA work, 90% of the battle is getting a good sound at source. Good mics produce better results than cheap ones, but more important by far is the way the drums are tuned and played, and where the mics are placed.

If you don't have any experience in tuning drums, leave the job to an experienced drummer, but if the drummer obviously needs a little help, here are a couple of basic tips. Firstly, keep in mind that a drum has a natural pitch, and if you over-tighten the skin or head, the tone will become "ringy" and lacking in power. If the skin is too loose, then the sound will lose its resonance, but you soon get an idea of which pitch sounds right. Secondly, ensure the head is evenly tensioned all round. You can check this by tapping around the edges of the head with a stick while adjusting the tensioners until you have the same pitch all the way round. Once you reach this stage, tune the head by making small adjustments to first one tensioner, then the one opposite before moving round the drum.

Single-headed toms are the easiest to tune, though if you prefer the sound of double-headed toms, the bottom may need a little damping to prevent it ringing. In the case of snare drums, the snare (bottom) head is generally tensioned slightly looser than the batter (top) head, though different drummers have different preferences. The snares will vibrate in sympathy whenever another drum is hit, and though this may be reduced by careful tuning of the snare drum, some buzzing is unavoidable. You'll inevitably have to live with a few rattles and buzzes, but most of these will be hidden by other instruments in the mix.

If damping is needed, this is usually achieved by taping folded tissue or cloth to the edge of the top head of the drum, but be careful not to overdamp the drums as they'll sound lifeless when the other members of the band are playing. It's easy to get paranoid about rings and rattles, but most will be inaudible during the actual performance.

Most rock and pop drummers will have a hole cut in the front head of their kick drums to produce a louder, more punchy sound, and this is far better then removing the front head completely, which risks distorting the drum shell. A wooden bass drum beater gives the most "smack" and the definition can be increased further by taping a piece of plastic to the head where the beater hits. Plastic token cards resembling credit cards work well for this purpose.

To damp the kick drum, just place a folded woollen blanket inside the shell; to increase the damping push the blanket so that it contacts more of the rear head. Noise gates are useful to tighten up bass drum sounds as a surprising amount of spill from the snare drum and toms gets into the bass drum mic. If you have enough gates, it can also be worth using them to clean up the toms, and in this application, gates with side-chain filters are easiest to set up as the filters help prevent false triggering from the cymbals.

useful drum eq frequencies

Boost at 80Hz to add weight to kick drums and low toms.
Boost at 120 to 150Hz to add punch to toms and snare.
Boost at 6kHz to add sizzle to cymbals.
Boost at 2 to 3kH to add definition to a snare drum.
Cut at 150 to 250Hz to reduce boxiness.
Cut at 1kHz to reduce harshness.

monitoring

Pop music relies on a mix of normally incompatible elements – for example, in an all-acoustic world, the vocalist and acoustic guitarist would be completely overwhelmed by the drum kit. It's only since the advent of amplification that all these disparate elements have been brought together with no need to take account of their natural relative levels. In the studio we have few problems, because we can exercise absolute control over relative sound levels, but on stage there's often a need to provide some form of monitoring so that the performers can hear a more useful balance. Even in small venues, the main PA speakers tend to be positioned forward of the band in an attempt to reduce spill, so the sound that does make its way back to the band is either reflected from walls and ceilings, or mainly low frequency sound from the rear of the PA enclosures.

A stage monitoring system is essentially a second PA system with the speakers directed back at the performers, and the complexity can vary enormously. At its simplest, everyone might hear the same monitor mix, while a more complex monitoring system might involve a dedicated monitor console capable of providing each performer with their idea of an ideal mix. Unfortunately, foldback can increase the risk of feedback.

The electric guitar, bass and keyboard, for example, can all be amplified to any practical level to balance the drums, but there is a limit to how much amplification can be applied to vocals before feedback becomes a problem. And, because miked drums sound quite different to the unamplified kit, drummers also tend to go through the PA system for all but the smallest gigs.

Without monitoring, the vocalist is at a particular disadvantage as he or she will have great difficulty hearing their own voice above the several hundreds of watts of back-line amplification only feet away. And as any singer knows, if you can't hear yourself sing, it's virtually impossible to keep perfectly in tune. This was exactly the situation at the end of the sixties where bands were playing relatively large gigs or even stadiums with no foldback monitoring.

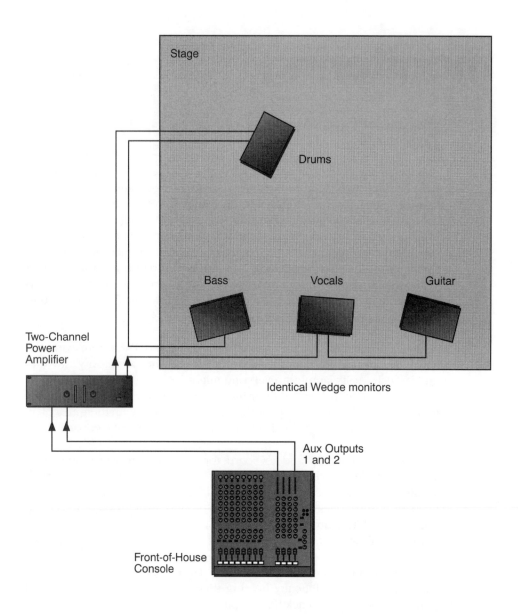

Figure 7.1: Typical monitor system

the floor wedge

The most familiar form of stage monitor is the floor wedge, a triangular speaker cabinet that sits at the feet of the performer, directing a foldback mix towards their position. Wedges are generally two-way speaker systems comprising either a 12-inch speaker or a 15-inch speaker with a horn driver handling the top end, though smaller systems are available for bands playing smaller venues. These wedges often include passive crossover systems, though it is also possible to buy active monitors with integral power amplifiers and crossovers.

In small-to-medium PA systems, stage monitors are driven from the pre-fade foldback sends of the main mixing console, though larger touring systems have the added sophistication of a separate monitor console, usually operated from the side of the stage. Separate monitor consoles and the systems in which they operate can be quite complicated and are really outside the scope of this book. The typical gigging musician generally has to make do with a relatively simple monitoring system, the complexity of which is limited by the number of pre-fade aux sends on the console and (in the case of passive monitors), the number of power amplifiers available. Figure 7.1 shows a system where two different monitor mixes are fed, via a two-channel power amplifier, to two pairs of floor wedges.

monitors and feedback

Putting loudspeakers on stage might seem like the perfect recipe for feedback, and if things aren't done properly, that is most certainly the case. However, if the monitor is well designed, with a good dispersion pattern, and it is positioned in the "blind spot" of a cardioid vocal mic, some of the vocal mix can be directed back at the singer without increasing the risk of feedback too much. Cardioid mics have their least sensitive region directly behind them whereas hypercardioids are least sensitive at around 45 degrees off the rear axis. Figure 7.2 shows the polar patterns of cardioid and hypercardioid mics in relation to the ideal monitor positions. Of course these dead spots aren't really dead because sound still reaches the mic by reflecting from nearby walls and other obstacles, and there's also the directivity of the monitor itself to consider.

wedge monitor design

There's a tendency amongst amateur bands to skimp on foldback speakers in the mistaken belief that the actual sound of the monitoring doesn't matter that much because the audience never gets to hear it.

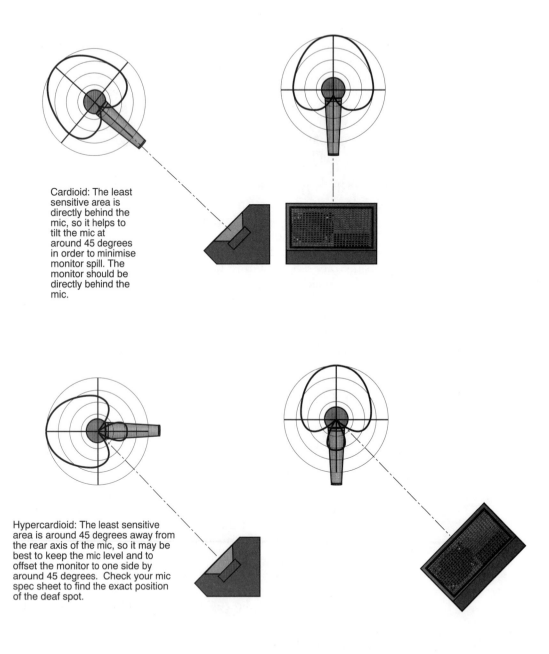

Cardioid: The least sensitive area is directly behind the mic, so it helps to tilt the mic at around 45 degrees in order to minimise monitor spill. The monitor should be directly behind the mic.

Hypercardioid: The least sensitive area is around 45 degrees away from the rear axis of the mic, so it may be best to keep the mic level and to offset the monitor to one side by around 45 degrees. Check your mic spec sheet to find the exact position of the deaf spot.

Figure 7.2: Mic and monitor positions

The problem is that by putting something like a 12-inch speaker in a box, then adding a cheap piezo-electric tweeter, the directivity of the 12-inch driver will be reduced to a narrow beam at the higher frequencies. This beaming greatly increases the risk of sound being reflected back into an open microphone, which in turn makes feedback problems much more likely.

Though it costs more money, the only way to do the job properly is to use a monitor with an integral crossover and a good quality high-frequency driver, though I hasten to add that piezo drivers can work quite well if they're fed from a suitable crossover. For small venue use, it's often more convenient to use a compact active monitor as these can be fed directly from a pre-fade send on the console.

A more typical passive budget system probably comprises a 12-inch driver complemented by a small horn-loaded, high-frequency unit driven from a passive crossover inside the cabinet. A separate power amplifier is needed to drive each monitor if everyone needs a different mix, but two 8 ohm monitors may be driven from a single 4 ohm power amplifier where two performers can work with the same mix.

causes of feedback

Even with a well designed monitor, the risk of feedback is increased because an amplified version of the vocal signal is being directed back into the general vicinity of the microphone. Feedback will always start to build up at just one frequency where the various parameters of directivity, room resonance and system frequency response conspire to provide most gain. If you've applied any EQ boost to the vocal, then the boosted section of the audio band is especially vulnerable to feedback.

The situation can be improved by using either a graphic or a parametric equaliser in the monitor feed to apply cut in the frequency bands that are causing problems, but this relies on the expertise of the user for its success. Some graphic equalisers are now available with LEDs above the sliders, which help pinpoint troublesome feedback frequencies, making setting up a lot easier. However, it is important not to try too hard to notch out all the feedback frequencies using a graphic EQ, because you'll probably find that you've also notched out most of what you wanted to hear in the first place! The problem is that even a 30-band graphic equaliser affects almost an octave when you move a single fader, yet the feedback frequency you're trying to combat may be less than a 20th of an octave wide. If you are using a graphic equaliser, it's probably best to ring out the system by increasing the system gain gradually until ringing starts, then cut only the worst offending bands by just a few dB.

Because of the location of the speakers, monitor systems may feed back at different frequencies to the main PA, so it's useful to have separate equalisers for the main PA and the monitor system. In larger PA rigs, there may be a separate graphic equaliser for each different monitor speaker, but each one is set up individually by ringing out the system as just described.

feedback eliminators in monitoring

In recent years, a number of companies have developed dedicated feedback suppressors which automatically identify the frequencies that are causing trouble, then apply appropriate filtering at those frequencies. These devices have two main advantages over simple graphic equalisers: firstly, they set themselves up automatically, which means the engineer doesn't need to be as experienced, and secondly, the filters used in these devices tend to be much narrower than those used in conventional graphic equalisers, which means more cut can be applied in more bands without significantly affecting the overall PA or monitor sound. Setting up is much like ringing out a PA system except as you increase the gain, the filters automatically lock onto, and remove, the feedback frequencies as feedback occurs. Most systems provide a set number of filters that lock onto feedback during ringing out, but additional filters are provided to tackle any feedback that may arise during the performance due to a singer moving a microphone. For more details on these devices, see the chapter on signal processing.

monitor positioning

Perhaps the most important factor – other than the quality of the monitors – is where you put them, especially when working in small venues such as pubs, where the stage area may not be exactly orthodox. Indeed, many pub venues are so cramped that there may be insufficient room for floor monitors to work properly at all, in which case it can be more effective to use just a pair of monitors or spare small PA cabs to cover the whole band. These can be positioned either on top of, or just behind, the main PA speakers, pointing backwards towards the opposite corner of the stage area. This effectively catches the whole band in the crossfire, and because the distance from the monitors is greater than usual, the sound is better dispersed before it gets reflected. This is pretty much the same principle as side-fill monitors in a large PA rig, but on a smaller scale. Figure 7.3 shows this setup.

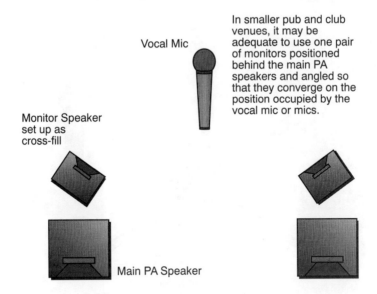

Vocal Mic

In smaller pub and club venues, it may be adequate to use one pair of monitors positioned behind the main PA speakers and angled so that they converge on the position occupied by the vocal mic or mics.

Monitor Speaker set up as cross-fill

Main PA Speaker

Figure 7.3: Monitors behind PA speakers

monitor spill

In a larger PA setup where all the band, rather than just the vocalist, has monitors, the setting up becomes a little more complex as not only do the vocal monitors have to be positioned to avoid feedback, but everybody else's monitors have to be arranged so as not to spill too much sound into the vocal mic, or the overall vocal sound through the PA will be seriously compromised and the engineer will have less chance of setting up a workable balance. In such a system, it is more likely that each monitor will have its own power amplifier and be fed from a different pre-fade foldback send. This enables different performers to hear different mixes. However, the best way to minimise spill is to get each monitor as close as possible to the person using it so that less overall level is needed. It is important that the monitors are angled correctly so that the sound is directed towards the performer's head, and not towards his knees!

mini monitors

Another practical approach is to use a much smaller monitor, still designed for good dispersion, and mount it on top of a mic stand very close to the person using it. These monitors are similar to miniature hi-fi

Figure 7.4: Mini monitor on stand

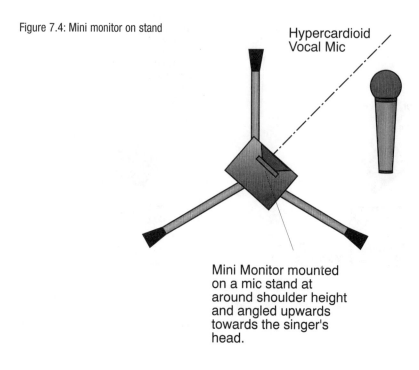

Hypercardioid
Vocal Mic

Mini Monitor mounted
on a mic stand at
around shoulder height
and angled upwards
towards the singer's
head.

speakers, generally with moulded plastic cases, but with a higher power handling, and many of the major PA companies make compact installation speakers that would do the job very well. Mic stand fittings are available for many of these speakers, and Figure 7.4 shows how a stand-mounted monitor might be positioned. Though they lack the low bass response of large floor monitors, this is no disadvantage for vocals and may actually help by preventing unwanted low-frequency sound being fed back onto the stage area. Furthermore, the low-end leakage coming from the rear of the main PA speakers will help increase the impression of bass. Again, in very small venues, this type of speaker can also be placed behind the main PA speakers and directed back towards the performers, their main advantage being that they are easy to position precisely.

in-ear monitors

In-ear monitoring is one of the more recent developments in PA technology, but the principle is very simple. Instead of using onstage loudspeakers to provide the monitoring signal, each performer wears a pair of in-ear phones, similar to those used with good quality personal hi-fi systems. These require only a small amount of amplifier power to drive, and singers who move around the stage take their monitoring with them rather than wandering out of range of a floor wedge. All the commercial systems I've tried come with a radio transmitter and receiver, exactly like those used for radio microphones but in reverse. Both VHF and UHF radio systems may be used depending on the budget and the requirements. VHF systems are more prone to interference than UHF systems, but they are cheaper and require no annual licensing fee.

On their own, in-ear phones allow too much sound leakage into the ear from back-line amplification and other sources, so the better systems involve custom ear moulds, where each phone is set into a soft rubber earplug moulded from the user's own ear canal. These are fairly expensive to have made, but they're infinitely better than struggling with off-the-shelf phones. Better models include an adjustable vent so that the performer can choose exactly how much spill to allow in from the outside world.

By excluding a large proportion of the spill from outside, the performer can monitor at a lower (and potentially less damaging) level, and in most professional systems, a limiter is included to prevent the monitoring from exceeding a safe level. In the small venue, there's the further advantage that the sound the audience hears is not being compromised by the leakage from the stage monitors.

Being small, these phones are more or less invisible in use and offer the added advantage that even performers working very close to each other can have quite different monitor mixes without conflict. As you might expect, the bass response is a little limited, so they won't satisfy the drummer who insists on 2kW of side-fills, but in all other respects, the concept is a good one and I'm sure it will become more widely used in the near future.

monitoring overview

Even in very small venues, some form of monitoring is desirable, but trying to use large wedges in a tiny pub can be disastrous. As stressed earlier, whatever monitor type you use should be properly designed with even dispersion characteristics, otherwise it will simply provoke feedback. Even with a well designed monitor, you have to use it carefully and position it where it is least likely to cause trouble.

If you don't want to buy a lot of extra gear for monitoring, then the simple expedient of using two wedge monitors or compact PA cabs as side-fills is often enough to get by, and if small speakers on stands aren't too much of a visual intrusion, the stand-mounted mini monitors are very useful for performers who don't need to move around too much.

In-ear systems have a lot going for them, but the initial investment is quite high as it includes the radio links and limiters. What's more, while some performers love working with them, others simply can't get used to them at all.

chapter 8

live sound practicalities

Assuming that you can play and you've rehearsed the songs, getting the best possible sound on stage starts with choosing the right equipment, both back-line and PA. Back-line is largely a matter of individual taste, but keep in mind that if it needs help from the PA, you'll need to ensure the PA is powerful enough to deal with it, especially when it comes to amplifying drums and bass guitar. This requirement has to be balanced against the space available for transport and available budget. You can achieve perfectly acceptable results using a fairly compact system (providing it's used within its design limitations), but to handle bass frequencies effectively, you'll need separate bass or sub-bass cabinets.

amplifier power

How much PA power you ultimately need depends on the size of venue you're likely to play, the type of music you play, and how much of the back-line is going to go through the PA. Furthermore, the level of sound a system produces isn't only dictated by the amplifier power, but also by the efficiency of the loudspeaker's drive units, and a 500-watt PA using very efficient drive units might well put out more actual volume than a 1500 watts PA built around less efficient drivers. It's also important to appreciate how much sound the back-line is contributing to the front-of-house sound – in small venues, this can be considerable.

Obviously a rock band with a drum kit is going to need a more powerful system than a folk band. If you're doing small pub gigs where the PA handles mainly vocals, then a system of just a few hundred watts per channel driven from a powered mixer is a practical choice. In most pub venues, getting the drums quiet enough is more of a problem than getting them loud enough. On the other hand, if you want to amplify everything, a couple of kilowatts is probably as small as makes any sense given that an acoustic drum kit can put out as much power as a 400w amplifier on its own. A good tip is that if you feel your amplification is being pushed to its limits most of the time, put a dedicated limiter before the power amp to prevent the peaks clipping. This will enable you to achieve a noticeably higher average power level without the risk of feeding distorted signals to your drivers. However, it is important to know that your drivers are capable of handling sustained levels of high average power.

don't forget loudspeaker efficiency

As explained in the chapter on loudspeakers, loudspeaker systems are often given a sensitivity rating quoted in dBs per watt measured at 1m, which tells you that if a 1w test tone or noise signal is applied to the system, the SPL or Sound Pressure Level measured 1m directly in front of the speaker will be so many dBs. This is a measure of how effectively the loudspeaker converts amplifier power into sound, but it only tells you what is going on directly in front of the speaker, not what's happening off-axis. If a loudspeaker has been designed with a very tight directivity pattern so that all the sound comes out as a narrow beam, then the sensitivity figures will obviously seem higher than for a similar speaker with a wider dispersion angle.

The other major weakness of this measuring system is that it only tells you how efficient the speaker is when dissipating 1w of power. Most PA speakers run at average powers considerably higher than this, and when speakers are driven hard, their efficiency tends to become reduced. This effect is known as power compression. What you really need to know is the maximum SPL the enclosure is capable of generating and over what coverage angle. In practical terms, this means that the only way to be really sure about the way a system will perform under real-life conditions is to try it. If you don't have friends with a similar system you can check out, then insist on hiring the system for a couple of gigs before you commit to buying it. Most dealers should allow you to deduct the hire charge from the purchase cost should you decide to buy. Because power compression can affect system performance so significantly, sizeably greater levels can sometimes be achieved by using two speaker cabinets (of the appropriate combined impedance) to share the load. In this situation, the use of a limiter is highly recommended as you will probably now have more loudspeaker capacity than amplifier capacity.

Whatever PA system you choose, it's vital that the loudspeakers have reasonably flat frequency responses, especially stage monitors that are used in close proximity to vocal mics. Any significant humps or spikes in the frequency response will increase the risk of feedback, not to mention compromising the sound.

coverage characteristics

Speakers also need to have properly controlled dispersion characteristics – a large cone loudspeaker used without a crossover will produce a much narrower beam of sound at high frequencies than it will at low and mid-range frequencies, which again increases the risk of feedback. These factors are explained in greater detail in the chapter on loudspeakers.

Unless a system is carefully designed, it is easy to end up having a very wide dispersion at low frequencies and a relatively narrow dispersion at higher frequencies. The outcome is that, although the high frequencies might make it to the back of the room, they tend to sound rather honky and don't blend well with the lower frequencies from the bass bins. Furthermore, because of the narrow dispersion pattern of the HF horns, it is likely that members of the audience who are close to the front, but off-axis from the speakers, will receive inadequate coverage.

To avoid this problem, PA loudspeaker systems and stage monitors generally comprise two or more loudspeakers, each handling only a part of the audio spectrum, and a crossover is used to direct the required part of the spectrum to the different drivers. In a typical portable, full-range speaker cab, a 12-inch or 15-inch speaker might handle the bass and mid frequencies while a horn-loaded tweeter handles the high frequencies. Larger systems may include a separate mid-range speaker, which necessitates a three-way crossover.

small system benefits

In smaller venues, full-range cabinets have the benefit of more predictable performance and greater ease of setting up, especially if they're small enough to put on tripod stands. They're also easy to transport if you have to rely on cars rather than a large van. What's more, because full-range cabinets can be designed and built using matched acoustic components, the system performance is likely to be more accurate than a system comprising bass, mid-range and horn cabinets from different sources. There's also less risk of making the wrong connection.

A typical full-range PA cab with an integral, passive crossover requires just a single, two-core speaker cable between it and the amplifier. Active systems are usually fed from an amplifier rack via a multi-way cable terminating in a multi-pin connector at the cabinet end, though for the ultimate in convenience, the new generation of moulded plastic full-range enclosures with integral power amps and active crossovers make a lot of sense. Be aware that although these may be small and light, they tend to be non-rectangular in shape, which can make them awkward to pack.

bass handling

Properly designed, even a relatively compact system can give adequately controlled directivity over the whole audio spectrum with a fairly flat frequency response, both of which are important for neutrality of tone and resistance to feedback. In fact the main compromise with portable, full-range cabinets is their bass handling capability, so for gigs where you're going to be relying on them to beef up the drums and bass, additional sub-bass speakers driven from separate power amplifiers are a good idea. These would be run from a crossover which removes all the low bass energy from the main speakers and directs only low bass energy to the bass speakers. Some systems do this with passive crossovers while others use an active crossover and an additional power amplifier for the bass cabinets. Not only does adding dedicated bass speakers improve the bass handling of the system, but by removing some of the low frequency burden from the main PA cabinets, it also allows the entire system to be used at a higher level.

If you're feeding bass through a system that doesn't have separate sub-bass speakers, use an equaliser or low-cut filter to ensure that the speakers don't receive any energy below their lower frequency limit. For example, a 1x12 speaker plus horn compact PA cabinet may only go down to 70Hz, so feeding in energy below this frequency will simply eat up your headroom and degrade the sound quality. By filtering out everything below, say 80Hz, the sound will remain much cleaner and you'll be able to get more level before distortion.

powered mixer benefits

Mixer amplifiers provide a convenient means of driving a small PA, and a number of more recent models also include digital reverb, which saves the cost of an external processor, reduces the amount of wiring to a bare minimum, and makes setup very fast. The obvious disadvantages are that if there's a serious failure, you've lost both your power amps and your mixer, and if you want more power than is available you have to buy external power amplifiers, which cancels out the main advantage of compactness. However, it may be possible to switch the internal amplifiers to run your stage monitor system, in which case adding external power amplifiers to drive the main PA is a sensible upgrade path. If you're intending to add sub-bass speakers at some stage, it's worth choosing one of the mixer amps that has an inbuilt active crossover (or the provision to fit one as an option) to cater for that eventuality. A limitation of powered mixers is that the speaker cables tend to be longer as they have to run all the way from the mixer to the speakers.

Good vocal mics are essential in any system as, like speakers, poor mics might have undesirable humps in the frequency response that encourage feedback. Most vocal mics have a deliberate presence peak at around 2 to 4kHz to aid clarity, but the rest of the response should be nominally flat with a gentle roll-off at the low end. For most applications, a good cardioid or hypercardioid dynamic vocal mic is fine.

setting up your pa system

Assuming you have a PA system suited to your requirements and to the size of venues you intend playing, the next most important factor is how you set it up. Sound levels diminish as you move further from the source, so it stands to reason that the further away your mics are from the speakers, the more level you can use before feedback becomes a problem. Because PA speakers are directional devices, they should be positioned in front of the mics, facing away from the performers. This may seem obvious, but I've played at venues where the organiser has tried to persuade us to put the PA speakers behind the band – and he's claimed that all the other bands do this without any problems! If somebody tells you this, don't believe them. Even if you have to compromise on the PA position because of the room layout, try to get the backs of the PA speakers facing your stage mics.

People are better at absorbing sound than reflecting or transmitting it, so it's pretty obvious that if the people at the back are going to be able to hear properly, the speakers need to be above the head height of the front rows of the audience. In a large concert system, separate speakers can be used to cover different sections of the audience, but in smaller venues, the same speakers are heard by front and back rows alike. Unfortunately, simply standing the speaker cabinets on tables, or putting them on stands that can't be tilted, isn't always the ideal solution, as Figure 8.1 illustrates.

Here the on-axis sound passes over the heads of all the audience until it hits the rear wall of the venue, whereupon it is reflected back into the room. In practical terms, this means your audience hears less level in the first place (because they are listening to the less powerful off-axis sound), and the reflections from the back wall will combine with the direct sound making it reverberant and unclear. It also means that more sound energy

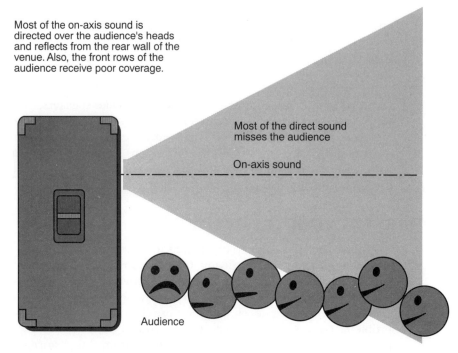

Most of the on-axis sound is directed over the audience's heads and reflects from the rear wall of the venue. Also, the front rows of the audience receive poor coverage.

Most of the direct sound misses the audience

On-axis sound

Audience

Setting the PA cabinets level

Figure 8.1: Speakers set up level

reflects back to the stage where there's a greater chance of your mics picking it up, causing the system to feed back.

angled cabinets

More effective use of the available sound is made by positioning the cabinets a little higher and angling them downwards so they point at a spot around two thirds of the way to the back of the audience. Figure 8.2 shows this arrangement. If you have speaker cabinets that use so-called top-hat adaptors to make them sit on top of tripod stands, the chances are that they won't have any facility for tilting. A DIY way to get around this is to fit a second top-hat adaptor to the speaker cabinet at an angle as shown in Figure 8.3.

By angling the speaker cabinets down slightly, the on-axis sound is directed towards the back of the audience, which helps compensate for the fact that they're further away. At the same time, those people at the front of the venue won't get deafened, because they're hearing the lower

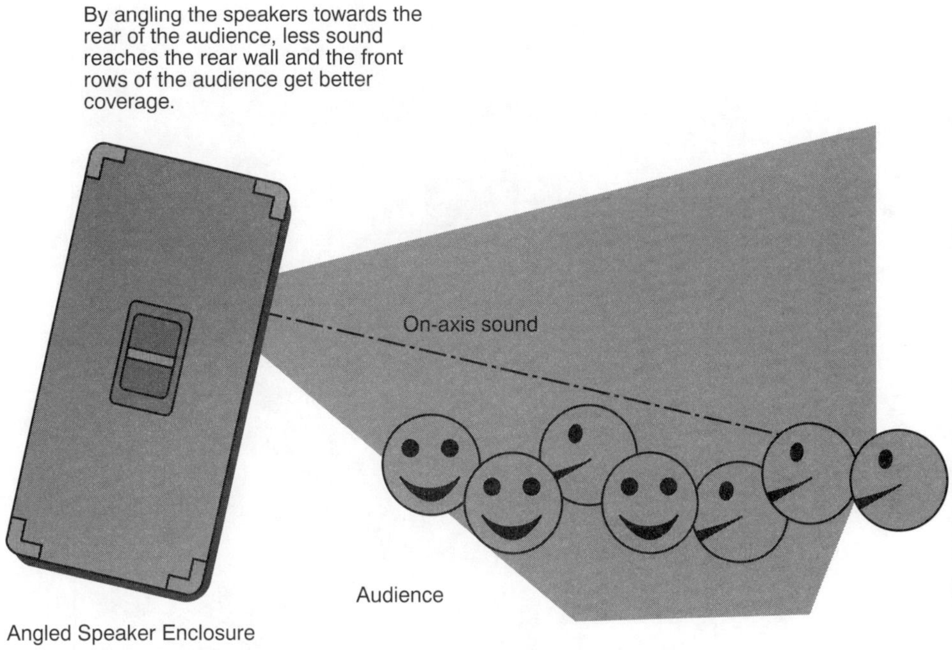

By angling the speakers towards the
rear of the audience, less sound
reaches the rear wall and the front
rows of the audience get better
coverage.

On-axis sound

Audience

Angled Speaker Enclosure

Figure 8.2: Speakers tilted downwards

level off-axis sound. The nearer you get to the front, the more off-axis the listeners are, but as they are proportionally nearer to the speakers, the actual sound level is more comparable with what's heard at the back. From this description, you can appreciate why an accurate off-axis response is important – relatively few of the audience are standing directly on the axis of the speakers. Ideally, the off-axis sounds should differ from the on-axis sounds only in level, though in practice, because of the longer wavelengths involved, the low bass end invariably has a wider dispersion than the mid and high areas of the spectrum.

wall reflections

Earlier in the book I mentioned the dangers of reflected sound getting back into the stage mics, so you should always position your speakers in such a way as to minimise unwanted reflections from walls or ceilings. Imagine the wall in front of the speaker is a mirror and try to figure out if you could see the reflection from the mic positions.

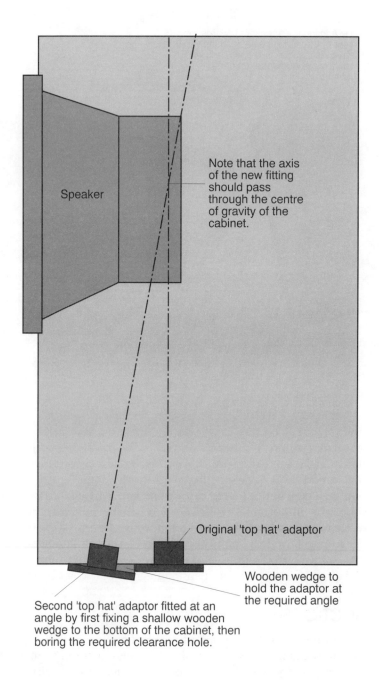

Speaker

Note that the axis of the new fitting should pass through the centre of gravity of the cabinet.

Original 'top hat' adaptor

Wooden wedge to hold the adaptor at the required angle

Second 'top hat' adaptor fitted at an angle by first fixing a shallow wooden wedge to the bottom of the cabinet, then boring the required clearance hole.

Figure 8.3: Modification for angled mounting

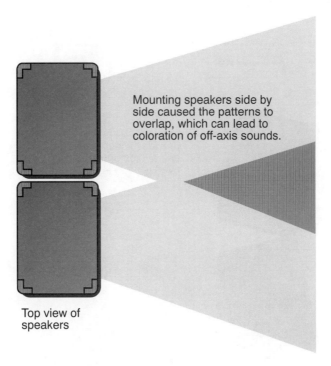

Mounting speakers side by side caused the patterns to overlap, which can lead to coloration of off-axis sounds.

Top view of speakers

Figure 8.4: Side by side cabinets reduce horizontal dispersion

In an ideal situation, all the front-of-house sound would be directed at your audience and none at the walls or ceilings, and even though this isn't possible in practice, you should aim to get as close to this ideal as you can. You can never eliminate all reflected sound, but the walls close to the speakers are the ones to worry about the most, so try to angle the speakers so that the reflections travel away from you, not bounce back onto the stage. Even rotating the speaker cabs by a few degrees can be enough to improve matters.

more power

There may come a time when you need to double up on your speakers and amplifiers to provide you with more power for larger venues, and you might imagine that to double the level of your system, all you need to do is add another power amp plus two more cabinets placed alongside the original pair. This isn't the best way to do things. Let's say for the sake of argument that these speakers have their -6dB point (the point is where the measured SPL is exactly half what it was when measured on-axis), at 15 degrees off-axis. If you visualise the sound

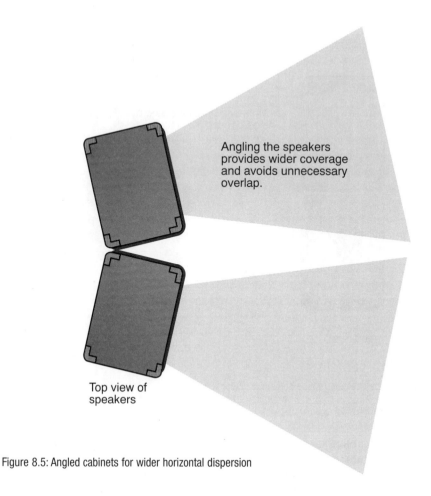

Angling the speakers provides wider coverage and avoids unnecessary overlap.

Top view of speakers

Figure 8.5: Angled cabinets for wider horizontal dispersion

coming out of the speakers in beams, as shown in Figure 8.4, the beams will overlap, causing an addition of power along an axis drawn between the two enclosures, but there will be both phase additions and cancellations at various frequencies in the off-axis sound. The result is that you actually narrow the useful angle of dispersion of the cabinets by standing them side by side.

A better way to use two speaker cabinets together is to stand them at an angle to each other as shown in Figure 8.5. The angle between the cabinets should be twice the -6dB dispersion angle of the speakers, and in our example where the -6dB point occurs at 15 degrees, the required angle would be 30 degrees. This way the dispersion patterns of the speakers overlap at the -6dB point providing a more even power coverage over a wider angle. The on-axis sound may be no louder than from a single cabinet, but the angle of coverage is wider so you get more sound energy into the room. Alternatively, you can stand one cabinet on top of the other as will be described shortly.

arrays

The business of positioning loudspeaker cabinets so that they work efficiently together is known as arraying, and as you might expect, this is vitally important in large concert systems where several tens of cabinets might be in use at one time. In such systems, the manufacturers are able to design individual enclosures to have a deliberately narrow dispersion angle, which means the on-axis sound is louder than for a standard cabinet, but the "beam" of sound produced is narrower. Multiple narrow dispersion cabinets of this type can be arrayed at more gentle angles to provide high intensity, wide-angle coverage, and while few gigging bands need to know about arraying in detail, the general principles will give you a better understanding of how your own system works. Where several rows of cabinets are to be stacked one above the other, the vertical angles are also calculated to give the desired coverage in the vertical plane, which is why the PA clusters at large concerts often curve both from side to side and from top to bottom.

controlled coverage

By now, the concept that sound reflections from walls is a major problem should be well learnt, so you have to develop a strategy to get as much direct sound as possible falling on the audience and as little as possible on the walls or ceilings. Low ceilings are a particular problem at smaller gigs, where it can be advantageous to try to narrow the vertical dispersion of your system so as to direct as little power as possible upwards. So far we've only really looked at angling and tilting the cabinets to direct the PA output in the most useful direction.

What we really could do with is some way of controlling the dispersion of the PA speakers, but sadly, enclosures don't come with a dispersion control knob. However, if you are using two or more identical cabinets per side, you can stack them in such a way as to achieve the desired end as shown in Figure 8.6. Intuitively, you might think that stacking one cabinet above the other would increase the vertical dispersion, but that's not the case. In this example, the top cabinet has been inverted so as to get the two high-frequency drivers as close together as possible. This produces a narrowing of the vertical dispersion of the mid and high frequencies without significantly affecting dispersion in the horizontal plane.

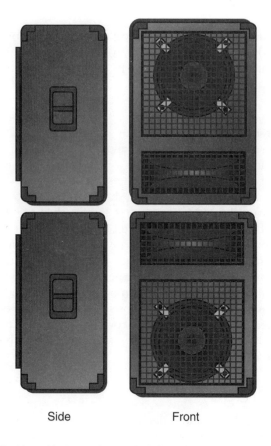

Inverting the top
speaker will
narrow the
dispersion
pattern in the
vertical plane.

Side   Front

Figure 8.6: Stacking cabinets to reduce vertical dispersion

early column speakers

In the early days of band PA, speakers were often built as vertical columns
containing four drivers (often with no HF units at all), not only to
maintain a narrow visual profile, but also because the tall, thin nature of
a column produces a good horizontal dispersion and a relatively narrow
vertical dispersion. In venues such as cinemas or theatres that combine
high ceilings with tiered seating, it may be desirable to increase the
vertical dispersion of the PA, and the easiest way to do this is to stack the
cabinets (both the same way up this time), with the top one angled back
slightly as shown in Figure 8.7. However, ensure that you have the
hardware to do this safely as falling speaker cabinets are no joke! It helps
if you check the vertical dispersion spec of your speakers so that you can
select an angle of tilt that will minimise the overlap between the two

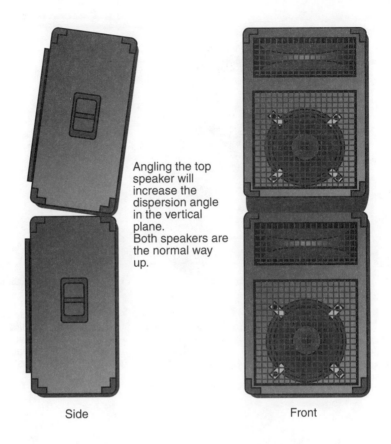

Angling the top speaker will increase the dispersion angle in the vertical plane.
Both speakers are the normal way up.

Side   Front

Figure 8.7: Stacking cabinets with top enclosure angled (to increase vertical dispersion)

cabinets, but if you don't have access to this information, or if such technical issues aren't your idea of fun, simply aim the top cabinet by eye so that it is directed somewhere towards the rear third of the audience.

pragmatism

So far I've covered a few basic techniques for positioning your speakers as effectively as possible, but in many small venues, you have to compromise because of space considerations. However, by understanding the nature (and possible consequences), of these compromises, it is often possible to improve matters dramatically.

Acoustic feedback is the number one enemy in small venues, and as explained earlier in the book, the likelihood of feedback is not directly

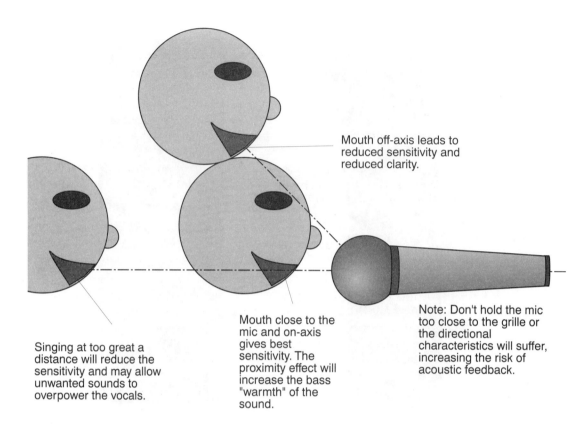

Mouth off-axis leads to reduced sensitivity and reduced clarity.

Mouth close to the mic and on-axis gives best sensitivity. The proximity effect will increase the bass "warmth" of the sound.

Note: Don't hold the mic too close to the grille or the directional characteristics will suffer, increasing the risk of acoustic feedback.

Singing at too great a distance will reduce the sensitivity and may allow unwanted sounds to overpower the vocals.

Figure 8.8: Singing directly into a cardioid mic

related to how loud the system is running, but to how much gain is being used. In other words, a loud singer working close to a microphone will be far less likely to encounter feedback problems than someone with a weak voice who doesn't keep close to the mic. There will always be some sound from the PA speakers that gets back into the vocal mics – even the pros can't prevent this entirely – but to keep it under control, the system gain must be kept below the point where feedback starts to build up. Unless you're miking quiet acoustic instruments, such as acoustic guitars, the major source of feedback problems is your vocal mic setup, so that's the first area to get right.

vocal mics and feedback

Feedback is related to gain, but you need a fair amount of gain to help a typical singer cut through over several hundred watts of back-line and drums. I've already stressed the importance of not skimping on microphone quality, but it is wise to be aware of the performance differences between cardioid and hypercardioid mics, as outlined in the chapter on microphone types. Essentially, hypercardioids have the most tightly controlled pickup pattern, but they are more sensitive to sounds coming directly from behind than cardioids. For this reason, the back of a hypercardioid mic shouldn't be aimed at a stage monitor or a PA speaker. Better to aim it at something absorbent, such as the audience. Though it is important to choose a microphone that has good feedback rejection characteristics, it is also important to buy one that suits your voice.

mic technique

Having got the right mic, you also need to develop good mic technique, and for rock work, the loudest results are obtained with the singer's lips almost touching the wire grille of the mic. It's also important to sing directly into the end of the mic, not across the top of it as so many club entertainers seem to do, though singing slightly off-axis can improve popping if that's a particular problem. Also switch in the low-cut filter on the mixing console to help reduce low frequency booming and popping.

Figure 8.8 shows the correct mic position for a cardioid microphone. However, the proximity effect associated with cardioid and hypercardioid mics causes a noticeable bass boost whenever the mic is used very close to the lips, and though experienced performers can vary their mic distance to make deliberate tonal changes, inexperienced singers may just end up with an uneven sound. A good way to practise mic technique is to set up some headphones at home so you can hear any tonal changes as you move the microphone relative to your mouth.

holding the mic

Another mistake you'll often see singers making is cupping the mic in their hands. It is very important to hold the mic so that your hand isn't touching the wire basket or blocking any of the small vents directly below the basket on some mics. These vents create the directional characteristic of the mic – covering them up stops them working and the mic picks up sound from all over the place rather than just in front. You must have seen at least one example of the performer who reacts to their mic feeding back by trying to cover it with their hands. The usual result is even more feedback!

If you're one of those singers who likes to take the mic off the stand and wander around the stage, make a few tests during the soundcheck to see if

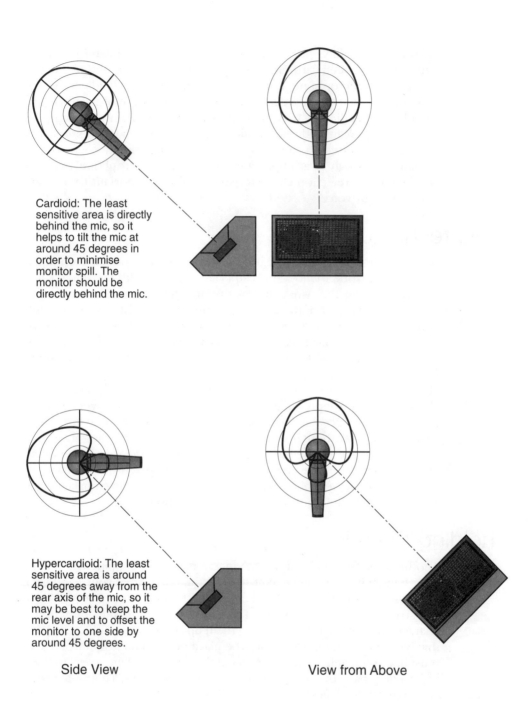

Cardioid: The least
sensitive area is directly
behind the mic, so it
helps to tilt the mic at
around 45 degrees in
order to minimise
monitor spill. The
monitor should be
directly behind the mic.

Hypercardioid: The least
sensitive area is around
45 degrees away from the
rear axis of the mic, so it
may be best to keep the
mic level and to offset the
monitor to one side by
around 45 degrees.

Side View

View from Above

Figure 8.9: Monitor positions relative to vocal mic

there are any "unsafe" areas where feedback is a particular problem. You must also be aware that if you're using conventional stage monitoring, you may move out of range of your own monitor so you may not be able to hear yourself as well as you'd like. What's more, moving into range of another musician's stage monitor might cause you feedback problems unless you make sure you keep the mic's dead axis pointing towards the monitor.

back-line spill

A vocal mic doesn't just pick up the singer – it picks up sound from everywhere, especially along its axis, so anything loud going on directly behind the singer will also be picked up and amplified through the PA so that it also competes with the vocals out front. Because of this, it's sensible to try to position the vocalist as far away as possible from back-line amplification or drums, and to ensure that no back-line is directly behind the mic unless it's at a lower level. For example, a guitar amp on a low stand or chair won't cause as much trouble as a speaker stack at microphone height. Apart from spill considerations, if you are being deafened by the back-line, you'll need more monitor level to hear yourself, and in turn, that increases the likelihood of feedback. If there is any room at all for manoeuvre, ensure that there's no back-line gear directly behind the singer, or too close on either side if at all possible. Position amplifiers as far back and to one side of the mics as possible.

pa spill

Having minimised spill from the back-line by careful mic positioning, there's also the spill from the main PA speakers to worry about. At low frequencies you can't do much about this other than use the low-cut filters on all your vocal mic channels, and minimising reflected sound by careful speaker placement has already been covered. However, spill can also bounce off the rear wall of the stage and into your vocal mics, and the closer the rear wall, the more likely feedback problems are. In small or cramped venues, consider hanging a temporary curtain behind the singer to absorb some of the sound. In general, use a heavy material and leave it partly pleated rather than stretched out.

stage monitors

Because of their necessary proximity to the singers, stage monitors are a common source of feedback problems, so careful positioning is essential. Ideally, they should be positioned at around 45 degrees to the rear of a hypercardioid mic, or directly behind a cardioid mic where the mics are least sensitive. This arrangement is shown in Figure 8.9.

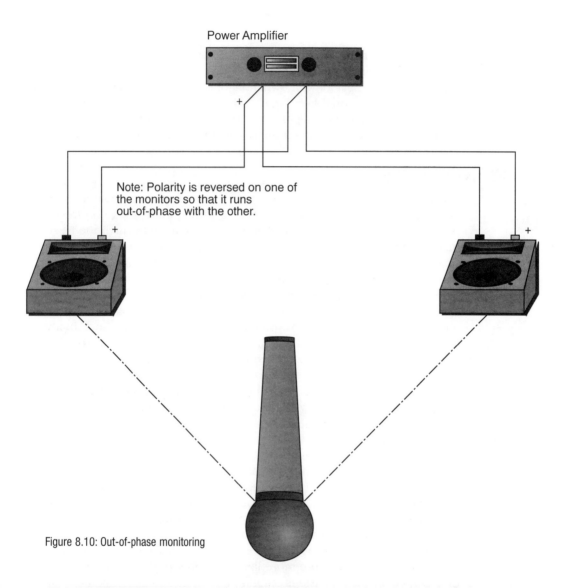

Power Amplifier

+

Note: Polarity is reversed on one of
the monitors so that it runs
out-of-phase with the other.

+

+

Figure 8.10: Out-of-phase monitoring

Where it is practical to use two stage monitors for one performer, it is
possible to feed them both the same signal but wire one monitor out-of-
phase with the other. As long as the monitors are placed symmetrically
about the mic stand, the direct sound from the monitors reaching the
mics will tend to cancel out, reducing the risk of feedback. However, the
singer, having the benefit of two ears, will still be able to hear the
monitors quite clearly. Figure 8.10 shows how this might be arranged in
practice. This arrangement can be very effective providing the vocal mic
stays in one place, but any benefits will be lost if the singer removes the
mic from the stand and starts to walk about.

monitor eq

To get the maximum level before feedback, you'll generally have to equalise your monitors to "notch out" troublesome frequencies where feedback is threatening to strike. Because of the physical parameters of a room and the equipment being used, feedback will always start at whatever frequency the system has the most gain, and the traditional remedy is to use a graphic equaliser as explained in the chapter on signal processing. However, automatic feedback reduction units (also described in that chapter) are more effective and have a less detrimental effect on the sound. If you can afford one of these, even if just for the monitor system, I can highly recommend them.

The EQ settings needed to tame feedback will vary from system to system and venue to venue as they depend on the PA speakers, the monitor speakers, the mics and the positions of all these components within the room. The shape and size of the room also has a significant influence, as do the nature and position of any reflective surfaces.

ringing out

If you're using graphic equalisers, you'll need to "ring out" the system during the soundcheck and then apply cut in the frequency bands where feedback is becoming a problem. The usual setting up technique is to start off with all the EQ faders flat, then increase the system gain during the soundcheck until feedback starts. Next, back off the level so that the system is just ringing when somebody speaks into a mic. Now you have to identify the frequency of this ring, which you do by pulling down the faders one at a time. If nothing happens, return the fader to zero and repeat with the next one. Eventually, you'll find one that makes the ringing stop. Pull this fader down by about 3dB, then turn up the system gain slowly until ringing starts again. If it's at the same frequency, apply another 3dB cut and continue with the process, otherwise identify the new ring frequency and pull that back by 3dB. If you don't have the experience to know roughly whereabouts the feedback is occurring, then either a spectrum analyser, or a graphic equaliser with feedback detection LEDs on each band, will help enormously. Repeat the process until all the worst rings have been killed. Eventually you'll reach a point of diminishing returns where no further adjustments help, or where you've moved the faders so far that the sound quality is starting to suffer. At this point, call it a day and pull the overall PA level down about 10dB from where ringing occurs so as to restore stability.

Ringing out applies both to the main PA and to the monitor system, and as you can imagine, it takes both time and experience to do well. As a rule, an automatic feedback reducer will do the job more effectively – it will do it in seconds rather than minutes, and it will have a far less obvious effect on the perceived sound due to the less intrusive nature of its very narrow filters.

Once you've set up the system EQ as best you can, turn up the gain until ringing starts again, then back it off by around 10dB. This may seem like a long way to back off, but if you stay too close to the feedback threshold, the sound will ring. What's more, you'll have virtually no scope for level adjustment as the gig progresses. If you're lucky, when the audience come in, the feedback threshold will rise by as much as 5dB purely due to sound being absorbed rather than reflected.

main pa eq

In all but the smallest systems, it is common to use a graphic EQ in the main PA as well as in the monitor system, not necessarily just to tame feedback, but to get the best possible sound. Again, each venue has different sonic characteristics so each will need a different EQ setting to make it sound good. It is seldom practical to try to EQ all the humps and bumps out of a PA system, and in reality, there's a limit to what a graphic EQ can do anyway, because it won't help reduce the clutter caused by strong echoes. Most room problems occur in the time domain (that is, they're caused by reflections that come after the original sound), whereas an EQ can only make changes in the frequency domain. However the judicious use of EQ can help you tame the worst booms and resonances by reducing the amount of energy fed into the room at those frequencies. Corrections should be made using EQ cut rather than boost and the changes should be as subtle as possible. The reason for using cut only is that the human hearing system is far less sensitive to missing frequencies than it is to having extra ones added – a few dB cut at one frequency may be quite unnoticeable, but the same amount of boost at that frequency will be very obvious.

Some powered mixers come with five- or seven-band graphic equalisers built in, but although these are useful for general tone shaping or for countering the worst anomalies of a room, they are too imprecise for feedback control or for precision room compensation. Ideally, a stereo 30-band, third octave equaliser should be used for more precise control, and many engineers use a pink noise source and a spectrum analyser to provide a visual display of the combined room/PA frequency characteristics. Using a graphic equaliser, the offending bands can be cut to produce a nominally flat response by simply watching the display as the equaliser is adjusted.

However, unless you're experienced in using a spectrum analyser, the results can be misleading, and moving the measurement microphone just a few feet may result in a quite different reading.

gigging practicalities

Once you turn up at a venue, try to assess where best to set up your gear before anyone starts assembling their kit. Find out where the main PA speakers can go, get them as far in front of you as is practical, and position them so as to produce the least problems with reflected sound. If the room is empty when you do the soundcheck, it may sound boomy and feedback may occur at a lower level than you might like, but in most cases, the situation gets better when the audience arrives.

The most important consideration is to direct as much sound as possible onto the audience by siting the speakers as recommended earlier. If possible, angle the speakers slightly downwards so that they are aimed at an imaginary point around two-thirds back along the room – the mod describer earlier will help you tilt your cabinets without them becoming mechanically unstable – putting boxes beneath the legs of a tripod speaker stand to change the angle is inviting an accident.

back-line position

Set the back-line up so that it's not directly behind the vocalists, and try to get the drums far enough back so that nobody has to have a cymbal ringing in their ear. If you're a guitar player using a small combo, a small stand to get it off the floor is a good idea, but don't set it so high that it spills into your vocal mic if you're also a singer. Another tip is to move your guitar amp a little to one side so that you're not masking all the sound with your body. If you stand between your amp and the audience, the sound heard out front will be rather duller than it should be.

If you mic any of the back-line, get all the mics in place and check each one is working before anyone starts to play their party pieces or warm-up exercises. Similarly, tune all the instruments to an electronic tuner after they have had a while to acclimatise to the temperature of the venue. If each band member has their own tuner, check to see they all read the same pitch. If tuners can be left connected in line with the instrument leads during the gig, tuning problems can be rectified quickly.

setting the mixer

Siting the mixer where you hear a representative sound from the speakers is important, but few small venues will want you in the middle of the room with multicore trailing along the ground for people to fall over. More often than not, you'll end up at one side, but avoid spots under balconies or in corners if at all possible, as these positions will cause you to hear more bass than is actually present in the room. Even mixing close to a side wall will cause a lift in perceived bass due to the boundary effect, so during the soundcheck, take a few steps into the room to see how much difference there is, and try to compensate for it when you mix.

When you turn on the system, make sure the mixer outputs are turned down, and turn the power amps on last, otherwise you might be greeted by a wall of feedback! Playing a known music tape or CD through the system is a good way to get a feel for the acoustics of the venue, and if you have a graphic equaliser connected to the main PA feed, now's the time to try to flatten out any major anomalies by applying a little cut to the offending frequencies – see "ringing out". If you're lucky enough to have an automatic feedback suppressor, you can set this up before the soundcheck.

Before embarking on the soundcheck, you need to verify that every mic and DI box is working and that the levels are optimised to leave you enough leeway in case the level creeps up during the gig. If you have a monitor system, also check that each monitor speaker is working properly. Try to work with the channel faders at around the three quarters up position so that you still have somewhere to go if you need more level. Also check that any connected effects units and processors are doing their jobs properly. Use a piece of masking tape stuck across the bottom of the console so that you can write on identifications for each channel.

use the groups

Mixing can be quite a difficult task, so use the mixer to help you simplify things. For example, if you have half a dozen drum mics around the kit, route those channels to a stereo group so that you can control the whole kit level using just one or two faders rather than six. Do the same for backing vocals, keyboards, and any other section where several sound sources need to be controlled without upsetting their relative levels.

soundcheck

There comes a point when you've done all you can do, and you have to make the best of what you have. The best way to tame an unruly system is to work at realistic sound levels – most audiences tend to think bands are too loud anyway. Quality will always be appreciated more than quantity. Now is the time to start your soundcheck, and the first thing to do is establish a safe maximum working vocal level. If you're really lucky, this will be far too loud and you'll have to turn it down, but more often than not, you'll have to run this near maximum to keep up with the rest of the band. However, do pull back a few dB from maximum so that you've got some power in hand if you need it. Always balance the back-line to the vocal level and not vice versa. I've seen too many bands balance the back-line first, then when they realise the singer can't be heard above it, they blame the sound engineer!

If the guitar amps are regularly too loud, consider using smaller combos or power soaks at smaller gigs so that they can be used at a lower level without sacrificing tone. It also helps to turn backing vocal mics down or completely off when not in use as system gain is affected by the number of live mics open at any one time. The more open mics you have, the more system gain there is and the more problems you'll have with feedback, not to mention spill from the back-line.

In venues where the main speakers can't be positioned symmetrically, consider panning everything into mono. Alternatively, if a mic close to one of the speakers is causing particularly bad feedback problems, try panning it slightly towards the speaker at the other side.

The drum kit will probably need some EQ to get it sounding good, but try to develop a technique for doing this as quickly as possible so you don't bore everyone to death with the kick drum going thud thud thud for minutes on end. The settings shouldn't change that much from gig to gig, so set up your default setting and fine tune that rather than working from scratch every time. However, you should use the EQ bypass button occasionally, just to make sure the EQ'd sound is better, not worse!

It's important to get the co-operation of the musicians during the soundcheck as the whole exercise will be rendered futile if everyone does their own thing. Each drum, vocal mic and instrument mic needs to be checked individually before you balance everything by running through a song. During this run through, you can fine tune the overall mix EQ using your graphic to make the best of the room acoustics, but remember the sound will probably dry up quite a little when the audience comes in. Also take this opportunity to check that the effect levels are okay.

If you have to accommodate a support act, it is important that you make a precise note of all your channel level, EQ and effect send settings before you change anything, and try to keep track of any mics that are moved.

mixing tips

Most types of music demand that the vocals be heard, so always make sure the vocals are sounding nice and are clearly audible. If not, pull the back-line level down until you have a good balance. It is possible to get the vocals too loud, but if you close your eyes and listen analytically, the performance should sound properly integrated with no one part swamping out the rest.

After the vocal sound, you need to get a good balance for the rhythm section as this is what holds the sound together. The drums and bass need to sit comfortably with each other, and if the drum sound is too boomy, you may need a touch of low-mid EQ cut to clean it up. If you can gate individual drums, it can help a lot in keeping the sound clean, but if you haven't had much mixing experience, I'd suggest you leave this until you've got the hang of basic balancing.

I find it helpful to close my eyes and listen from time to time as the visual impact of a show can completely change your perception of what's really going on. Keep notes on who takes the solos in which songs and where, because you'll probably need to push their levels by a couple of dB to give them the necessary lift. You may also need to increase the effects level for solos. Finally, don't forget to turn off the vocal effects when somebody is announcing the next song.

It can help keep the sound clean if you pull down the level of mics in songs where they're not being used, but make sure they're back on again when required. If you're working with an unfamiliar band, pull unused mics down by 5 or 6dB rather than turning them off altogether so that if somebody does suddenly start singing or playing, they won't be completely silent. This gives you a second or two to get their mic back to normal level and hopefully nobody will notice.

concentration

Perhaps the most important element in live sound mixing is to keep your eye on the ball all the time. You shouldn't be constantly moving faders, but you'll probably need to push levels by 3dB or so for solos, you'll need to cut mics that aren't being used, and you'll need to change effects patches as required. You must also make sure you kill any vocal reverb between songs to keep the announcement clear, and don't push it back up until the next song starts – performers have a habit of announcing a song, then coming back to say something else, and if the reverb is back up, it sounds bad.

Keep an ear open for creeping back-line levels, and if this is causing you a problem, ask the band to reset their levels as soon as there's a convenient break in the set. If you're not familiar with the band, you can tell a lot from body language, and with just a little practice, you'll be able to tell who's about to play a solo or who's about to start singing.

folk music

Mixing folk music or other ensembles where the instruments are mainly acoustic is no more difficult than working with electric instruments, though because of the number of mics that may be in use, you do have to be very certain that you're working well below the feedback level. Sound will tend to leak from one mic to another, but that can sometimes help you, because if a mic is accidentally turned down when it's needed, the chances are that the performer will still be audible via the other mics, giving you time to reset the correct level. Providing you make level changes slowly, nobody will realise that you made a mistake!

Pay particular attention to mic placement as the closer the performers are to their mics, the fewer feedback problems you will have and the better the overall separation will be. Watch during the performance for people moving out of range of their mics, and if necessary, send a helper to move a mic back into place if the situation gets really difficult. Again body language will tell you a lot about what's going on as most players go through some kind of little ritual before starting to play. Wind players wet their reeds, fiddle players position their bows, percussionists pick up sticks and so on.

When two instruments are playing together, perhaps with one performing a harmony part to the other, ensure they are reasonably balanced with each other. Close your eyes and confirm that both are clearly audible. Also, don't be afraid to drop the level of instruments if they are getting in the way of a vocal part or a lead instrument.

the self op pa

If you're operating you own mix from onstage, balance it while one of you listens out front, then make as few changes as possible during the performance. Set up the mixer within arm's reach so you can address any feedback problems simply by pulling down the master faders a touch. If any friends of the band who come to your gigs regularly have a good ear for balance, get them to report back on the sound during the show so that you can make changes if necessary. A few simple hand signals to indicate who's too loud and who's too quiet is all that's needed.

Another useful tip I've learned the hard way is that if you use an effects footswitch to turn the vocal reverb on and off, try to get one with a status LED as it's sometimes difficult to tell whether the reverb is on or off in some venues. More than once I've sung a song dry, then turned on the reverb to announce the next number!

If the sound doesn't work out as well as you'd like, still play as though you're having a good time. If you don't look as though anything is wrong, the chances are your audience won't notice. When you've finished playing, don't hang around too long before packing up at the end of the night, because the organiser isn't going to thank you for keeping him out of bed. Besides, if you do pack up quickly, you're more likely to be offered a free drink.

be resilient

If you're the guy who does the PA, the one thing you soon learn is that if there's a problem with the sound – any sort of problem – it's all your fault. It doesn't matter that the drum kit actually does sound like cardboard, or if the acoustics of the venue are impossible, or if one of the speakers is broken, it's up to you to make the band sound good. In many ways it's a thankless job, but if you're a masochist with a skin like a rhino, then maybe a live sound engineer is what you ought to be!

common problems

Without doubt, the most common problem is not being able to get the vocal levels loud enough without feedback. However, it is essential that when you optimise your gain structure you leave enough safety margin to push the vocal levels up during the gig, otherwise you might find console overload distortion becomes a problem before feedback does. If feedback really is the problem, then your only course of action is to reduce the level of the other band members, but you don't have to do this simply by pulling down level faders. Vocals occupy mainly the mid-range of the audio spectrum, so by pulling some of the mid-range out of the guitars and drums, you should be able to increase the vocal clarity without robbing the overall mix of too much power. There's also the option of using an aural exciter or other form of enhancer on the vocals to increase clarity without increasing level.

Yet another approach to pushing the vocals forward in the mix is to put a compressor across the whole mix, and set the threshold so that compression kicks in only when the vocalist sings. Using a compression ratio of around 6:1, the result should be that the whole PA level will drop slightly whenever there's any singing, helping the singing get heard above the back-line.

room boom

A generally boomy sound is another common problem, especially in venues with poor acoustics. Assuming you've done your best with speaker placement, make sure all the mics other than the kick drum have their low-cut filters switched in, and if that doesn't work, try to identify the frequency where the problem is worst and pull it down some more on your graphic EQ. Before you do this, however, make sure it's not just an effect that occurs at your mixing position – walk a little way into the room and see if the problem is still as bad.

inaudible monitors

Another very familiar complaint is that the monitors aren't loud enough. This is a particular problem if somebody in the band has a quiet voice, but check the relative positions of the monitors and the mics anyway, and see if there are any drapes or curtains that can be used to mask off the back and side of the stage area to reduce reflections. If this problem occurs every time you play, give serious thought to getting an automatic feedback suppressor. They aren't magic, but they should get you around 6dB more vocal level without feedback. As vocals are generally mono, a single-channel unit in the vocal group insert point may be all you need, providing your mixer will allow you to route your groups to the centre as well as hard left and right. An in-ear monitor system for the singer with the quiet voice could also help.

anticipating disasters

Modern equipment is very reliable, but it still breaks down from time to time. The most likely casualties are leads, so check yours regularly and keep spares. In particular, check all mains plugs, especially the tightness of the terminal screws holding the cable ends, and the cable clamp. Also carry a long mains extension lead for those occasions where the nearest power point is 30 feet away, but use one with a sufficient current rating, and uncoil the cable fully regardless of how much cable you actually need. If you draw a high current through a partially-coiled mains cable, it will get very hot, and I've actually seen them melt and catch fire!

Never trust the mains wiring at a venue. You can buy inexpensive devices that indicate the state of the mains, including the ground integrity, by means of a simple LED display, but it's also a very sensible move to use individual RCB trips (Residual Current Breakers) on the back-line amplification and on smaller PA systems so that if a fault does occur mid performance, the power will shut off before you receive a lethal shock. Inexpensive units are available from garden suppliers for use with electrical garden tools.

You should also try to imagine the worst case scenario for equipment failure and then come up with a contingency plan to allow the show to go on. For example, if a guitar amp fails, you could plug directly into the PA mixer, but only if you have an overdrive device (assuming you use overdrive that is), and a speaker simulator. Some so-called recording preamps combine both, plus basic guitar EQ, in a single unit for little more than the cost of a decent fuzz box, so having one of these in your gig bag is good insurance.

improvisation

Of course the PA may break down, so what then? If it's a speaker fault, you may be able to shut down one channel and carry on with the other, but what if it's a mixer or a power amp that dies? A dead mixer leaves you in trouble because you've nowhere to plug your mics in, but again, you can get inexpensive mixers with just basic EQ and maybe four mic inputs that will bail you out in case of an emergency. Alternatively, a low-to-high impedance mic transformer in your gig back will enable you to plug a low-impedance stage mic into an instrument amplifier. Bass amps have the flattest response, so sharing the vocals with the bass player and turning everyone down a bit might save the day. Guitar amps also often have a second input, but the sound is likely to be rather nasal.

If a power amp fails, there's again a possibility of using the bass amp to drive the PA speakers, then using the mixer to feed the bass amp. If there isn't a second input on the bass amp, the bass player can go through the mixer along with the mics, and if the PA doesn't cope with bass too well, just roll off some low end using the EQ on the bass channel (or via the system's graphic EQ if you have one), and put up with a more middly bass sound. There's generally more scope for improvisation in a system with active crossovers as there will be more than one power amplifier. For example, you could redistribute the components of a stereo, two-way system to run just one speaker stack from the surviving amplifiers. In a three-way system, you could leave out the mid-range cabs and then switch the crossover frequency to run the bass speaker cabinet so it covers both the bass and mid-range. There are usually options if you think hard enough – the main thing to ensure is that by changing crossover settings or by removing crossovers, you're not feeding any tweeters with frequencies lower than they're designed to take. In an emergency, it's even possible to use graphic equalisers or the side-chain filters of frequency-conscious gates to improvise crossovers.

gig diplomacy

Many of the typical problems that you can run into at small venues can be avoided if you make an effort to establish a relationship with the venue manager. This is especially important at pub and club gigs where there is no proper stage area and you have to negotiate for floor space, but on a more practical note, the manager is most likely the guy who's going to decide whether or not to have you back again. It's surprising how many people expect you to be able to set up in an odd corner with the PA speakers in a totally inappropriate place, but they may not be as aware of the laws of physics as they relate to acoustic feedback as you are. Your job is to explain politely that there may be problems, and explore alternatives. However, if changing your setup leaves cables all over the floor, tape them down safely so you don't end up on the wrong end of a law suit for damages when a drunk punter trips over them!

be on time

One important prerequisite is to arrive at the venue in plenty of time and identify any potential problems before you go too far with the setting up. If you can arrange your speakers so they are not pointing directly at the bar, you are less likely to get complaints about the noise, and if you have a multi-cabinet PA system, don't use more than you need for the size of the venue. Above all, don't take a belligerent stance when the landlord tells you that you can't set up the mixing console in the middle of the floor – that's hardly likely to make him change his mind. Try to see his point of view and suggest a compromise that won't inconvenience either party too much. If you come over as friendly and co-operative, you're more likely to get asked back. Being polite, and tactfully suggesting that a few simple changes might result in better sound quality is far more likely to get results.

backing tracks

A very large number of performers, ranging from top festival acts to solo club performers depend on the use of backing tapes or other pre-recorded backing material. Many people still use cassette tapes because they're cheap, easy to copy and the machines to play them are cheap.

Furthermore, commercially available backing tapes are often released only on cassette. But as the public's awareness of sound quality continues to increase, side-effects such as hiss, wow and flutter, tonal dullness and pitch errors are no longer acceptable. There are technically superior alternatives to cassette, each with its own strengths and weaknesses.

cassette tapes

Cassette tapes are definitely the poor relations in today's digital world, but it is still possible to achieve surprisingly good results providing the equipment is of good quality, well maintained, and used with good quality tapes. As mentioned in the introduction, there are several weaknesses in the cassette format, so I'll address those first.

Tape hiss is a common problem, and many people still misunderstand tape noise reduction systems, which makes the problem worse. All tape noise reduction systems (Dolby being by far the most popular on commercial units) work by processing the signal in some way during recording and then by applying an opposite process during replay. This ostensibly recreates the original sound but with less tape noise. I say ostensibly, because noise reduction can have side-effects which are most noticeable when recordings are made on one machine but played back on another. It is imperative that the same noise reduction system be used both when recording and playing back tapes – you can't, for example, record a tape using Dolby B and then play it back using Dolby C without experiencing some tonal changes. More importantly, you can't use noise reduction to process a tape that was recorded without it – the result will be a very dull sound.

tape types

For the best performance, use a high quality type II (sometimes called chrome type), preferably one of the brands recommended in the machine's handbook, and use a machine with either Dolby C, or better still, the newer Dolby S noise reduction system. It is equally important that the tapes are recorded at a proper level – the meters should always go a little way into the red on signal peaks. If you record at too low a level, the recording will be noisy, whereas working at too high a level will result in audible distortion. The idea is to record as loud as you can without getting distortion.

It's vital to clean the tape machine before making a recording and it's also a good idea to clean it prior to each gig. All you need do is use a cotton bud moistened in head cleaner (isopropyl alcohol), to rub away any dirt from the tape heads and guides. In practice, you just keep wiping until no more brown gunge comes off on the cotton bud, then wipe the parts again with a clean, dry cotton bud. Leave the machine to dry out for a couple of minutes before inserting a tape. The whole business takes no more than a couple of minutes.

tape machine pitch

Assuming that your tapes now sound clean and bright, there's the problem of pitch to worry about. Tapes made on one cassette deck seldom play back in pitch on a different machine, and even the same machine can drift in speed from one day to the next. Using the same machine for both recording and playback helps, both as far as speed consistency is concerned and for making sure the noise reduction system behaves as well as possible, but because some speed drift is still possible, it is advisable to record a tuning tone at the start of the tape so that you can tune your instrument (or recalibrate your guitar tuner) to the tape prior to the performance.

A better solution to the speed (and hence pitch) problem is to use a cassette deck with a variable speed control, but these are few and far between. However, most decks have an internal preset to allow the speed to be calibrated, and any competent service technician should be able to replace this with a conventional pot which could be mounted on the rear panel. If you can do this, then record a tuning tone at the same time as you record your backing tapes, then when you get to the gig, use the speed control to precisely tune the tape to your instrument or guitar tuner rather than vice versa. If you find a good service engineer, he should also be able to fit start and stop footswitch jacks to any machine that has "soft touch" transport button controls, though you can't do this if the machine has mechanical transport keys. Having footswitch control makes your performance look a lot slicker and it saves you having to walk to the recorder every time you want to start and stop playing.

Another practical problem faced by most types of tape machines is that they take longer than you'd like to wind through, so unless your songs are recorded in a fixed running order, finding and cuing up individual songs can be a nightmare. If you're in the habit of changing your running order, then putting each song, or just a small group of songs, on a separate cassette might be the simplest option.

Always keep backups of your tapes, because even the best tape player has been known to eat the occasional cassette. To be fair, this is usually due to the tape being loosely wound or to the machine being dirty, so always keep a clean machine (transport it in a dust-proof case), and keep your cassettes in the type of storage boxes that include small tabs in the lid to lock the reels. If the reels aren't locked, the vibration involved in driving to a gig will almost certainly leave you with several inches of loose tape inside the cassette shell – which is the cassette equivalent of holding up a sign saying "Eat Me". If in doubt, use a pencil through the tape hub to take up the slack before you put the tape in the machine.

ADVANTAGES: *Very cheap, reasonably reliable.*
DISADVANTAGES: *Prone to pitch instability; high background noise; slow wind speed.*

alternatives to cassette

Digital tape formats offer the very real benefits of virtually hiss-free recording, the elimination of concerns over noise reduction systems and rock solid speed stability. Several record/playback systems are commercially available, the most common probably being DAT.

dat

DAT (Digital Audio Tape) machines offer the same sound quality as the CD format and have incredibly fast wind speeds, allowing you spin through a complete album in well under a minute. Start IDs can be placed before each song so that you can cue up new songs quickly and precisely, and because DAT is a "single-sided" tape format, you don't have the problems associated with turning the tape over. The maximum playing time for a DAT tape is 120 minutes, and though the blank tapes cost more than cassette tapes at between £7 and £10 each, they are still very cost effective.

The down side to DAT machines is that good ones are quite expensive while cheap ones are often unreliable. You also need to get the machines serviced after every 500 hours of use or so, otherwise you may start to suffer from mysterious dropouts and glitches. You'll also need to find a source of backing material on DAT as copying from cassettes will lose most of the sound quality benefits of DAT. DAT machines can be cleaned with special head cleaning tapes in much the same way as video recorders, though thorough cleaning is best carried out by a qualified repair technician. Tape might seem like old technology, but you can at least be sure it's not going to "jump" if somebody knocks the machine!

ADVANTAGES: *High sound quality; speed stability; fast winding.*
DISADVANTAGES: *High cost; regular servicing is needed to maintain reliability.*

dat cassettes

DAT tapes are physically compact and have door mechanisms which offer some protection against dust, though they should still be stored in their library cases when not in use. Even so, they should not be stored or transported in humid, damp or dusty environments and, like any tapes, they should never be left inside a vehicle during warm weather or left on a window ledge in direct sunlight. Tapes should always be removed from the machine after use, and wound to the start or end before storing. Again, this applies to all tape formats.

dcc

Philips' DCC system (Digital Compact Cassette) is a consumer digital tape format designed to offer a high-quality, affordable alternative to the traditional analogue cassette, but unlike DAT, you still have to reverse the cassette's playing direction to play the other side. Because DCC never made a big impact as a consumer product, prices are low, though the number of suppliers is limited, both for the hardware and the tapes. The subjective sound quality is very similar to that of DAT, even though a digital data compression system is used to cram more information onto the tape, and unlike DAT which uses rotating heads similar to those in a video recorder, DCC uses a fixed head, which may bode well for long term reliability. The machine can be cleaned in the same way as a conventional cassette machine and will even play back (but not record) conventional cassette tapes.

DCC cassettes are comparable in price to DAT tapes, but although you can use track IDs to locate songs precisely, the fast wind speed is closer to that of conventional cassettes than it is to that of DAT.

> **ADVANTAGES:** *CD quality sound; speed stability; immunity to jumping if knocked.*
> **DISADVANTAGES:** *Fast wind is no faster than for a regular cassette.*

recordable compact disc

Having material transferred onto CD-R (recordable CDs that can be recorded once only) costs little more than the shop price of a music CD, though you should consider any copyright implications in doing this (to CD or any other recording format) if you're not working exclusively with your own material.

CD-Rs may be treated in much the same way as conventional CDs, though exposure to bright sunlight for extended periods can damage them. All CDs should be treated with care – they're not indestructible, and as with tapes, it's prudent to get a backup copy made in case of unforeseen damage to your working copy. CD players are cheap, many come with useful remote controllers, and access to tracks is extremely fast. In most respects, using CD-Rs is the best option based on convenience, sound quality and cost, but they have a weakness – like vinyl records, they can jump if knocked or subjected to excessive vibration, and occasionally a dirty or scratched disc will jump with no provocation. Because of the floor vibrations present due to your sound system and the (hopefully) dancing feet of your audience, some sort of vibration isolation system should be considered essential if the risk of jumping is to be minimised. At the very least, you should sit your CD player on a thick slab of foam rubber.

> **ADVANTAGES:** *Low cost; high sound quality; near instant access to tracks.*
> **DISADVANTAGES:** *The tendency of CDs to jump when subjected to vibration or when dirty.*

minidisc

Sony's MiniDisc is yet another consumer recording format, and like DCC, data compression is used to get more data onto the disc than would otherwise fit. However, the subjective sound quality is very similar to that of regular CD. As the name suggests, MiniDisc uses recordable discs rather than tape (built into a cartridge like a computer disk), but unlike CD-R, where the disc can only be recorded onto once, MiniDiscs can be recorded onto multiple times in much the same way as tape.

The main benefits of MiniDisc are the same as for CD-R, with the added bonus that you can record your own discs if you change your repertoire. MiniDisc recorders are more costly than CD players, but a further benefit (other than the fact that CD players can't record while MiniDisc recorders can) is that MiniDisc incorporates a powerful buffering system to minimise the risk of jumping in the case of vibration. This was included to make MiniDisc suitable for in-car use, jogging, rollerblading and so on, but it's just as welcome for live performance. I've seen demonstrations where the disc has been completely removed from the machine while music was playing, then returned a couple of seconds later with no disruption in the music whatsoever! Even so, I believe paranoia to be an essential survival trait for live performance, so I'd still stand the player on a foam slab. The discs are quite small, so losing them is probably just as great a risk as damaging them.

ADVANTAGES: *Near CD sound quality; pitch stability; virtually instant access to tracks; good resistance to jumping.*
DISADVANTAGES: *High hardware costs.*

MIDI files

While many performers buy prerecorded backing tapes, there's a strong case for using commercially available MIDI files, either to create your own tapes, or to create a "live" synthesised backing from a General MIDI sound module. Better still, create your own tracks using a MIDI sequencer and keyboard if your arranging skills are up to it. The great beauty of MIDI files is that they only contain data, they don't produce any sound on their own, so the sound of the end result can be changed depending on what synthesiser module (or computer soundcard) you use to play the file back.

Perhaps more important is that you can customise the performance by changing the tempo, or by changing the key of the song, both of which may be adjusted independently, unlike tape recordings where playing back at a faster tempo causes the pitch to increase too. What's more, anyone with editing experience on a MIDI sequencer can modify the song arrangements – for example, to add or subtract verses, or to mute the part or parts that you want to add live.

Unless you have your own MIDI sequencer and synth (or PC with suitable soundcard and software), you'll need to buy your MIDI files, then take them to a MIDI studio to get them turned into backing tracks. Depending on the studio, and on your budget, you can use the files as they come or you can experiment with different sounds and different effects to make your version of the song in some way distinctive.

MIDI backing live

The alternative to backing tapes is to use a MIDI file player plus synth on stage, and the safest bet is to use a hardware (as opposed to computer-based) system as computers tend not to enjoy a life of travel. There are systems that combine synthesiser and MIDI file player in the same box, and these are very attractive to the performer wanting to travel light. Having tried both approaches in the past, I find having a finished backing tape or disk rather more reassuring as there's less to go wrong. MIDI file players and sequencers can occasionally be disrupted by mains-borne interference, and if you happen to be connected to a sound level cutout, your song will evaporate from the machine's memory if you trip the system.

click tracks and cues

Things start to get more complicated when you want a backing tape or disc that also provides a click track for your drummer. Using any of the previously mentioned stereo systems would mean recording the click track on one audio channel and your audio on the other, meaning your audio would then be in mono only. If that's okay, then fine, but if you require stereo audio, then you need a tape/disc machine with three or more tracks. Options here include budget eight-track digital machines, such as ADAT or Tascam's DA88/DA38 where you'll have tracks to spare – you could press these into service to provide surround sound backing tracks. A less costly alternative is to consider one of the new MiniDisc four-track recorders designed for home studio use, though the maximum playing time per disc is limited to a little over 35 minutes in this application. There's also the possibility of using MIDI files on stage with a hardware system that provides either a metronome output or runs an extra synth/drum machine module that can be dedicated to providing a click track.

chapter 9

the technical stuff

The aim of this book has been to be as practical as possible, yet without getting too technical. However, a little technical understanding can go a long way, which is why I'm including this chapter. Even so, I've done my best to keep it simple. Possibly the most confusing term in audio is the word decibel, so I'll start there.

Most of us know that mixer or tape recorder VU meters are calibrated in decibels, or dBs for short, but even the most experienced engineer can start to fumble when asked to explain exactly what they are, and how they are related to the likes of dBu, dBm, dBv and dBV. Fortunately, it's not as complicated as it sounds.

the decibel

The name decibel means a tenth of a Bel, the Bel part being named after that well-known inventor of telephones, Alexander Graham Bell (hence the capital B in dB). The first hurdle is to grasp that the dB doesn't have to relate to any fixed level of signal; it is simply a convenient way of expressing the ratio between two different signal levels. I say convenient because the decibel expresses a logarithmic mathematical relationship, and our ears are also logarithmic in the way they perceive sound level.

The method of calculating dBs for both voltage and power ratios is shown below. We can pick any power or voltage to be our 0dB level and then express all other values relative to that. For example, the nominal maximum operating level for a mixing desk may be shown as 0dB on the meters, regardless of what that means in terms of output voltage. If a signal is lower than optimum, it reads as minus so many dBs, whereas if the signal pushes the meters into the red, it is shown as plus so many dBs.

calculating dbs

When comparing two power levels, the number of dBs difference may be calculated by the equation:

Number of dBs = 10 log (P1/P2) where P1 and P2 are the two powers being compared and where the log is to the base 10.

If you don't understand how logs work, don't worry because few people actually work out dB levels in this way. However, there are some useful figures that you should remember, the most common being that 3dB represents a doubling in power. It follows then that a 10-watt amplifier can produce 3dB more power than a five-watt amplifier. Similarly, a 20-watt amplifier can produce 3dB more power than a 10-watt amplifier. So, how much more powerful is a 20-watt amplifier than a five-watt amplifier? Simple, just add two lots of 3dB, which gives you 6dB.

Because of the mathematical relationship between power and voltage, the calculations are slightly different when it comes to working out voltage ratios in dBs. Here the equation is:

Number of dBs = 20 log (P1/P2) where P1 and P2 are the two powers being compared and where the log is to the base 10.

Note that we now have a 20 in the equation instead of a 10 which means the answer is twice what it would be for a ratio of powers. In other words, double the voltage and the level goes up by 6dB; halve the voltage and the level goes down by 6dB.

Some of the more common ratios are shown in the table below.

AMPLIFIER POWER	LEVEL IN DB
(Watts)	(Relative to 1 Watt = 0dB)
1	0dB
10	10dB
100	20dB
200	23dB
400	26dB
800	29dB
1,000	30dB
2,000	33dB

SIGNAL VOLTAGE	LEVEL IN DB
	(Relative to 1V = 0dB)
1	0dB
2	6dB
4	12dB
8	18dB
10	20dB
100	40dB
1,000	60dB
10,000	80dB
100,000	100dB

From the table, it can be seen that a voltage amplifier having a gain of 60dB amplifies the input signal 1,000 times. The same is true of specifications such as dynamic range: a 100dB dynamic range means that the largest signal a circuit can handle is 100,000 times bigger than the smallest signal it can handle.

the dbm

While dBs express only general ratios, the dBm is a fixed value where 0dBm equates to 1 milliwatt of power. This is of little direct relevance in the world of modern audio, but was vitally important in the pioneering days of telephone when small amounts of electrical power needed to be transmitted over long distances. In the world of telephones and 600 ohm line impedances, 0dBm tended to mean a signal of 0.775 volts applied to a load of 600 ohms, which results in 1mW of power being dissipated.

Today, the term dBm is often abused to signify a signal level of 0.775 volts, but unless the load impedance is exactly 600 ohms, this is incorrect. Because exact load impedances are less of an issue in modern audio systems, the new term dBu (u meaning unloaded) was introduced to signify a voltage level of 0.775 volts, regardless of the load impedance. In other words, while the dBm is a measure of power, the dBu is a measure only of voltage. The term dBv (lower case v) also means the same thing as dBu, though the term dBu is more commonly used.

So far so good, but a reference voltage level of 0.775 volts is pretty clumsy – 1 volt would be far neater. That's where the more recently introduced dBV (note the upper case V) comes in. This simply signifies a signal level of 1V without regard to the load impedance.

standard levels

Most live sound (and studio) audio equipment is specified as working at either "Plus 4" or "Minus 10", but what does that mean in practice? "Plus 4" means +4dBu, an operating level adopted in pro audio due to historic rather than purely logical reasons, and corresponding to an RMS signal level of 1.23 volts. This is a fairly convenient operating level for use with modern op-amp circuitry as it leaves a sensible amount of headroom before the circuitry runs into clipping.

The so-called "Minus 10" level was introduced along with semi-pro recording gear and is largely a Japanese concept. Correctly stated, this is -10dBV, which corresponds to 0.316 volts – roughly a third of a volt. Again this is reasonable for use with op-amp circuitry, but many purists feel the +4dBu system provides a better balance between noise and headroom.

resistance & impedance

Loudspeakers, amplifiers, microphones, mixing consoles – even cables – exhibit electrical resistance and electrical impedance, and the reason they're important is that they matter once you start to connect different pieces together. If the impedance match isn't correct, you could end up with signal loss, distortion, excess noise, or you could even damage something. Fortunately, the concept is reasonably simple, as are the rules for matching. As with almost everything else in this book, this is the non-technical version of the story.

Electrical resistance is simply a means of describing a circuit's opposition to DC current flowing through it; the higher the resistance of a circuit, the more voltage you need to push a given current through it. Copper cable has a low electrical resistance, hence current flows through it easily, whereas something like plastic has a much higher electrical resistance and it's very difficult to get current to flow through it. Materials with very high resistances, such as rubber, are known as insulators.

ohm's law

Resistance is measured in ohms, and a simple formula known as Ohm's law establishes the relationship between current, voltage and resistance. If you know any two of these parameters, you can easily calculate the third using the formula R = V/I, where V is the voltage across the circuit and I is the current (in amps) flowing through the circuit. Furthermore, because electrical power is defined as current multiplied by voltage, a subset of equally simple equations can be derived relating power to current, voltage and resistance, the most useful of which are probably Power = V (squared)/R watts, and Power = I (squared) x R watts.

impedance

Knowing how to calculate resistance in a DC circuit is fine in theory, but in audio, we're dealing with alternating currents right up to 20kHz or beyond – the upper threshold of human hearing. At these frequencies, circuitry ceases to behave as a pure resistor and instead is said to exhibit an impedance. Think of impedance as being AC resistance and you won't go far wrong.

Impedance is still measured in ohms, and in a purely resistive circuit, resistance and impedance are the same thing, but in a circuit that has electrical capacitance and inductance as well as resistance, things starts to get more complicated. For example, a circuit which presents a capacitive load will fall in impedance as the frequency rises, so you can't just quote a single figure and expect it always to apply. However, impedance is also useful, because by using capacitors, resistors and inductors, we can construct circuits that offer a higher impedance to some frequencies and a lower impedance to others. We call these circuits filters, and they are used to build devices such as equalisers and crossovers.

In the case of audio equipment, it is desirable to keep the impedance reasonably constant over the entire audio range, though this isn't always possible. For example, loudspeaker impedance varies with frequency, and when the speaker is in a cabinet, the acoustic loading affects the electrical impedance. This latter point isn't always appreciated, so always go by the impedance marked on the speaker cabinet, not necessarily by the ratings of the drivers inside. The same is true of horn-loaded loudspeakers – a four-ohm driver might actually present an impedance closer to eight ohms when driving into a horn flair.

input impedance

Input impedance is related to how much current the input terminals of a device draw from the device feeding it, and the lower the impedance, the more current is required. If a circuit needs more current than the circuit feeding it can provide, you have a mismatch. The input impedance of a circuit is determined by the electrical components used in that circuit, and when we're dealing with line-level audio signal, or signals from microphones, it is necessary to make sure that the receiving device demands less current than the maximum the source device can supply, otherwise signal loss and distortion will result. In mechanical terms, a mismatch of this kind is exactly the same thing as trying to operate a machine from a motor that isn't powerful enough to turn it.

Output impedance is a measure of how much current an output can supply; the lower the output impedance, the more current the unit can supply. It stands to reason then that to pass a signal from one piece of equipment to another, the output impedance of the source must be equal to, or lower than the input impedance of the source.

impedance matching

If the aim is to transfer the maximum power from one device to another, the optimum matching conditions occur when a circuit with a given output impedance is feeding an input which has exactly the same value input impedance. Exact matching is important where we're concerned with transferring the maximum amount of power from one circuit to another. I like to describe impedance matching as being the electrical equivalent of a gearbox – to make the most efficient use of an engine, you have to choose an appropriate gear ratio.

When dealing with line-level audio signals, we're not concerned about transferring lots of energy – we are more concerned with transferring the signal voltage from one piece of equipment to another with as little loss as possible. To achieve this, it's usual for the source impedance (the output impedance of the equipment providing the signal) to be significantly lower than the load impedance it feeds (the device accepting the signal). A factor of around five or ten times lower is not uncommon. Not only does this prevent the source signal from being unduly loaded, it also enables a single source to drive multiple loads simultaneously if required. Note that a simple splitter lead may be used to feed one output into two or more inputs, but you can't do the same in reverse – you can't join two outputs to feed one input. For that you need a mixer.

mic matching

The mic input stage of a typical mixing console has an impedance of around 1 kohm, while a typical low-impedance dynamic microphone will have an impedance of between 150 and 200 ohms or thereabouts. This obviously provides a good match. Similarly, most pro audio line-level equipment has an input impedance of several tens of kohms – 47 kohms is a common figure, whereas output impedances tend to be made as low as possible so that long cables can be driven without significant loss. Budget equipment (such as effects units) will typically have an output impedance of 10 kohms or less while professional equipment may have an output impedance of only a few tens of ohms.

basic rules of matching

When connecting amplifiers to loudspeakers, the rated output impedance of the amplifier (an amplifier's actual output impedance is many times lower than its rated impedance) should be equal to the impedance of the loudspeaker cabinet to which it is connected. If more than one cabinet is connected to the same amplifier, then the combined impedance must still be the same as the amplifier's output impedance.

NOTE: Even though speaker impedances vary with frequency, good amplifiers are designed to take this into account, so you can treat the impedance figures on the spec sheets at face value when it comes to matching speakers and amplifiers.

If the amplifier's rated output impedance is lower than that of the speaker, the system will still work, but because the matching (electronic gear ratio) is incorrect, the amplifier will deliver less than the optimum power to the speakers. As a rough guide, doubling the speaker impedance halves the power delivered to the speaker. Conversely, if the speaker impedance is lower than the rated output impedance of the amplifier, the amplifier will attempt to deliver more current than it was designed to do, and depending on the magnitude of the mismatch, either the amplifier will overheat, or the protection circuity will step in and shut it down.

When connecting mic or line-level audio equipment, the source impedance should be significantly lower than the load impedance, ideally by a factor of five or more. If the load impedance is lower than the source impedance, the signal level will drop and there may also be audible distortion.

NOTE: Never run valve amplifiers without a speaker connected as damage may result. Solid state amps usually survive this treatment.

When using cables in excess of 10 metres, use low impedance sources to avoid signal degradation caused by cable impedance and external interference. Balanced systems offer greater immunity to interference than unbalanced systems, and on very long cable runs, onstage line drivers may be required.

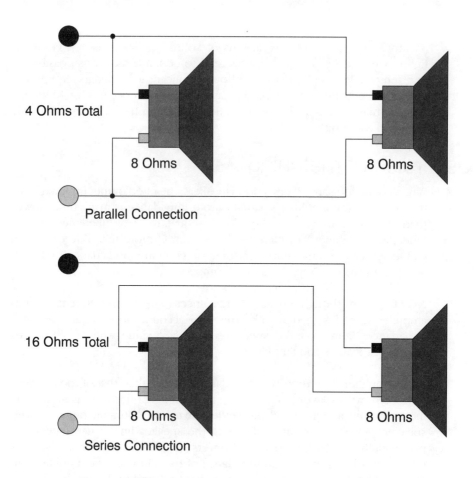

4 Ohms Total

8 Ohms

8 Ohms

Parallel Connection

16 Ohms Total

8 Ohms

8 Ohms

Series Connection

Figure 9.1: Series and parallel speaker connections

With very high impedance sources such as on an electric guitar, keep the cable length as short as is practical and choose a cable designed for guitar use.

the importance of matching

Impedance matching is important, but thanks to the degree of standardisation that has been adopted by our industry, you can safely assume that the majority of line-level equipment will work together without too many problems. However, correct speaker/amplifier matching is important, and in a situation where you may be using a different number of cabinets depending on the size of gig, and where one amplifier may be required to drive more than one speaker cabinet, it is important that the amplifier's rated output impedance and the combined speaker impedances are the same.

calculating speaker impedances

Speakers may be wired in series or parallel, as shown in Figure 9.1, and in such situations, only speakers of the same impedance should be used together. The formula for resistance or impedance where devices are daisy-chained in series is simply: $R = R1+R2+R3$ and so on.

Parallel connections take a little more working out from the formula: $1/R = 1/R1 +1/R2 + 1/R3$. However, if the speakers are all the same impedance (as they should be), then the impedance of any number of parallel speakers is simply the impedance of one of the speakers divided by the total number of speakers. For example, two eight-ohm speakers in parallel produce a total load of 8/2 or four ohms.

frequency response

Putting it rather formally, frequency response may be defined as the relationship between the input level and the output level of an electrical or electronic device taking into account the frequency of the input signal. In other words, it tells us something about how the device behaves at different frequencies. Every piece of audio equipment has a measurable frequency response, from the most sophisticated digital signal processor to the jack sockets in your patchbay, but what does a frequency response look like on paper, how does it affect the sound, and what is considered an acceptable figure? Before answering any of these questions, it helps to consider the human hearing system; all audio technology is directed towards satisfying the human ear/brain combination, so it stands to reason that we need to know something about how this performs.

The commonly quoted 20Hz to 20kHz frequency response of "technically acceptable" audio equipment goes back to early research on human hearing which indicated that a set of young, healthy ears could, typically, hear frequencies as low as 20Hz and as high as 20kHz. Sounds below 20Hz may still be "felt", even though they aren't heard, though frequencies above the range of human hearing, are as far as we are aware, not registered in any meaningful way. This 20Hz-20kHz figure varies from individual to individual and is not the flat response curve shown for "perfect" power amplifiers, but is in fact a complex curve making us more sensitive to sounds in the middle of the frequency range than to those at

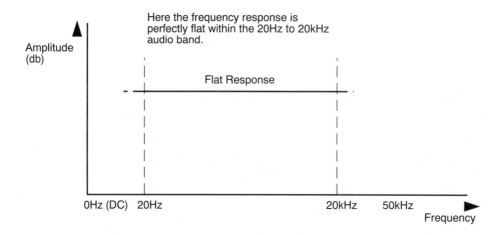

Figure 9.2: Flat frequency response

the extreme high and low end. However, because we perceive the world around us through the "filter" of this inbuilt response curve, we can treat it pretty much as though it wasn't there. On the other hand, audio equipment, such as amplifiers, is required to pass audio signals as accurately as possible, which means that it needs to amplify all frequencies to the same extent. If a graph were to be plotted of level against frequency for a theoretically perfect audio device, the result would be a straight line – or a flat frequency response – between the upper and lower frequency limits of human hearing. Figure 9.2 illustrates this point.

As we get older, our sensitivity to high frequencies diminishes, and this process can be considerably accelerated by constant exposure to loud noise or music. A typical adult's frequency range goes up to 16kHz or so with many people not managing to get far beyond 12kHz. Because the best ears can manage 20Hz to 20kHz, that figure has been adopted as a benchmark for certain critical components such as power amplifiers and loudspeakers, though as we shall see, it doesn't have to apply to all audio devices.

frequency specifications

In practice, no electrical device, whether analogue or digital, is perfect, so when we say that such and such a device has a frequency response flat from 20Hz to 20kHz, we mean that it is flat within certain limits or

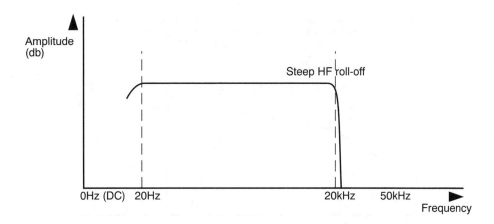

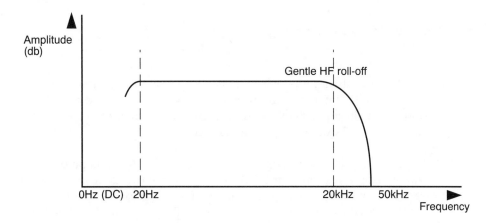

Figure 9.3: Sharp and gradual high-frequency roll-off

tolerances. For example, a power amplifier might be specified as having a frequency response of 20Hz to 20kHz plus or minus half a dB. This means that if a fixed level input signal is swept across the specified frequency range, the output won't change in level by more than half a dB either way. Beyond the upper and lower limits, the response will normally "roll off" or fall away, though the basic 20 to 20 spec doesn't tell us in what way – it's only concerned with what happens between the upper and lower frequency limits. For example, a CD player's response drops away very quickly above 20kHz to avoid aliasing which would occur if any audio was allowed to exist above 22kHz (half the sampling frequency of 44.1kHz).

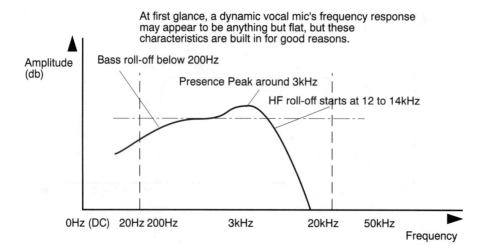

Figure 9.4: Response of a typical vocal mic

On the other hand, a power amplifier with exactly the same "20 to 20" spec might exhibit a more gently falling response and still be providing an output, albeit diminished, at 30 or even 40kHz. Figure 9.3 shows these two theoretical examples for comparison.

If we can't hear above 20kHz, does it matter if the equipment has a sharply falling response or a brick-wall cutoff above 20kHz? If we can't hear it, why worry? There are a couple of answers to this question – and possibly a couple of new questions too. First off, any filtering, either natural or intentional, which affects the frequency response of a system also affects its phase response – the accuracy with which the relative timing of the various harmonics that make up a sound are preserved. It was once thought that these phase relationships were unimportant, but current research seems to indicate that an accurate phase relationship goes hand in hand with the subjective perception of tonal accuracy – a fact exploited in many psychoacoustic enhancing devices.

Another consideration is that when two or more pieces of equipment are cascaded (one device feeding into another, to form a chain), their combined frequency response always suffers slightly; cascade half a dozen units with seemingly impressive specs and you could find the high end rolling off audibly. Alongside this, the overall phase response of the combination will also suffer. That's one of the reasons why top mixer manufacturers give their desks apparently ludicrously wide frequency responses. At least their desk isn't going to significantly compromise the performance of whatever is plugged into it.

how much bandwidth?

Does this mean that all audio equipment has to have an ultra-wide bandwidth? Not necessarily. There are devices, such as guitar loudspeaker systems that only sound the way they do because their frequency response is limited – and usually far from flat. Similarly, certain microphones have humps and dips in their frequency response curves which helps them emphasise certain frequencies and attenuate others. A vocal mic, for example, may have a presence peak at around 3 or 4kHz to help intelligibility, but the bass end is likely to roll off below 200Hz to reduce the effect of sounds occurring below the normal frequency range of the human voice. Figure 9.4 shows the frequency response of a typical vocal mic.

effects unit specs

You may have noticed that some effects units have two different frequency response specs – one for the direct sound and another for the processed sound. While it's easy to pass the direct sound through with a generous bandwidth, the frequency response of digital processing is limited by the sampling rate used which, in turn, is linked to factors such as processor speed, available RAM memory and component cost. Until recently, most digital reverb units had an upper limit for the processed sound of far less than 20kHz with some being as low as 10kHz, but because natural reverb doesn't usually contain much high-frequency energy, this didn't affect the subjective quality of the sound. As processor chips and converters have become faster and cheaper, units offering a respectable performance over the full 20 to 20 range have become far more common.

limits and tolerances

For a frequency response specification to have meaning, it must include not only the lower and upper frequency limits of the equipment, but also the maximum level deviation which occurs between these limits. For example, a quoted response of 20Hz to 20kHz +1dB/-3dB tells us that the gain between these limits may rise by up to 1dB or fall by up to 3dB, but it doesn't tell us whereabouts in the spectrum these deviations occur. In practice, because the frequency response falls away at both the low and high ends, it can usually be assumed that the -3dB points occur at the frequency extremes, and indeed, it is common practice to measure the response of amplifiers between their "3dB down" points. The point is that the specifications must include the number of dBs of possible deviation; if you read a spec that just says 20Hz to 20kHz, it doesn't tell you anything – the signal could be 30dB down at these points for all you know.

gain structure revisited

Gain structure was touched upon in the chapter on mixers, but the concept is so important that it's worth going into in more detail. The nature of sound is that it covers a vast dynamic range, from the dropping of a pin to the exploding of a tank shell, and to reproduce this range using an equivalent analogue electronic signal results in a signal level that might vary from less than a microvolt (millionths of a volt) up to 10 volts or so. In a typical PA mixer, the signal from a microphone is amplified to bring it up to what we call line level (the nominal operating level of the system, for example, +4dBu), and then the signal is passed through a whole chain of circuitry where it is equalised, routed, mixed and effected before being passed on to the power amplifiers.

The main problem when processing analogue signals is that each and every piece of circuitry adds noise to the signal – there's no such thing as noise-free circuitry. This noise is actually due to the random movement of electrons, and until we find some way around the limitations set by quantum mechanics, we're stuck with it. Fortunately, a well-designed circuit adds only a tiny amount of noise, and this noise is largely constant. This being the case, it's pretty obvious that if you feed a very low-level signal through the circuit, the ratio of the noise to the wanted signal is going to be worse than if you feed a strong signal through the circuit. However, there is a limit to how hot your signal can be, because if it's too high in level, it will cause the circuitry to clip and you'll hear distortion.

optimum level

The secret is to find a compromise, where the signal level is kept reasonably high but still leaving a little safety margin or headroom to accommodate any unexpected signal peaks. If you visualise the VU meters on a mixing console, this whole concept makes more sense. The nominal operating level is where the signal peaks at around the 0VU mark (where the red area starts) and the safety margin or headroom is how far you can push the level into the red before you hear distortion.

Most analogue circuits don't suddenly clip when the level gets too high – instead, the amount of distortion rises gradually as the last few dBs of headroom are used up, then hard clipping occurs.

setting digital levels

Digital circuits have similar limitations to analogue ones; if the signal is too high in level, it will still clip as the maximum numerical value the system can handle is exceeded. However, there's no safety margin or area of progressive distortion as there is with analogue circuitry – one moment the signal is perfect, but push it up another dB and you're into clipping. For this reason, the nominal operating level for digital equipment is usually chosen around 12dB or so below the actual 0VU or clipping point in order to leave a useful amount of headroom. This is important when setting up the send level to digital effects.

If too small a signal is fed into a digital system, it is represented by fewer bits which, in practical terms, means that the signal suffers from quantisation distortion which sounds very much like noise. In other words, digital circuitry doesn't mean you don't have to worry about noise – you still have to feed it the right level.

optimising gain structure

The whole idea behind optimising gain structure is to ensure that every circuit in your system is running at, or close to its optimum signal level. When it comes to the inside of your mixer, you don't have too much control over what goes on, but the designers will have done their best to ensure that the internal gain structure is right. However, this carefully planned gain structure can be compromised if you, for example, plug something into a channel insert point that significantly reduces the level of the signal passing through it. A compressor with the output gain set too low would be a good example. Now the signal fed back into the mixer is too low so you have to restore the level by turning up a gain control somewhere further on in the signal path, and as you might expect, when you turn up the level, up comes the level of the background noise too. The golden rule when using insert points is that your peak signal level should be roughly the same whether the external piece of gear is connected or not.

using pfl

Perhaps the most important place to get the gain structure right is at the start of the audio chain, especially if you're using microphones. Always use the channel PFL buttons on your mixer to help you set individual input gain trim controls so that the peak signal is just going into the red on the console PFL meters. It takes a few minutes to go around all your mics individually, but it's something that you really have to do religiously if you're after the best possible sound. If you always use the same mics in the same channels, and if the PA is only for the use of your band, then you could mark the input gain trim settings to save you repeating the performance every gig.

send levels

Another potential source of trouble is the external effects unit. If you have your console effects send controls turned to a low setting, then you turn up the input stage of your effects unit to compensate, you'll end up with more noise than if you had the console levels set higher and the effects input level set lower. The best scenario where line level signals are concerned is to maintain a unity gain situation wherever possible – in other words, the signal stays at nominally the same level instead of being constantly built up and then knocked down again, or vice versa. On most mixers, a send setting of around seven corresponds to unity gain and the same is true of the master send control. If you make sure that the channel with the highest send setting is set to around seven, then you won't go too far wrong. Of course it helps if the unity gain setting is marked on the mixer controls, and some manufacturers are considerate enough to do this for you.

If your effects unit has an output level control, this should also be set at around seven or to the unity gain position, which means that the actual level of effect is determined by the effects return control on your desk. If you set your gain structure first and then use the effects return to fine tune the amount of effect on the most heavily effected channel, you'll end up with the best possible signal-to-noise ratio.

gain structure overview

Gain structure is important, simply because once noise or distortion is added to a signal, it is amplified by circuits further along the line in exactly the same way as the wanted signal, so there's no way to get rid of it.

The most vulnerable level matching stage is the mic amplifier, because it's here that the tiny signal from the microphone is brought up to line level before its journey through the rest of the mixer. If you take the time to optimise your mic levels, you're far more likely to end up with low noise and adequate headroom.

When it comes to effects and processors, try where possible to use unity gain settings because every time a signal level is changed, it has to be changed back again later on in the system, which again leads to a build-up of noise.

Finally, don't have anything feeding noise into your system that's not being used. For example, if you have an effects unit patched in that isn't being used, make sure the appropriate mixer inputs or returns are turned right down. Disconnecting unwanted items of equipment also applies to bits of your mixer that aren't being used, so if you have unused channels, don't just mute them – make sure they're not routed anywhere either as even a muted channel adds a little noise. The same applies to aux sends, and while most of the smaller PA desks don't allow you to unroute your sends, you may have the option of routing them to an unused alternative mix buss, which has exactly the same effect.

You may be surprised to know that a lot of the noise you blame your effects unit for adding comes from the aux send mix buss and not from your effects unit at all. So, if you have an effect that you only need to add to one channel, consider connecting the effects via the insert send point instead – you'll be surprised at how much cleaner it sounds.

cables and connections

One of the less glamorous aspects of live sound is the amount of cabling required to get a system up and running, and while there's little I can do to reduce the amount of cabling you need, it is important to choose the right cable for the right job.

screened cable

In a typical audio system, all the signal cables, other than those linking the power amplifiers to the speakers, should be screened. Screened cable can be recognised by its coaxial construction where one or more inner conductors are surrounded by a tube-shaped screen so as to minimise the effects of external interference. The purpose of the screen is to intercept electrostatic interference and drain it away to earth before it can affect the signals passing along the inner wires. In the case of an unbalanced cable, the screen also forms the signal return conductor, whereas in a balanced cable, the signal is carried by the two cores and the screen does not constitute a part of the audio signal path.

The screen may comprise woven copper braiding, layers of multi-strand wire wrapped around the inner cores in a spiral-like fashion, a thin layer of metal foil, or conductive plastic. Each type of cable has its own

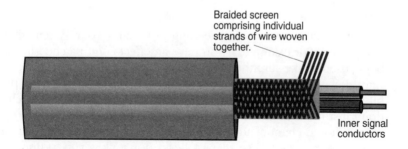

Braided screen comprising individual strands of wire woven together.

Inner signal conductors

Figure 9.5: Braided screen cable

strengths and weaknesses, which has implications for screening efficiency, flexibility, cable capacitance, ease of termination, and so on.

braided screen coax

Braided screen coax is probably the most common type of screened cable and combines good screening efficiency with durability and reasonable flexibility. Braided screen cables are available in a variety of thicknesses, but tend to be time-consuming to terminate. To make a connection, you have to strip the outer plastic sleeve, then either unpick a short length of screen, or part the strands sufficiently so as to allow you to pull the inner conductors through the side of the screen. Once this is done, you have to twist together the strands of screen so that you can solder them, and if the cable is heavy duty, you can end up with a fairly thick bunch of screen that has to be soldered to a relatively small connector.

The screening efficiency of a cable is dictated in parts by the dimensions of any gaps in the screenings. The shorter the wavelength of the potential interference, the smaller the gap it can leak in through. Loosely woven screened cable may seem to be more flexible and easier to terminate, but it can be more susceptible to high frequency interference, such as is generated by the sparking electrical contacts inside motors and so on. It's also generally true that the longer the cable, the better the screening needs to be.

Because of their good screening properties, braided screen cables are often used as instrument or mic cables. Figure 9.5 shows the construction of a typical braided cable.

wrapped screen coax

Wrapped or lapped screen cable is similar in construction to woven screen types, except the wire screening (actually multiple fine wires) is simply wrapped around the inner core rather than woven. The result is a flexible, easy-to-terminate cable, but as the cable is bent, there's a possibility that gaps may open up in the screening, compromising its effectiveness. What's more, any movement of the screen relative to the core, caused by bending, tends to change the cable capacitance slightly, and in low signal applications (such as mic leads) this can generate noise. We've all had experience of mic or guitar leads that crack when they're moved or bent.

Larger diameter types sometimes include a cotton filler to separate the screen from the core, though in my experience, this seems to make the cable even more prone to kinking. Because of these limitations, cheap wrapped screen cable is best avoided, If you specifically want to use it, pick a good quality cable. Figure 9.6 shows how wrapped screen cable is put together.

foil screening

Foil screening provides the best immunity to interference of all the screened cable types and has the advantage of being very easy to terminate. The screening foil is usually made from aluminium, and is spiral-wrapped around the inner cable core with a degree of overlap between turns. Inside the wound foil screen (and in electrical contact with it) is an uninsulated length of wire used to make the screen connection. You can't solder directly to aluminium.

To make a connection, the outer insulation is stripped as normal and the foil screen is also peeled back and cut off to the same length as the outer insulation. The inner cables are then stripped and soldered as required while the exposed uninsulated screen connection wire is soldered to the screen terminal.

While this type of cable exhibits excellent screening properties, it is relatively stiff and it is possible to break the foil screen if very tight bends are made in the cable. Foil screened cable is, therefore, best suited to wiring the insides of equipment racks or other applications where little flexibility is required. Figure 9.7 shows the construction of a foil-screened cable.

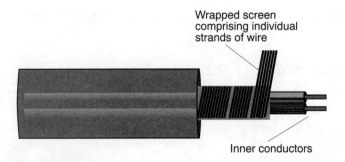

Wrapped screen
comprising individual
strands of wire

Inner conductors

Figure 9.6: Wrapped screen cable

multicores

The type of multicore cable used to feed mic signals from the stage to the mixer comprises a number of small-diameter, individually-screened twin core cables constrained within a common outer sleeve. Multicores are used in fixed installations and for connecting the mixing console to the stage box in conventional PA applications. Multicores that employ foil screening may be used for this latter purpose so long as the cable isn't bent further than the manufacturer's specifications permit. While it is possible to wind the cable onto a large diameter drum, most users tend to coil it "freehand" in a large packing case so as to avoid kinks or tight bends. There are two types of foil screen construction; one where the foil is wrapped around the inner core as a continuous tube, and the other where it forms an overlapping spiral. Spiral-wrapping is less likely to suffer damage through bending. In mobile multicore applications, it is especially important to choose connectors with properly designed strain relief systems, and to fit these in accordance with the manufacturer's instructions.

Note that it is possible to use multicores to feed signals in both directions – mic feeds from the stage and power amp feeds back to the stage. Though this often works, I don't feel entirely comfortable with it as even a very small amount of capacitive coupling between the conductors can result in sufficient crosstalk to make high frequency feedback a possibility. You may end up with an oscillation above the range of human hearing, in which case the first you'll know about it is when your tweeters no longer work. HF oscillations can burn out a tweeter coil in a second, and short of plugging the output of the bass bin amp into the HF cab by mistake, HF oscillation is probably the most common cause of HF driver damage.

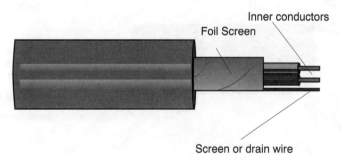

Figure 9.7: Foil-screened cable

conductive plastic

Conductive plastic screening is a relatively new innovation where the traditional metal screening is replaced by a sheath of carbon-loaded plastic. Constructionally, the conductive plastic cable is much like the foil-screened cable discussed earlier, and because you can't solder to plastic, the same uninsulated drain wire runs inside the screen. To make a termination, you strip back both the outer jacket and the plastic screen and make the connections to the inner cores and the drain wire.

Most conductive plastic cables also use very soft, rubbery outer jackets available in a range of colours. Screening efficiency isn't generally as good as for the other types of cable because of the higher resistance of the plastic screen, so it may be unwise to use this type of cable for very long runs or in unduly hostile interference environments. It is, however, ideal for instrument leads and fairly short microphone cables. Figure 9.8 shows a cross section of a conductive plastic cable.

speaker cables

While hi-fi fanatics seem happy to pay fortunes for esoteric speaker cables, what really matters in live sound is that the cable is durable and has as low an electrical resistance as possible. The function of a speaker cable is to provide a low resistance path between the amplifier and the loudspeaker, and if the cable resistance is significant compared to the impedance of the speakers to which it is connected, the power will be shared between the speaker and cable. Take the extreme case of an amplifier capable of delivering 100 watts into four ohms or 50 watts into eight ohms: if the cable has a resistance of four ohms, the total of the speaker and the cable is eight ohms, so already the amplifier is delivering only 50 watts instead of 100 watts. Furthermore, the 50 watts is shared equally between the speaker and warming up the cable, so only 25 watts

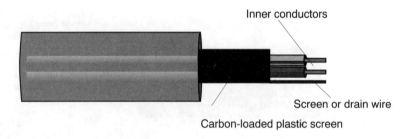

Inner conductors

Screen or drain wire

Carbon-loaded plastic screen

Figure 9.8: Conductive plastic screen cable

actually reaches the speaker. In reality, cable resistance is unlikely to be anywhere near this high, but you can see from this example why it must be kept as low as possible – and low resistance invariably equates to thick cable.

Using inadequate cable will also reduce the damping factor of the amplifier – where the damping factor is defined as the output impedance of the amplifier divided into the impedance of the speaker connected to it. This is important, because the higher the damping factor, the greater the amplifier's ability to sink any current produced by a loudspeaker voice coil when it overshoots its position and starts to work as a generator rather than a motor. By sinking the current produced by the driver in this way, the cone movement is effectively damped, producing a tighter, more accurate bass end. When calculating damping factor, the cable resistance must be added to the output impedance of the amplifier, so the higher the cable impedance, the lower the effective damping factor becomes.

Use the shortest, thickest speaker leads you can, make sure speaker cables are roughly the same length, and use low-resistance connectors such as Speakons or XLRs. Jack connectors are a pretty poor compromise, even on low-powered systems.

connectors

An audio link is only as good as its connectors, and in a touring situation, connectors get a lot of abuse. Make sure the connectors are soldered on properly, and that whatever cable clamping system is fitted is properly used to provide the necessary strain relief on the individual conductors. Most connector failures occur as a result of stress on the cable due to inadequate strain relief. Avoid, where possible, using jack connectors for loudspeakers, even on low-power systems, and clean dirty jacks and contact pins using isopropyl alcohol whenever necessary. Using name brand connectors may cost more than buying no-name budget equivalents, but cheap alternatives often fail to mate correctly with their professional counterparts. You tend to get what you pay for, and knowing what trouble faulty cables can cause, this is one area where it's not worth skimping. Also make sure that you carry sufficient spares, and that any faulty cables are clearly identified so you don't keep trying to reuse them!

signal cable capacitance

Signal cables usually feed into high- or medium-impedance loads, so the cable resistance is seldom a problem unless the cable run is extremely long. However, the capacitance of cable is significant, especially in high-impedance circuits such as exist between guitars and amplifiers. Cables exhibit electrical capacitance by virtue of the close proximity of the inner cores and the outer screen of a coaxial cable, and the longer the cable, the higher the capacitance. A capacitor is former when any two conductors are brought close together; the value of capacitance is proportional to surface area and inversely proportional to the separation of the two surfaces.

A capacitor and a resistor effectively form a 6dB/octave, low-pass filter – and in an audio connection, the cable capacitance combines with the impedance of the circuitry connected to the cable to do just that. For example, the capacitance of a guitar lead 20 or 30 feet long may introduce audible tonal changes. Indeed, guitar pickups are designed to sound their best with an average length guitar lead connected.

Mic cables running back to a mixer desk cause a much less noticeable change in level and tonality because of the lower impedances involved. Though short cable runs are unlikely to produce audible capacitance-related effects, it's generally best to buy the lowest capacitance cable of the appropriate type that you can get. Cable lengths should also be no greater than necessary. Figure 9.9 shows some common cable connection details.

balanced wiring

Analogue audio signal connections can either be balanced or unbalanced. An unbalanced connection relies on a two-conductor cable, and in the case of screened audio cable, this comprises a central core surrounded by a conductive screen. Though the screen (which is generally connected to ground) offers a degree of protection against electromagnetic interference, it is still possible for traces of outside interference to become superimposed on the wanted signal.

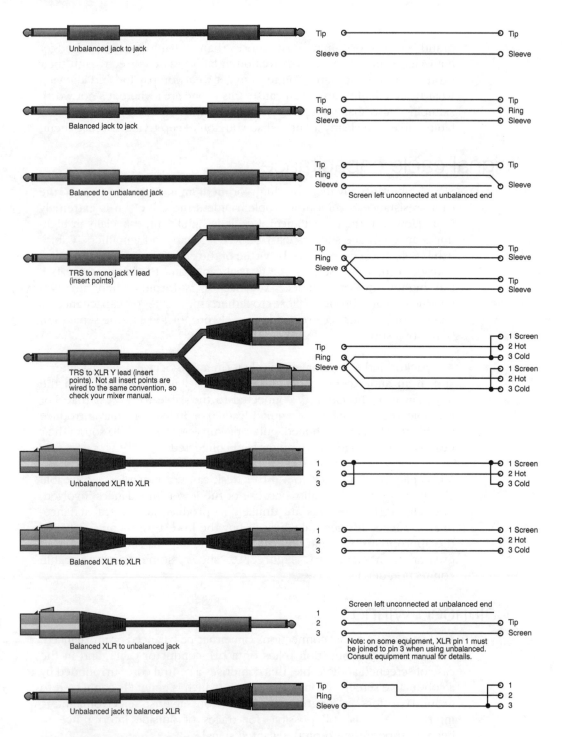

Unbalanced jack to jack

Tip — Tip
Sleeve — Sleeve

Balanced jack to jack

Tip — Tip
Ring — Ring
Sleeve — Sleeve

Balanced to unbalanced jack

Tip — Tip
Ring —
Sleeve — Sleeve

Screen left unconnected at unbalanced end

TRS to mono jack Y lead (insert points)

Tip — Tip
Ring — Sleeve
Sleeve — Tip
 — Sleeve

TRS to XLR Y lead (insert points). Not all insert points are wired to the same convention, so check your mixer manual.

Tip — 1 Screen
Ring — 2 Hot
Sleeve — 3 Cold
 — 1 Screen
 — 2 Hot
 — 3 Cold

Unbalanced XLR to XLR

1 — 1 Screen
2 — 2 Hot
3 — 3 Cold

Balanced XLR to XLR

1 — 1 Screen
2 — 2 Hot
3 — 3 Cold

Balanced XLR to unbalanced jack

Screen left unconnected at unbalanced end
1 —
2 — Tip
3 — Screen

Note: on some equipment, XLR pin 1 must be joined to pin 3 when using unbalanced. Consult equipment manual for details.

Unbalanced jack to balanced XLR

Tip — 1
Ring — 2
Sleeve — 3

Figure 9.9: Common cable connections

Balanced systems were developed to provide increased immunity to electromagnetic interference, and the principle is very simple. Instead of a two-conductor system, balancing involves using three conductors, one of which is still an outer screen, the other two being inner wires used to carry the signal. The reason for having two signal cables is that one has to be fed with a phase-inverted version of the signal, and if you look at the wiring details for a balanced connector (usually an XLR or stereo jack), you'll see that the normal signal connection is usually referred to as "plus" or "hot" while the inverted signal is "minus" or "cold".

At the receiving piece of equipment, the "minus" signal is inverted once again to bring it back into phase with the "plus" signal and the two are added together. Why does this help? As the two signal wires are physically very close to each other, it's reasonable to assume that any interference will affect both conductors pretty much equally. When the "minus" signal is reinverted at the receiving end, any interference on that line will also be inverted, so when the "plus" and "minus" signals are added, the overall result is that the two interference signals cancel each other out, while the wanted signals combine. Even this isn't quite perfect as you don't get exactly the same interference signal on each conductor, and the phase inverting circuits at either end of the line aren't 100% accurate either, but even so, the amount of interference remaining on the final signal is a tiny fraction of what it would be on an unbalanced connection in similar conditions. Figure 9.10 shows both balanced and unbalanced connection systems.

ground loops

Ground loops are a potential problem in any complex audio system where there are multiple earth paths between pieces of equipment and between multiple pieces of equipment and the mains supply ground. Individually, your effects, processors, mixers, power amplifiers and back-line may function perfectly, but connect them together and the chances are you'll hear at least some background hum. If you're lucky, this will be quiet enough to live with, but at worst, it may be so intrusive as to make your system unusable.

This is the point at which some people start disconnecting the earth cables from various mains plugs in the hope that the hum will go away, but this is not a good idea from the safety point of view, especially in live situations where performers are in proximity to both grounded metalwork and mains-powered amplification.

unbalanced audio systems

Simple audio systems rely largely on unbalanced audio connections

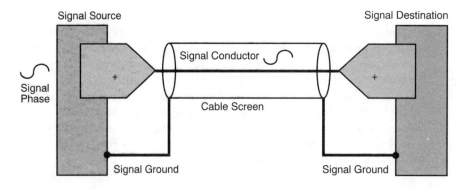

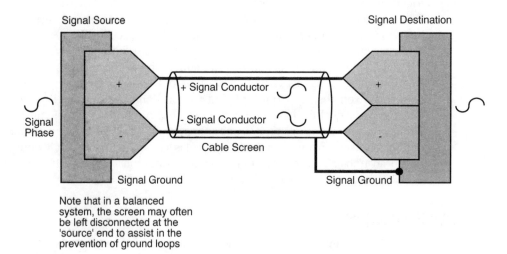

Note that in a balanced
system, the screen may often
be left disconnected at the
'source' end to assist in the
prevention of ground loops

Figure 9.10: Balanced audio connections

where the signal travels along screened cables, each one comprising a single insulated core surrounded by a screen. The screen is grounded so as to prevent outside electrical interference from reaching the signal on the centre conductor, but this isn't a foolproof arrangement. An audio signal is really the voltage difference between the centre (hot) conductor and the outer screen, so if the screen isn't held firmly at zero volts, any audio frequency voltages that find their way onto the screen will end up superimposed on the audio signal. But if the screen is earthed, how come hum interference from the mains still gets into our systems?

All cable has an electrical resistance, and though this may be fairly low, it is nonetheless finite. If you pass an electrical current through any material that has an electrical resistance, a voltage will be produced between the two points of contact, its magnitude depending on the strength of the current and the resistance of the material – as stated by Ohm's law. It follows then that if you pass a current through the screen of a cable, there will be a difference in voltage between one end of the screen and the other. If this all sounds a little academic at this point, bear with me, because all ground loop hum problems stem from this simple fact, and the same knowledge can be used to cure the problem.

the ground loop

Any audio system includes numerous mains-powered pieces of equipment joined to each other via cables, and if all or part of this system uses unbalanced connections, there can be problems. All the signal screens and mains earths interconnect, and because cable does have a finite resistance, there's a real danger that interference signals will cause current to flow in the cable screens resulting in audible signal contamination. While most interfering signals, such as signals from distant radio transmitters, are pretty feeble, the 50/60Hz mains supply is a different matter. If you were to place a closed loop of wire inside a studio, you'd be able to measure a 50/60Hz current flow in the wire because the loop acts exactly like an inefficient transformer.

Because audio signals are measured in millivolts rather than volts, even the most inefficient coupling of the mains supply into our wire loop will produce enough current to generate a voltage which, when added to a typical audio signal, will be audible as hum. Unfortunately, power transformers and other equipment radiate mains frequency energy.

While the loop of wire in my example is purely hypothetical, Figure 9.11 clearly illustrates how the earth and screen connections between just two pieces of equipment can form a closed loop which will be affected by induced mains hum. In reality, the wiring in a typical system is likely to create many ground loops, all of which interact with each other.

In Figure 9.11, the circuit is completed by the mains lead grounds and the signal cable screens to form our single-turn transformer. The resulting "hum" voltage is effectively in series with the signal path and is sometimes known as "series mode interference".

breaking the loop

To reduce or eliminate the effect of ground loops, each piece of equipment should have only one ground current path between it and the

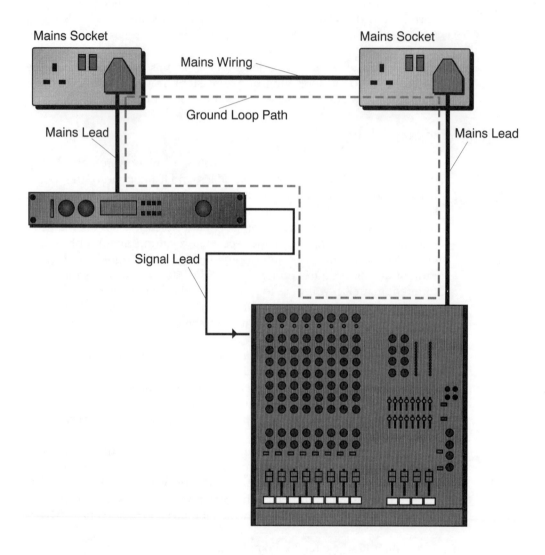

Figure 9.11: Anatomy of a ground loop

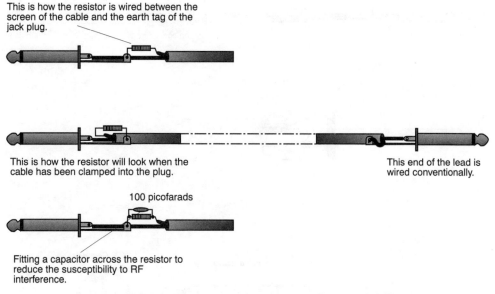

This is how the resistor is wired between the screen of the cable and the earth tag of the jack plug.

This is how the resistor will look when the cable has been clamped into the plug.

This end of the lead is wired conventionally.

100 picofarads

Fitting a capacitor across the resistor to reduce the susceptibility to RF interference.

Figure 9.12: Making a ground lift lead

rest of the system to which it is connected. To comply with this rule, it is necessary to locate any ground loops and break them in some way, which creates a dilemma; either we have to disconnect a signal screen at some point to break the loop, or we must remove the mains earth and keep the signal screens connected.

While the latter approach may work, removing the mains ground connection is potentially dangerous and quite possibly illegal. What's more, if the signal lead is unplugged, the earth protection is completely removed. Note that equipment operating from external mains two-pin mains adaptors is designed to be used unearthed and so may be less susceptible to ground loop problems. This is often the case with effects units powered by adaptor plugs. However, if the unit is bolted to a metal rack, a ground loop may be created via the casework of the unit.

remedies

In professional studios where everything is balanced, disconnecting the screen at one end of a signal cable will usually cure any hum problems because the screen isn't used as a return path for the signal – it's purely a protective screen. In an unbalanced system however, disconnecting one end of a screen can cause difficulties because then you're relying on the mains cable earth to act as a return path for the audio signal. This

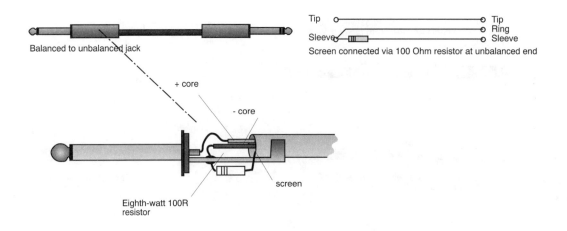

Balanced to unbalanced jack

Tip ○─────────────────────○ Tip
                                                    ○ Ring
Sleeve ○──▭▭▭───────────────○ Sleeve
Screen connected via 100 Ohm resistor at unbalanced end

+ core

- core

screen

Eighth-watt 100R resistor

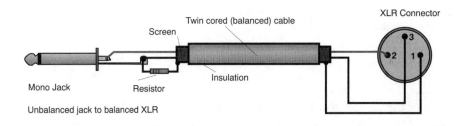

XLR Connector

Twin cored (balanced) cable

Screen

Mono Jack   Resistor   Insulation

Unbalanced jack to balanced XLR

Figure 9.13: Unbalanced to balanced connection

can lead to RF interference problems, and in the event that the mains cable is removed you've no return path at all and you'll be greeted by a very loud hum!

A simple remedy is to connect a small resistor in series with the screen at one end of the cable as shown in Figure 9.12. In a typical audio system, a resistor of around 100 ohms will be high enough to significantly reduce any induced hum currents while still being low enough not to affect the level of the signal passing through the cable. Using a resistor alone slightly increases the risk of RF (Radio Frequency) interference. Usually this isn't a problem, but if you do experience high frequency whistles or breakthrough from radio stations, a 1nf (1 nanofarad) capacitor connected in parallel with the resistor should help. Because the current flow we're dealing with is very small, low wattage resistors may be used, and a quarter- (or even eighth-) watt metal oxide film resistor can be mounted inside most plastic-bodied jack plugs without difficulty. Figure 9.12 also shows how the capacitor is wired should you decide to add one.

This method of tackling ground loops is a compromise because the induced current isn't eliminated, merely reduced. Nevertheless, it can bring about a dramatic improvement in the level of background hum, and in a system which uses unbalanced cables, it can be very difficult to get rid of hum by any other means.

unbalanced to balanced

If you have a desk with balanced line inputs, but your outboard gear is unbalanced, you can go one better as shown in Figure 9.13. A balanced input only "sees" the difference between the + and - input lines, so if both carry identical interference signals, the interference cancels out – a concept known as "common mode rejection". This can be exploited when connecting unbalanced sources to balanced inputs, and to prevent significant earth currents flowing in the cable screen (which in extreme conditions could compromise the common mode rejection of the input stage allowing hum back in), we can insert a series resistor of around 100 ohms in series with the screen connection. This is more satisfactory than putting a resistor in series with the screen in a completely unbalanced circuit because we're not relying on the screen to act as a signal return path – it works purely as a protective screen against interference.

ground compensation

Some mixing consoles use a pseudo balancing system know as "ground compensation". Details of how to connect both balanced and unbalanced signals to these mixers are included in the handbook and in most instances, the additional effort involved in making or adapting cables to take advantage of these inputs is well worthwhile.

patchbays

Larger PA systems may include unbalanced jack patchbays to handle effect and processor connections, and though this doesn't present any great problem, there are one or two points to keep in mind. In the interests of avoiding unnecessary connections between one ground point and another, avoid the type of patchbay where the socket grounds are all linked together along the length of the patchbay – this is simply asking for trouble. If your patchbay provides the option of removing the

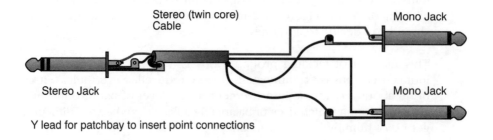

Stereo (twin core)
Cable

Mono Jack

Stereo Jack

Mono Jack

Y lead for patchbay to insert point connections

Figure 9.14: Y lead for use with insert points

ground link between upper and lower socket pairs, then do so wherever a patchbay is being used in a non-normalised application – such as for providing remote console inputs or for bringing the inputs and outputs of effects and processors to the patchbay.

Normalised patch sockets are usually fed from console insert points, and providing the distance between the console and patchbay is less than 10 feet or so, you can get away with using a stereo cable to carry both the insert send and return connections as shown in Figure 9.14. The fact that both signals share a common screen means that there can't be a ground loop between the insert point and the patchbay, even if the upper and lower patchbay socket pairs are ground-linked. However, with very long cable runs, sending both signals down the same cable runs the risk of crosstalk which may lead to high frequency instability.

problem solving

Even once you know what causes ground loops, it can be very difficult to track down the source of the problem in a large system, and while a studio installer might have the luxury of a few day's troubleshooting time, PA rigs are installed and de-installed every time they go out. However, it is wise to set up the system and check it through for possible problems before you take it on tour with you.

You might think that the best way to find problems is to set up the whole system and see if it buzzes, but if you do this, you might find that you fix one loop and the hum actually gets louder. This can occur when multiple ground loops interact and one ground loop is in antiphase with another! The right way to do it is to build the system a few components at a time and check at every stage. If a problem occurs, track it down and deal with it before moving onto the next stage. Fortunately, the main parts of even a modest PA system are balanced, so disconnecting the signal screen at one end is normally all that's needed.

The starting point is to connect just the mixer, the power amplifiers and the speakers. If you have active crossovers, those will obviously need to be plugged in too. Once you're happy that the system doesn't hum, you can connect any signal processors such as graphic equaliser, limiters and effects, then check again. If hum does rear its ugly head when you patch in an unbalanced piece of gear, make up special cables with resistors in the screen connector as described earlier and make sure these are clearly labelled so they always get used. Some hiss and hum is inevitable if you turn the monitoring system up far enough, but providing the hum is at a lower level than the natural background hiss of the circuitry, it's probably as good as you can hope for.

Finally plug in any DI feeds from the back-line and see if you have any problems there. DI boxes with ground lift switches will generally solve the problem, but be aware that hum problems can occur in building with three-phase mains supplies where the back-line is fed from one phase and the main PA from another. Such a connection can also increase the amount of voltage applied to live equipment in the case of a fault condition. It is vital therefore that the whole system is fed from the same electricity phase, and if you're unsure, use suitably rated extension cables to make sure the whole system is powered from the same part of the building.

ground lift

If you draw out a wiring diagram for your system including all the signal cables and mains leads (only those with earths, not mains adaptors), you'll soon see where potential ground loop problems lie. However, as intimated earlier, problems also arise when a ground signal path is completed by another route – say the metalwork of a rack system. Some rack equipment is fitted with an internal ground lift, either fixed or switchable, and this reduces the risk of ground loops when unbalanced connecting cables are used. Conversely, balanced equipment should always have the metalwork grounded.

How do you tell if a piece of equipment is ground-lifted or not? In a ground-lifted unit, there is no direct signal path between the "cold" or screen side of the audio circuitry and the casework of the box. Instead, the box is earthed and the "cold" side of the circuitry connected to the

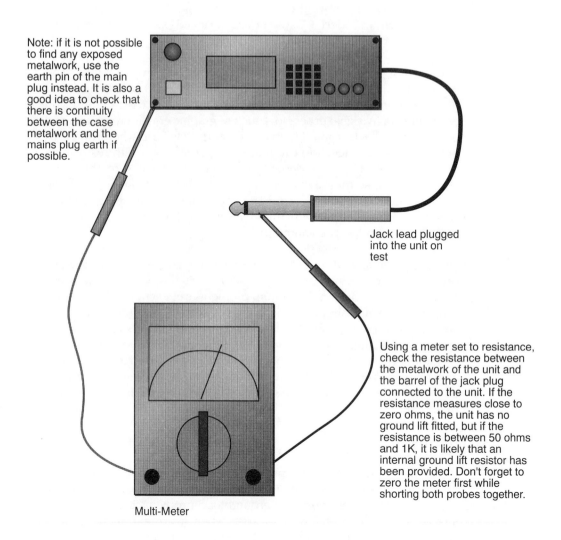

Note: if it is not possible to find any exposed metalwork, use the earth pin of the main plug instead. It is also a good idea to check that there is continuity between the case metalwork and the mains plug earth if possible.

Jack lead plugged into the unit on test

Using a meter set to resistance, check the resistance between the metalwork of the unit and the barrel of the jack plug connected to the unit. If the resistance measures close to zero ohms, the unit has no ground lift fitted, but if the resistance is between 50 ohms and 1K, it is likely that an internal ground lift resistor has been provided. Don't forget to zero the meter first while shorting both probes together.

Multi-Meter

Figure 9.15: Using a multi-meter to check ground lift

case via a resistor, usually between 50 and several hundred ohms. If the manual doesn't make it clear whether a ground lift is fitted or not, simply unplug the unit, plug in a lead, and use a multi-meter (set to resistance). to measure the resistance between the metal case and the barrel of the jack plug as shown in Figure 9.15. If the resistance measures close to zero, there's no ground lift, but if it measures over 50 ohms, a ground lift is almost certainly fitted.

If no ground lift is evident, then you could run into trouble when fitting unbalanced units into a metal rack; the metal frame creates yet another earth current path between different pieces of equipment. The only solution here is to use nylon mounting bolts and washers so that the case is isolated from the rack. You may also need to leave extra space to ensure that the device doesn't touch the units above or below it, though a thin insulating spacer will normally do the trick.

ground loop overview

Having painted a pretty grim picture of ground loops and the annoying hum they cause, you'll probably find that only a few pieces of equipment give you any real trouble. Providing you test your system as you assemble it, you should have little difficulty in identifying the areas that need attention and the things you can leave alone.

When laying out your cables, try not to run signal cables alongside mains cables for any distance as this can also induce hum. Crossing cables at right angles is no problem, but the further signal cables and mains cables travel side by side, the greater the amount of hum that's likely to result. Also be aware that anything containing a large transformer is liable to radiate a strong hum field, so mount power amps and mixer power supplies away from other processors. At the very least, leave a few U of empty rack space between these items and your effects processors.

ground loop check list

● Don't disconnect the earth leads from pieces of equipment that are designed to be used grounded.

● Build up your system a piece at a time checking for hum at every stage. Cure any ground loop problems before connecting any more equipment. If you experience no hum problems when using standard leads, don't feel you have to fit ground-lifted cables – move onto the next piece of equipment.

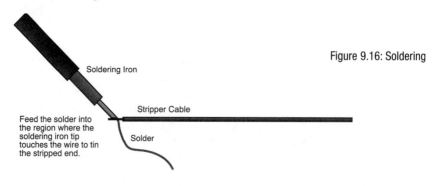

Figure 9.16: Soldering

Soldering Iron

Stripper Cable

Feed the solder into
the region where the
soldering iron tip
touches the wire to tin
the stripped end.

Solder

Thread the tinned wire end through
the hole in the connector cable and
bend the end over with your pliers.

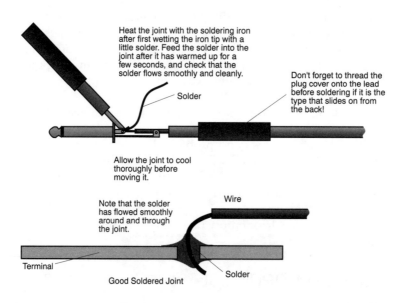

Heat the joint with the soldering iron
after first wetting the iron tip with a
little solder. Feed the solder into the
joint after it has warmed up for a
few seconds, and check that the
solder flows smoothly and cleanly.

Don't forget to thread the
plug cover onto the lead
before soldering if it is the
type that slides on from
the back!

Solder

Allow the joint to cool
thoroughly before
moving it.

Wire

Note that the solder
has flowed smoothly
around and through
the joint.

Terminal

Solder

Good Soldered Joint

The solder has not flowed smoothly around
this joint but instead has formed into blobs.
This is a sign that either the joint was not hot
enough, or all the flux has been boiled away
before the joint could be made. If this
happens, simply apply fresh solder and start
again.

Terminal

Solder

Bad Soldered Joint

- Use balanced wiring where practical.

- When working with unbalanced equipment, use ground-lifted leads to ensure that each piece of equipment has only one direct earth path, either via a mains earth or via a signal cable screen. For connecting unbalanced sources to balanced destinations, use a modified balanced cable as shown in Figure 9.13.

  In the case of two-pin mains equipment or that running from mains adaptors, treat as you would for ground-lifted equipment and ensure that just one of the signal cables provides a true ground. Additional connections should be ground-lifted (via resistors in the case of unbalanced units) if problems arise. If you don't find a problem, don't feel you have to provide a cure.

- Check individual items of equipment with a meter to see which have built-in ground lift resistors. Those that are ground-lifted should be grounded both via the mains and via one signal cable.

- Beware of case-to-case contact causing problems. This is common in metal racks and may usually be cured using nylon mounting hardware.

- Make sure that any special cables, such as those with resistors in them, are clearly marked.

soldering

Running even a small PA system involves a certain amount of maintenance, most of which comprises checking and repairing cables. If you're putting together a new system, you may also find it advantageous to make some of your own cables in instances where suitable off-the-shelf cables are unavailable. At the heart of cable maintenance is soldering, and despite having heard protests from people that they simply can't do it, I still maintain that anyone can learn to solder reasonably well within half an hour if they approach it the right way.

To start with, you need the right tools, and a soldering iron of around 30 watts with a plated bit (the soldering tip), rather than a plain copper one, is ideal. Plated tips last much longer than copper ones, and they can be cleaned during use by simply wiping away excess or oxidised solder with a piece of cotton rag or a special moistened sponge (not foam rubber!). Other than the iron, you'll need some wire cutters, a pair of small electrical pliers (the type that taper to a point), a pair of wire strippers and a reel of multicore solder. These can join the rest of your travelling tool kit, which should at the very least include a torch, multi-meter, some spare fuses and connectors, assorted screwdrivers, an adjustable spanner and a reel of insulation tape, not to mention gaffa tape (duct tape in the US).

Multicore solder isn't, as you might expect, solder specifically designed for soldering multicores – the name refers to cores of chemical flux sealed inside the solder itself. This flux is vital to keep the joint free of oxide while it is being made. You may also need a miniature vice, but when soldering jacks or XLRs, I usually plug them into my cable tester to hold them firm while I solder them.

tinning

If a connector has holes for a wire to pass through, as jack plugs often have, the easiest way to work is to first strip the end of the wire, then tin it using the soldering iron. Tinning is the process of applying solder to each of the two parts to be joined prior to final assembly. Bring the soldering iron, the wire end and the solder together, and you should see the solder melt and flow onto the wire end. The individual strands of wire should soak up the solder like a sponge, so that what you're left with is a single, solder-coated strand.

NEVER TRY TO CARRY SOLDER TO THE JOB ON THE END OF THE IRON – this is where most beginners go wrong. All that will happen is that the flux will boil off, then when you try to get the solder to flow onto the wire, it will produce a pasty blob – or it will refuse to flow at all. It is vital that the solder is melted at the location of the joint so that as soon as the flux in the solder is heated, it can flow onto the job. You'll find that you need to wipe the iron fairly frequently to keep the tip clean.

Most connectors are either pre-tinned or have a surface plating that doesn't need tinning, so now you can push the tinned wire ends through the holes in the connector terminals, then bend them over with your pliers so that they don't fall out as you complete the joint. With the connector held firmly in a vice or spare socket, apply just a little solder to the tip of the iron to wet it, bring the iron to the joint to heat it up for a few seconds, then feed in a little solder between the iron tip and the joint. If the joint is hot enough, the solder will flow smoothly and creep to fill any gaps between the wire and the terminal. As soon as this happens, remove the heat and keep the joint very still for 10 seconds or more until the solder has solidified. If you move the joint as the solder is setting, the solder may crystallise, causing a dry joint. If the joint isn't hot enough, or if you've tried to carry solder on the tip of the iron, the solder won't flow and you'll either end up with no joint at all or a dry joint. A dry joint is one where you've managed to get some solder to stick, but it hasn't joined the two parts to make a good electrical contact. A good joint should be shiny and the solder should have flowed smoothly along the terminal, away from the joint in all directions as shown in Figure 9.16.

soldering coax

Before you can solder the screen of a braided screen coax cable, you either need to "unpick" a little of the end of the screen to free the inner core, or make a hole in the side of the braid and pull the inner core through using your fine nose pliers. Lapped screen coax simply needs unwrapping after the outer sheath is stripped, and both conductive plastic and foil-screened cables have tinned copper drain wires, which makes connecting very simple.

Soldering the screen of a coax cable is the same as soldering any other cable once you've twisted the end and tinned it. The only difference is that braided or lapped screens are thicker than a regular wire, so it may take a little more heat to solder, and the tinned end will probably be too thick to poke through the hole in the jack plug terminal. Sometimes there is a small metal tag on the screen terminal of a jack plug around which the tinned screen can be wrapped using pliers. This is preferable to soldering the wire straight to the terminal as you start from the basis of a sound mechanical joint rather than relying on the solder to act like glue! Though solder can make quite a strong joint, it's always better, where possible, if the joint is mechanically sound before soldering.

soldering xlr connectors

With XLRs and similar connectors, there's no way to fix the wire in place while you solder as the terminals are generally formed like small tubes, and you simply poke the tinned wire down the end of the tube. In this case, the technique is to hold the tinned wire inside the tube, then heat the tube from the outside with a freshly tinned iron until the tube itself is hot enough to melt your solder. Once it is, push the end of the solder into the tube next to the tinned wire whereupon solder should automatically flow down into the tube and fill it. Again, keep the joint quite still until it hardens, and resist the temptation to blow on it. The larger the metal terminal you're soldering to, the longer it will take to heat up to temperature and the longer it will take to cool down. As a general guide, a jack plug will solder in three or four seconds, while an XLR or Speakon may take a little longer.

If you make a mess of a joint, simply heat it up and bang it on a hard surface to remove the excess solder, then using fresh solder, make the joint again. It won't take you long to learn to solder properly if you're prepared to try.

glossary

ac:

Alternating Current.

active:

Describes a circuit containing transistors, ICs, tubes and other devices, that require power to operate and are capable of amplification.

a/d converter:

Circuit for converting analogue waveforms into a series of equally spaced numerical values represented by binary numbers. The more "bits" a converter has, the greater the resolution of the sampling process. These converters are used at the inputs of digital effects units, digital mixing consoles and digital audio recorders.

afl:

After Fade Listen; a system used within mixing consoles to allow specific signals to be monitored at the level set by their fader of level control knob. Aux sends are generally monitored AFL rather than PFL (see PFL).

ambience:

The result of sound reflections in a confined space being added to the original sound. Ambience may also be created electronically by some digital reverb units. The main difference between ambience and reverberation is that ambience doesn't have the characteristic long delay time of reverberation – the reflections mainly give the sound a sense of space.

amp:

Unit of electrical current.

amplifier:

Device that increases the level of an electrical signal.

amplitude:

Another word for level. Can refer to sound levels or electrical signal levels.

analogue:

Circuitry that uses a continually changing voltage or current to represent a signal. The origin of the term is that the electrical signal can be thought of as being 'analogous' to the original signal.

attenuate:

To make lower in level.

attack:

The time taken for a sound to achieve maximum amplitude. Drums have a fast attack, whereas bowed strings have a slow attack. In compressors and gates, the attack time equates to how quickly the processor can change its gain.

audio frequency:

Signals in the human audio range:
nominally 20Hz to 20kHz.

aux:

Control on a mixing console designed to route a proportion of the channel signal to the effects or cue mix outputs (aux send).

aux return:

Mixer inputs used to add effects to the mix.

aux send:

Physical output from a mixer aux send buss.

balance:

This word has several meanings in recording. It may refer to the relative levels of the left and right channels of a stereo mix, or it may be used to describe the relative levels of the various instruments and voices within a mix.

balanced wiring:

Wiring system which uses two out-of-phase conductors and a common screen to reduce the effect of interference. For balancing to be effective, both the sending and receiving device must have balanced output and input stages respectively.

band-pass filter (bpf):

Filter that removes or attenuates frequencies above and below the frequency at which it is set. Frequencies within the band are emphasised. Band-pass filters are often used in mixer mid-range tone controls.

bandwidth:

A means of specifying the range of frequencies passed by an electronic circuit such as an amplifier, mixer or filter. The frequency range is usually measured at the points where the level drops by 3dB relative to the maximum.

boost/cut control:

A single control which allows the range of frequencies passing through a filter to be either amplified or attenuated. The centre position is usually the "flat" or "no effect" position.

bpm:

Beats Per Minute.

buss:

A common electrical signal path along which signals may travel. In a mixer, there are several busses carrying the stereo mix, the groups, the PFL signal, the aux sends and so on. Power supplies are also fed along busses.

capacitor:

Electrical component exhibiting capacitance. Capacitor microphones are often abbreviated to capacitors.

capacitor microphone:

Microphone that operates on the principle of measuring the change in electrical charge across a capacitor where one of the electrodes is a thin conductive membrane that flexes in response to sound pressure.

cardioid:

Meaning heart-shaped, describes the polar response of a unidirectional microphone.

cd-r:

A recordable type of compact disc that can only be recorded once – it cannot be erased and reused.

cd-r recorder:

A device capable of recording data onto blank CD-R discs.

capacitance:

Property of an electrical component able to store electrostatic charge.

channel:

A single strip of controls in a mixing console relating to either a single input or a pair of main/monitor inputs.

chip:

Integrated circuit.

chord:

Three or more different musical notes played at the same time.

chorus:

Effect created by doubling a signal and adding delay and pitch modulation.

chromatic:

A scale of pitches rising in semitone steps.

click track:

Metronome pulse which assists musicians in playing in time.

clipping:

Severe form of distortion which occurs when a signal attempts to exceed the maximum level which a piece of equipment can handle.

common mode rejection:

A measure of how well a balanced circuit rejects a signal that is common to both inputs.

compressor:

Device designed to reduce the dynamic range of audio signals by reducing the level of high signals or by increasing the level of low signals.

conductor:

Material that provides a low resistance path for electrical current.

console:

Alternative term for mixer – also desk or mixing desk.

contact enhancer:

Compound designed to increase the electrical conductivity of electrical contacts such as plugs, sockets and edge connectors.

cutoff frequency:

The frequency above or below which attenuation begins in a filter circuit.

cycle:

One complete vibration of a sound source or its electrical equivalent. One cycle per second is expressed as one Hertz (Hz).

damping:

In the context of reverberation, damping refers to the rate at which the reverberant energy is absorbed by the various surfaces in the environment.

damping factor:

Ratio of loudspeaker impedance to the output impedance of the amplifier driving it.

dat:

Digital Audio Tape. The commonly used DAT machines are more correctly known as R-DAT because they use a rotating head similar to a video recorder. Digital recorders using fixed or stationary heads (such as DCC) are known as S-DAT machines.

db:

Decibel. Unit used to express the relative levels of two electrical voltages, powers or sounds.

dbm:

Variation on dB referenced to 0dB = 1mW into 600 ohms.

dbv:

Variation on dB referenced to 0dB = 0.775 volts.

dbV:

Variation on dB referenced to 0dB = 1 volt.

db/octave:

A means of measuring the slope of a filter. The more dBs per octave, the sharper the filter slope.

dc:

Direct Current.

dcc:

Digital Compact Cassette. Stationary head digital recorder format developed by Philips. Uses a data compression system to reduce the amount of data that needs to be stored.

ddl:

Digital Delay Line.

decay:

The progressive reduction in amplitude of a sound or electrical signal over time.

de-esser:

Device for reducing the effect of sibilance in vocal signals.

deoxidising compound:

Substance formulated to remove oxides from electrical contacts.

detent:

Physical click stop in the centre of a control such as a pan or EQ cut/boost knob.

di:

Short for Direct Inject, where a signal is plugged directly into an audio chain without the aid of a microphone.

di box:

Device for matching the signal level impedance of a source to a tape machine or mixer input.

digital:

Electronic system which represents data and signals in the form of codes comprising 1s and 0s.

digital delay:

Digital processor for generating delay and echo effects.

digital reverb:

Digital processor for simulating reverberation.

din connector:

Consumer multipin signal connection format, also used for MIDI cabling. Various pin configurations are available.

direct coupling:

A means of connecting two electrical circuits so that both AC and DC signals may be passed between them.

disc:

Used to describe vinyl discs, CDs and MiniDiscs.

disk:

Abbreviation of Diskette, but now used to describe computer floppy, hard and removable disks.

dolby:

An encode/decode tape noise reduction system that amplifies low-level, high-frequency signals during recording, then reverses this process during playback. There are several different Dolby systems in use: types B, C and S for domestic and semi-professional machines, and types A and SR for professional machines. Recordings made using one of these systems must also be replayed via the same system.

dry:

A signal that has had no effects added.

dsp:

Digital Signal Processor. A powerful microchip used to process digital signals.

ducking:

A system for controlling the level of one audio signal with another. For example, background music can be made to "duck" whenever there's a voiceover.

dynamic microphone:

A type of microphone that works on the electric generator principle, where a diaphragm moves a coil of wire within a magnetic field.

dynamic range:

The range in dB between the highest signal that can be handled by a piece of equipment and the level at which small signals disappear into the noise floor.

dynamics:

Way of describing the relative levels within a piece of music.

early reflections:

The first sound reflections from walls, floors and ceilings following a sound created in an acoustically reflective environment.

effect:

Device for treating an audio signal in order to change it in some creative way. Effects often involve the use of delay circuits, and include such treatments as reverb and echo.

effects loop:

Connection system that allows an external signal processor to be connected into the audio chain.

effects return:

Additional mixer input designed to accommodate the output from an effects unit.

electret microphone:

Type of capacitor microphone utilising a permanently charged capsule.

enhancer:

A device designed to brighten audio material using techniques such as dynamic equalisation, phase shifting and harmonic generation.

envelope:

The way in which the level of a sound or signal varies over time.

equaliser:

Device for selectively cutting or boosting selected parts of the audio spectrum.

exciter:

An enhancer that works by synthesising new high-frequency harmonics.

expander:

A device designed to decrease the level of low-level signals and increase the level of high-level signals, thus increasing the dynamic range of the signal.

fader:

Sliding potentiometer control used in mixers and other processors.

feedback suppressor:

Device designed to increase the amount of usable level from a system before acoustic feedback occurs.

ferric:

Type of magnetic tape coating that uses iron oxide.

fet:

Field Effect Transistor.

figure-of-eight:

Describes the polar response of a microphone that is equally sensitive both front and rear, yet rejects sounds coming from the sides.

filter:

An electronic circuit designed to emphasise or attenuate a specific range of frequencies.

flanging:

Modulated delay effect using feedback to create a dramatic, sweeping sound.

flutter echo:

Resonant echo that occurs when sound reflects back and forth between two parallel, reflective surfaces.

foldback:

System for feeding one or more separate monitor mixes to the performers so that they can hear what they (and the other musicians) are playing more clearly.

frequency:

Indication of how many cycles of a repetitive waveform occur in one second. A waveform which has a repetition cycle of once per second has a frequency of 1Hz (pronounced Hertz).

frequency response:

A measurement of the frequency range that can be handled by a specific piece of electrical equipment or loudspeaker.

fx:

Short for effects.

gain:

The amount by which a circuit amplifies a signal.

gate:

An electronic device designed to mute low-level signals so as to improve noise performance during pauses in the wanted material.

general midi:

An addition to the basic MIDI spec to assure a minimum level of compatibility when playing back GM format song files. The specification covers type and program number of sounds, minimum levels of polyphony and multitimbrality, response to controller information and so on. Backing tracks for MIDI sequencer use are often provided in General MIDI or GM format.

graphic equaliser:

An equaliser whereby several narrow segments of the audio spectrum are controlled by individual cut/boost faders. The name comes about because the fader positions provide a graphic representation of the EQ curve.

ground:

Electrical earth or 0 Volts. In mains wiring, the ground cable is physically connected to the ground via a long conductive metal spike.

ground loop:

A condition likely to lead to the circulation of currents in the ground wiring of an audio system. When these currents are induced by the alternating mains supply, hum results.

group:

A collection of signals within a mixer that are mixed, then routed through a separate fader to provide overall control. In a multitrack mixer, several groups are provided to feed the various recorder track inputs.

harmonic:

High-frequency component of a complex waveform.

harmonic distortion:

The addition of harmonics that were not present in the original signal.

headroom:

The safety margin in dBs between the highest peak signal being passed by a piece of equipment and the absolute maximum level the equipment can handle.

high-pass filter (hpf):

A filter which attenuates frequencies below its cutoff frequency.

hiss:

Noise caused by random electrical fluctuations.

horn:

Flared "sound pipe" used in front of a loudspeaker driver to increase its efficiency.

hum:

Signal contamination caused by the addition of low frequencies, usually related to the mains power frequency.

hz:

Short for Hertz, the unit of frequency.

ic:

Integrated Circuit.

impedance:

Can be visualised as the "AC resistance" of a circuit which contains both resistive and reactive components.

inductor:

Reactive component that presents an increasing impedance with frequency.

insert point:

A connector that allows an external processor to be patched into a signal path so that the signal now flows through the external processor.

insulator:

Material that does not conduct electricity.

intermittent:

Usually describes a fault that only appears occasionally.

intermodulation distortion:

A form of distortion that introduces frequencies not present in the original signal. These are invariably based on the sum and difference products of the original frequencies.

i/o:

The part of a system that handles inputs and outputs, usually in the digital domain.

isopropyl alcohol:

Type of alcohol commonly used for cleaning and de-greasing electrical connectors, tape machine heads and tape guides.

jack:

Commonly used audio connector. May be mono or stereo.

jargon:

Specialised words associated with a specialist subject.

k:

Abbreviation for 1,000 (kilo). Used as a prefix to other values to indicate magnitude.

kHz:

1,000Hz.

kOhm:

1,000 ohms.

led:

Solid-state lamp.

limiter:

Device that controls the gain of a signal so as to prevent it from ever exceeding a preset level. A limiter is essentially a fast acting compressor with an infinite compression ratio.

linear:

A device where the output is a direct multiple of the input.

line level:

A nominal signal level which is around -10dBV for semi-pro equipment and +4dBu for professional equipment.

load:

Electrical circuit that draws power from another circuit or power supply. Also describes reading data into a computer.

low-pass filter (lpf):

A filter which attenuates frequencies above its cutoff frequency.

mA:

Milliamp or one thousandth of an amp.

machinehead:

Another way of describing the tuning machines of a guitar.

meg:

Abbreviation for 1,000,000.

mic level:

The low-level signal generated by a microphone. This must be amplified many times to increase it to line level.

midi:

Musical Instrument Digital Interface.

mixer:

Device for combining two or more audio signals.

monitor:

A type of loudspeaker used for onstage foldback.

noise reduction:

System for reducing analogue tape noise or for reducing the level of hiss present in a recording.

normalise:

A socket is said to be normalised when it is wired such that the original signal path is maintained unless a plug is inserted into the socket. The most common examples of normalised connectors are the insert points on a mixing console.

nut:

Slotted plastic or bone component at the headstock end of a guitar neck used to guide the strings over the fingerboard, and to space the strings above the frets.

octave:

When a frequency or pitch is transposed up by one octave, its frequency is doubled.

ohm:

Unit of electrical resistance.

open circuit:

A break in an electrical circuit that prevents current from flowing.

opto electronic device:

A device where some electrical parameter changes in response to a variation in light intensity. Variable photoresistors are sometimes used as gain control elements in compressors where the side-chain signal modulates the light intensity.

oscillator:

Circuit designed to generate a periodic electrical waveform.

overload:

To exceed the operating capacity of an electronic or electrical circuit.

pad:

Resistive circuit for reducing signal level.

pan pot:

Control enabling the user of a mixer to move the signal to any point in the stereo soundstage by varying the relative levels fed to the left and right stereo outputs.

parallel:

A means of connecting two or more circuits together so that their inputs are connected together, and their outputs are all connected together.

parameter:

A variable value that affects some aspect of a device's performance.

parametric eq:

An equaliser with separate controls for frequency, bandwidth and cut/boost.

passive:

A circuit with no active elements.

patchbay:

A system of panel-mounted connectors used to bring inputs and outputs to a central point from where they can be routed using plug-in patch cords.

patch cord:

Short cable used with patchbays.

peak:

Maximum instantaneous level of a signal.

pfl:

Pre Fade Listen; a system used within a mixing console to allow the operator to listen in on a selected signal, regardless of the position of the fader controlling that signal.

phantom power:

48V DC supply for capacitor microphones, transmitted along the signal cores of a balanced mic cable.

phase:

The timing difference between two electrical waveforms expressed in degrees where 360 degrees corresponds to a delay of exactly one cycle.

phaser:

Effect which combines a signal with a phase-shifted version of itself to produce creative filtering effects. Most phasers are controlled by means of an LFO.

phono plug:

Hi-fi connector developed by RCA and used extensively on semi-pro, unbalanced recording equipment.

pickup:

The part of a guitar that converts the string vibrations to electrical signals.

pink noise:

Noise source used for testing sound system where each octave contains the same level of sound energy.

pitch:

Musical interpretation of an audio frequency.

post-fade:

Aux signal taken from after the channel fader so that the aux send level follows any channel fader changes. Normally used for feeding effects devices.

power supply:

A unit designed to convert mains electricity to the voltages necessary to power an electronic circuit or device.

ppm:

Peak Programme Meter; a meter designed to register signal peaks rather than the average level.

pre-fade:

Aux signal taken from before the channel fader so that the channel fader has no effect on the aux send level. Normally used for creating Foldback or Cue mixes.

preset:

Effects unit patch that cannot be altered by the user.

processor:

Device designed to treat an audio signal by changing its dynamics or frequency content. Examples of processors include compressors, gates and equalisers. PA system processors may combine EQ, limiting, crossovers and system protection.

pzm:

Pressure Zone Microphone. A type of boundary microphone. Designed to reject out-of-phase sounds reflected from surfaces within the recording environment.

Q:

A measure of the resonant properties of a filter. The higher the Q, the more resonant the filter and the narrower the range of frequencies that are allowed to pass.

release:

The time taken for a level or gain to return to normal. Often used to describe the rate at which a synthesised sound reduces in level after a key has been released.

resistance:

Opposition to the flow of electrical current. Measured in Ohms.

resolution:

The accuracy with which an analogue signal is represented by a digitising system. The more bits are used, the more accurately the amplitude of each sample can be measured, but there are other elements of converter design that also affect accuracy. High conversion accuracy is known as high resolution.

resonance:

Same as Q.

reverb:

Acoustic ambience created by multiple reflections in a confined space.

rf:

Radio Frequency.

rf interference:

Interference significantly above the range of human hearing.

ribbon microphone:

A microphone where the sound-capturing element is a thin metal ribbon suspended in a magnetic filed. When sound causes the ribbon to vibrate, a small electrical current is generated within the ribbon.

rms:

Root Mean Square. A method of specifying the behaviour of a piece of electrical equipment under continuous sine wave testing conditions.

roll-off:

The rate at which a filter attenuates a signal once it has passed the filter cut-off point.

safety copy:

Copy or clone of an original tape for use in case of loss or damage to the original.

sample:

The process carried out by an A/D converter where the instantaneous amplitude of a signal is measured many times per second (44.1kHz in the case of CD).

short circuit:

A low-resistance path that allows electrical current to flow. The term is usually used to describe a current path that exists through a fault condition.

sibilance:

High frequency whistling or lisping sound that affects vocal recordings, due either to poor mic technique or excessive equalisation.

side-chain:

A part of the circuit that splits off a proportion of the main signal to be processed in some way. Compressor use the side-chain signal to derive their control signals.

signal:

Electrical representation of input such as sound.

signal chain:

Route taken by a signal from the input to a system to the output.

signal-to-noise ratio:

The ratio of maximum signal level to the residual noise, expressed in dBs.

sine wave:

The waveform of a pure tone with no harmonics.

snake:

Another term for stage multicore systems used to connect the mixer to the onstage mics. The snake invariably terminates in a stage box.

spectrum analyser:

Device for measuring the level of an audio signal over a number of narrow frequency bands.

spl:

Sound Pressure Level measured in dBs.

stage box:

Metal box containing a number of XLR sockets at the stage end of a multicore or snake.

stereo:

Two-channel system feeding left and right loudspeakers.

sub-bass:

Frequencies below the range of most compact, full-range speaker systems. Some define sub-bass as those frequencies that can be felt rather than heard. In general, frequencies from 25Hz to 50Hz might qualify as sub-bass.

surge:

Sudden increase in mains voltage.

synthesiser:

Electronic musical instrument designed to create a wide range of sounds, both imitative and abstract.

test tone:

Steady, fixed level tone recorded onto a multitrack or stereo recording to act as a reference when matching levels.

thd:

Total Harmonic Distortion.

transducer:

A device for converting one form of energy to another. A microphone is a good example of a transducer as it converts mechanical energy to electrical energy.

transparency:

Subjective term used to describe audio quality where the high frequency detail is clear and individual sounds are easy to identify and separate.

transpose:

To shift a musical signal by a fixed number of semitones.

tremolo:

Modulation of the amplitude of a sound using an LFO.

trs jack:

Stereo type jack with Tip, Ring and Sleeve connections.

truss rod:

A metal bar within a guitar neck which is tensioned so as to counteract the tendency for the neck to bend under the tension of the strings.

uhf:

Ultra High Frequency. Radio band used for professional radio mics.

unbalanced:

A two-wire electrical signal connection where the inner or hot or +ve conductor is usually surrounded by the cold or -ve conductor which forms a screen against interference.

unison:

To play the same melody using two or more different instruments or voices.

valve:

Vacuum tube amplification component, also known as a tube.

vhf:

Very High Frequency. The radio band used by semi-pro radio microphones that need no licence in the UK.

vibrato:

Regular, pitch modulation.

vu meter:

Meter designed to interpret signal levels in roughly the same way as the human ear, which responds more closely to the average levels of sounds rather than to the peak levels.

wah pedal:

Guitar effects device where a band-pass filter is varied in frequency by means of a pedal control.

warmth:

Subjective term used to describe sound where the bass and low mid frequencies have depth and where the high frequencies are smooth-sounding rather than being aggressive or fatiguing. Warm-sounding tube equipment may also exhibit some of the aspects of compression.

watt:

Unit of electrical power.

waveform:

A graphic representation of the way in which a sound wave or electrical wave varies with time.

white noise:

A random signal with an energy distribution that produces the same amount of noise power per Hz.

xlr:

Type of connector commonly used to carry balanced audio signals including the feeds from microphones.

MUSIC TECHNOLOGY – A SURVIVOR'S GUIDE
Paul White
£14.95 ● 1-86074-209-2

RECORDING AND PRODUCTION TECHNIQUES
Paul White
£12.99 ● 1-86074-188-6

HOME RECORDING MADE EASY
Paul White
£11.95 ● 1-86074-199-1

MIDI FOR THE TECHNOPHOBE
Paul White
£11.95 ● 1-86074-193-2

CREATIVE RECORDING PART I – EFFECTS & PROCESSORS
Paul White
£11.95 ● 1-86074-229-7

GUITAR WORKOUT FOR THE INTERMINABLY BUSY
David Mead
£19.99 ● 1-86074-239-4

GIANTS OF BLUES
Neville Marten
£19.99 ● 1-86074-211-4

LEGENDS
Adrian Clark
£19.99 ● 1-86074-220-3

HOT COUNTRY
Lee Hodgson
£19.99 ● 1-86074-138-X

RHYTHM
David Mead
£19.99 ● 1-86074-198-3

FOR MORE INFORMATION on titles from Sanctuary Publishing Limited visit our website at www.sanctuary-publishing.com or contact Sanctuary Publishing Limited, 32-36 Telford Way, London W3 7XS. Tel: +44 (0)181 749 9171 Fax: +44 (0)181 749 9685.

To order a title direct please ring our credit card hotline on 0800 731 0284
(UK only) or write to Sanctuary Direct, PO Box 2616, Great Dunmow, Essex CM6 1DH.
International callers please ring +44 (0)181 749 9171 or fax +44 (0)181 749 9685.
To order via e-mail contact spub@mail.easynet.co.uk

also available from sanctuary techniques